A World of Difference

Every Student's Guide To Off-Beat Work, Travel and Study Opportunities / third edition

LISA YARMOSHUK AND CHRISTOPHER COY

A World of
Difference

A World of Difference

Every student's guide to off-beat work, travel and study opportunities

third edition

Lisa Yarmoshuk &
Cris Coy

broadview press • 1993

Canadian Cataloguing in Publication Data

Yarmoshuck, Lisa
A world of difference: every student's guide to off-beat work, travel and
study opportunities
3rd ed.
ISBN 1-55111-020-2

1. Students, Interchange of — Canada — Directories.
2. Students, Interchange of — Directories.
3. Foreign study — Canada — Directories.
4. 3. Foreign study — Directories.
5. Students — Employment — Canada — Directories.
6. Students — Employment — Directories.
7. Youth travel programs — Canada — Directories.
8. Youth travel programs — Directories.
I. Coy, Chris. II. Title.

LC6681.Y37 1993   370.19'62'025   C93-094689-8

Broadview Press
Post Office Box 1243
Peterborough, Ontario, Canada, K9J 7H5

in the United States of America
Post Office Box 670,
Lewiston, NY 14092

in the United Kingdon
c/o Drake Marketing,
Saint Fagan's Road,
Fairwater, Cardiff, CF53AE

Broadview Press gratefully acknowledges the support of the Canada Council,
the Ontario Arts Council, and the Ontario Publishing Centre.

PRINTED IN CANADA

Contents

Acknowledgements

This book would not have been possible without the assistance and support of many people. We are deeply indebted to all the organizations, program coordinators, and students who replied to our questionnaire, responded to our phone calls, and patiently answered our questions, and to all those people who gave us food and shelter as we travelled the country. Many thanks to Dr David Johnston for his support and encouragement when this book was but an idea and a bundle of notes and to Terry Tesky for her keen editorial eye. Special thanks are also due to all those teachers, employers, advisors, and friends who took the time and effort to guide us into "off-beat" endeavours throughout our education. Above all, we are indebted to our parents who supported our idea from beginning to end. Without their encouragement we would never have decided to take the leap.

Foreword

Many students complete high school and university without venturing far from the conventional path. Most students attend their neighbourhood high school and, if university is an option, many choose to attend the institution in vogue among classmates. These "conventional" students will find summer jobs either listed in classified ads or posted in the local employment centre. Conventional students will not fir extensive travel into their school years. Chances are that most students you know will fit this conventional mold. It is also probably true that most of these students would welcome more daring experiences. What often holds them back is lack of information and the belief that such experience is unattainable or financially impossible. That is why we wrote tis book.

Throughout high school and university we felt a need to sample a broad range of activities. Over the years we worked in political offices, historical museums, and research labs. We participated in language and cultural exchanges, studied exotic plants with the U.S. government and researched humpback whales in the North Atlantic. We also travelled extensively in North America, Europe, and Asia, and found full-time jobs in Japan and the United States. We were always on the lookout for exotic opportunities. However, most of the time, we simply stumbled across the information that we needed to turn our interests into experiences. We often learned of opportunities by happening across a pamphlet in the library or hearing that a friend of a friend just participated in some exiting program. Occasionally, a teacher would matter-of-factly mention the existence of an exchange or scholarship. All too often we heard of these programs after we were too old to participate or long after the deadlines had passed.

Looking over own high school and university experiences, we realized how much easier it would have been to get involved with off-beat programs if they had been listed in one comprehensive book. So, after months of researching all sorts of programs, interviewing directors and employers, and talking with students — here it is! At your fingertips you have a multitude of work, travel, and study options, as well as all the practical information (names, addresses, deadlines, and phone numbers) you'll need to pursue them. Research for this third edition was undertaken during the summer of 1993, so all the information is as current as possible.

Many of the programs appeared in the first and second editions, but all addresses, phone numbers, and prices have been checked and changed where necessary. Program directors were once again interviewed and in many cases new students were asked to comment on their experiences. Programs no longer in operation were removed, and many new programs were added. Several new "special features" and "student profiles" complete the updating and expansion of this new edition.

Why take the risk of trying something different? Involving yourself in unusual types of employment and special education or travel programs will set you apart from the "conventional" student. Employers and scholarship committees screen hundreds of applicants for single positions and they are often searching for the student who has done something a little bit different. Consider too, that by being daring and participating in a fairly off-beat program, you'll encounter other students who took the same risk. Meeting these students and comparing notes invariably opens up new horizons. Along with these specific benefits comes a lasting feeling of self-confidence. it feels good to have taken a chance and accomplished something rare. Whether you decide to teach English in Czechoslovakia, spend grade 11 on a tall ship, travel in Nepal or work on a sheep farm in New Zealand, you'll come away with a sense of confidence in your adventurous spirit and new knowledge.

As we've stressed, there are hundreds of great established programs to choose from. However, organized programs do not always offer exactly what a student is looking for. That is why an important part of this book offers practical advice on how to turn ideas into experiences using your own initiative. Often, finding the perfect employment position or travel opportunity comes down to persistence. It is surprising how many doors are opened by asking the right question or approaching a key individual. In our "Student Profile" sections, enterprising students will let you in on how they arranged valuable experiences for themselves.

In short, this guide is here to help you channel your thirst for the off-beat into opportunities. It gives you access to hundreds of very different programs; it exposes you to a positive approach to planning a unique and exciting high school and university career. You'll only get one chance to live these years—make the most of them!

Preface

As we completed the last items for the third edition of this book we found ourselves trying to remember how the entire project had begun. How had we managed to come to the point where we were preparing to meet with our publisher and hand him our third manuscript? Thinking back, we realized that the putting together of the book was a story in itself—a story we wanted to share with our readers.

One evening back in the summer of 1986, the summer after our first year of university, we found ourselves reminiscing about our high school years. We had been guinea pigs together in a newly founded French Immersion Program, had competed in local, national, and international science fairs, and had been on exchanges to la belle province. We both had friends who had also done interesting things. When the time came to go to university, we both chose to go out of the province—one of us selected McGill University and the big city sights and sounds of Montréal and the other chose Mount Allison, a small, residential liberal arts university in New Brunswick. Now, after our first year, we found ourselves with a couple of hours to swap experiences and stories. But the conversation gradually drifted to life's opportunities and how we had missed out on some really neat ones simply because we had had no idea that they existed. We had discovered that while our own high school years had been fairly satisfying, they could have been even better. As we talked, we found ourselves saying, "Wouldn't it have been great if we'd had a comprehensive guide to unique student programs when we started high school." We realized that there was a real need for such a guide. The idea was again mentioned at Christmas and we decided that we would each prepare a rough outline of what we envisioned would go into such a guide. In March of 1987, we decided to find out if a publisher would see any merit in our idea.

To our amazement, a leading Canadian publisher agreed to meet with us to discuss the book. By now it was May, and we each had full-time summer jobs in Montréal and Toronto. So, armed with several pages of sample writing and a proposed outline, we met with the V.P. Publishing and an acquisitions agent. To our repeated surprise, the response was very encouraging. For a while there was even talk of their offering us a contract to write the book; but reality soon presented itself. After a couple of weeks of anxious waiting the publisher rejected our idea. It was now late May. We had spoken to many parents and students about the project and they thought it sounded great, but we had no publisher—we were faced with a dilemma and a big decision. After much discussion, many long distance phone calls, and much hesitation, we decided to devote the rest of the summer to writing the book. Admittedly, it was a risk and a very big one. We had no money for the project, little idea of how or where to begin such a task, and, assuming all went well, we had no guarantee that we would ever find someone willing to publish the completed work. We had three months of summer left. It was the perfect time to apply the saying "nothing ventured, nothing gained."

So we jumped in head first, spending a couple of weeks making up a data base of possible feature programs. We went to every library, resource person, and student guide we could find. Our biggest fear was that we would find out that what we wanted to produce had already been done. Another concern was that we might lack credibility when it came to approaching organizations for information or interviews. In anticipation of this problem, we solicited letters of support from both Dr. Johnston (Principal of McGill) and Dr. Wells (President of Mount Allison). Their highly encouraging letters were included in the package we sent to organizations in which we requested information. Everything seemed to be going smoothly and then disaster struck. Just as we prepared to send out our first mass mailing, Canada Post went on strike and mail service became very unpredictable. The strike was potentially disastrous to our project since we relied heavily on rapid mail service. As the mail began to drift in, we began arranging interviews with all program directors. Over the course of the summer we spent many days in Toronto, Montréal, and Ottawa. We were also able to conduct interviews in Halifax and Charlottetown and contact other locations from St. John's to Victoria by phone. Travel costs were kept to a minimum by using available car pools and staying with friends wherever our research took us. At the same time we attempted, unsuccessfully, to secure some sort of grant or funding for our project and also approached some twenty publishers with our proposal.

A word here about our search for a publisher might prove useful to aspiring authors. Overall we found publishers to be a helpful and encouraging group. One polite rejection letter we received concluded, "Nonetheless, we urge you to pursue publication since we all felt it would find a solid market with the right publisher—one which handles both trade and educational." This helpful advice was followed with some names and addresses of suggested houses. An early inquiry to the Book and Periodical Development Council elicited a lengthy reply full of ideas. They recommended we look through *The Book Trade in Canada*, a directory of all Canadian publishers which gives a brief description of their operation. This book proved very useful to us. The search for a publisher is potentially one of the most frustrating, but equally, one of the most exciting aspects of being an author. We suggest that if you have an idea for a book which you believe in, don't let your lack of a publisher keep you from writing it. If your project has merit, writing enough letters and talking to enough people will eventually see it to press.

The August long weekend marked the start of the third phase of our project—the writing of the manuscript. With all of the notes, flyers, and student feedback we had collected, it was now time to put pen to paper. It took us a while to get into the swing of it, but once we got started there was no stopping. We each wrote up programs and then edited the other's work. All copy was put on the computer and soon we were running off our first completed chapter. At about the same time, we received four serious inquiries from publishers who wanted to "see more". We immediately sent each of them our first chapter. By the end of August, all interviews had been finished and only our last section remained unfinished. But time had run out and school was starting. After spending our summer vacation in a basement and working 17 hours a day, we were relieved to be returning to the more relaxed pace of university life. Unfortunately, we were returning without a finished manuscript and, even worse, without a publisher!

However, in late September the picture brightened as we received one confirmed contract offer and a reply from another publisher who was still interested, but needed more time to decide. At a meeting just before Thanksgiving, we agreed to sign with Broadview Press. Ironically, we never did approach Broadview about our book; they heard about it through another publisher who had rejected our proposal and they contacted us about taking a look at it. Over the fall term the manuscript was completed and delivered to the publisher by the set deadline. We received advance cheques that guaranteed that we'd be able to pay off all of our phone bills and left us with the hope that royalty cheques would soon be coming our way.

As we entered the final stage, which involved editing the text, preparing a cover design, and planning promotional and marketing strategies, we began to see the fruits of our efforts. Over the summer we said over and over again that the book would be a success as long as we could make it available to the students for whom it had been written. That happened in March 1988. Looking back at the experience, it was frustrating, exciting, and challenging without question it was a lot of long hours, hard work, and fun.

In September of 1989 we received a call from our publisher indicating their interest in producing a second edition. And now in 1993 we are again researching new programs and updating those already in the book. The need for a third editon indicates that the book has been well received and that there is still a need for such a guide. Updating the book for a third edition has involved shorter hours, less stress, but an equal amount of fun. We've uncovered some great programs which we missed the first two times around. The off-beat opportunity scene has changed quite a bit since we did the first edition. Budget cuts have unfortunately eliminated some excellent programs, but at the same time, there is more and more interest in unique student opportunites. We have featured over a dozen brand new opportunities, some of which make us green with envy of today's high school and university students.

Our hope is that this book will make a difference in your life. Let's face it, writing this book was a big risk—but the risk paid off and you are now holding it in your hands. And that is really the message we want you to take away from the book—that risk-taking can be exciting and worthwhile. Choose one of the challenges we suggest, or come up with one of your own, just be sure to make the most of your youth.

Work

Introduction

Most people, whether they like it or not, will spend most of their adult life working. If you're reading this book, chances are you're not yet a member of the full-time work force, but in a matter of years you will be. In the meantime, why should you spend your working hours deep-frying chicken gizzards while sporting an orange polyester suit? What can you possibly gain (aside from minimum wages and an oily complexion) from that sort of experience! At this stage of life, while you still have some room to manoeuvre and time to play with, you should try a variety of different jobs. The more off-beat, the better! By exposing yourself to a wide range of fields, you'll have a clearer idea of the career paths available out there. You'll acquire a wide range of skills and make every job an experience. You'll also make important contacts and meet interesting people.

The bulk of the chapter previews established, Canadian-based programs which offer work-related experience. The programs are divided into two main sections: those programs which offer work in Canada and those which offer work abroad. Program offerings include, among other things, the chance to restore castles in France, spend a summer on a dairy farm, teach English in Japan or do community work in Africa. Sound exciting? Read on!

Along with the necessary addresses and phone numbers, you'll be able to read thorough descriptions of the operation of each program. In the "Overview" to each program, you'll learn about the official aims of the programs and get a basic feeling for what they involve. Under the heading "Inside view", you'll get a behind-the-scenes discussion of the organization. After speaking with hundreds of coordinators and directors, as well as to countless students who have recently participated in these programs, we've gathered information which isn't always printed in official brochures, such as what the selection committee looks for, exactly how tough the work is, and how much money you can realistically expect to earn. Along with the two program sections, you'll find helpful features such as "How to find the job you want", "Volunteering your Services" and "Au Pair Survival". These sections will assist you in creating your own opportunities, as well as leading you to find available jobs without the aid of an established program. For inspiration, we have also included some "Profiles" of individual students who have been successful in creating work experiences that really stand out. Your appetite for the exotic work opportunity will probably be well established after reading this section, and chances are you will want to read more. At the end of the chapter we have listed many other interesting work guides.

We hope that you will be able to make your work experience as exciting and enriching as possible.

Work Within Canada

How To Discover Little-known Jobs

So it is time to find a job. In the past, you may have found work by going through the classified ads or visiting your local employment centre, although the jobs you find there represent only a tiny fraction of those available. Also, in today's economy you are no doubt aware that summer and part-time jobs are increasingly hard to come by. Budgets have been slashed, eliminating many student employment programs. As a result, you will have to look even harder and be more inventive in your search. By starting your search a couple of months early and doing a little bit more investigating on your own, you will probably succeed in finding a job and hopefully one that is just a little bit different. It might mean making a few phone calls or writing a couple of letters (and investing in a couple of stamps to send them), but the time you spend at this stage could pay off with an interesting or fun job that you won't be bored with after two weeks.

There are still many governmental and private organizations which hire students for the summer. These positions are often not widely advertised. Although information sheets on available positions are sometimes circulated, frequently they are not well posted and stumbling across them is a matter of chance. Our advice is: if there is a place you would like to work, ask if they hire students for the summer (or part time during the year). Phone or write the Personnel Director, express an interest in their operation and inquire about employment opportunities. The worst that can happen is that you'll find out that they don't hire. But, you may also discover that you now have a job. You might have an even better chance if you direct your letter to the Executive Director or President! Take the time to get names and titles. This is easily done by making a quick call to the organization.

Many provincial and federal government ministries hire summer students, which can be a terrific way to learn about the inside workings of our political system and can often provide you with a wide range of new experiences and new ideas. Unfortunately, these jobs often go to students who "know someone" in government or whose parents have political connections. In situations such as this, don't be afraid to talk to people you know about your job-search. This is often how job opportunities are discovered. If you are looking for a job in government and know your MP, MPP, or MLA well, ask them to assist you in your job-search. Even if you don't have connections it is still worth your while to write to the Ministry where you wish to work. Be sure to include your resumé whenever you write to ask about employment opportunities. Also, be sure that your cover letter is well written and neat. First impressions, in this case your letter, are very important.

If you happen to live in Ontario, look for the Ontario Government's 'Experience' guide to summer opportunities. (Québec has the equivalent Placement Etudiante and similar programs exist in other provinces.) Through this program students returning to full-time studies in the fall can obtain practical or study-related jobs in Ontario's government ministries and associated organizations. Over 1,000 opportunities exist. More information and application forms are available at Canada Employment Centres.

Ontario, Alberta, the Yukon, Nova Scotia, Prince Edward Island and Newfoundland also have new employment programs called Environmental Youth Corps and Conservation Corps which provide full- and part-time jobs for thousands of students. These programs are fully discussed on pp 14–16.

Tourism is a very important industry in Canada, an industry that provides jobs for many Canadians—especially students. There are an endless number of tour guide positions available across the country. The experience of being a tour guide can help you develop many skills that future employers will look for. This type of job builds confidence and sharpens your oral and interpersonal skills. In many cases, it also allows you to work in both official languages.

In our established work program section we have included some specific examples of guide positions, but many others are available. Unfortunately, detailing them on a national scale is a book in itself. Instead, we will provide a list of suggestions for you to follow-up.

---

1. Parliament Hill—Ottawa

- hires university students as tour guides for the summer
- hires students to perform in the "changing of the guard"
- contact House of Commons Information for details

For more help in finding a guiding position in Ottawa you might want to contact a company called Conference Aide. This operation places bilingual high school graduates in full- and part-time tour guide positions. They supply guides primarily to bus tour companies, but are also responsible for staffing Rideau Hall. Conference Aide can be reached at:

Conference Aide
275 Bay Street
Ottawa, Ontario
K1R 5Z5
(613) 238-3700

Another useful job-hunting organization is the National Capital Commission. They hire a large number of young people each summer to give walking tours of Ottawa. They can be reached at the following address:

National Capital Commission
14 Metcalfe Street
Ottawa, Ontario
KIP 6J6
(613) 239-5555

2. Provincial Legislatures

- hire students as summer tour guides and to work with visitor information
- contact your provincial legislature for more information

3. Historical Forts

- all forts hire students in the summer as tour guides
- contact the fort you are interested in
- your employment centre may be able to give you more information, selection criteria and application procedures

4. Provincial Tourist Information Offices

- most of these are staffed by university students
- contact your Provincial Department of Tourism for more information

5. Tourist Attractions

- most museums, historical homes and sites and other attractions hire students as tour guides
- depending on where you live, there may be several opportunities right in your backyard
- for more information on opportunities, contact the attraction directly

6. Jobs at Resorts

Most resorts across Canada hire students year round, but particularly in the summer, to work as waiters/waitresses, bartenders, chambermaids, lifeguards, bell-hops and other service personnel. These may seem like Joe-jobs, but if you've ever seen Caddyshack you'll have an idea of how much fun they can be. Students usually live in staff residences where room and board costs are minimal. Students come from all over the world to work at these resorts, so it's a great way to broaden your horizons. You can get more information, as well as application forms, by writing directly to the resort of interest to you.

Some possibilities are:

Banff Springs Hotel
P.O. Box 960
Banff, Alberta
T0L 0C0
(403) 762-2211
(800) 828-7447

Pines Resort Hotel
Shore Road, P.O. Box 70
Digby, Nova Scotia
B0V 1A0
(902) 245-2511

Mont Tremblant Lodge
Mont Tremblant, Québec
J0T 1Z0
(819) 425-8711

Cleveland's House
Minett Post Office
Muskoka, Ontario
P0B 1G0
(705) 765-3171

Nottawasaga Inn
Highway 89, Box 1110
Alliston, Ontario
L0M 1A0
(705) 435-5501

Le Chateau Montebello
392 Notre Dame Street
Montebello, Québec
J0V 1L0
(819) 423-6341

Le Chateau Frontenac
1 rue des Carrieres
Québec City, Québec
G1R 4P5
(418) 692-3861
(800) 828-7447

The Algonquin
184 Adolphus Street
St. Andrew's, New Brunswick
E0G 2X0
(506) 529-8823
(800) 828-7447

Fairmont Hotspring Resort
Box 10
Fairmont, British Columbia
V0B 1L0
(604) 345-6311

Lake Okanagan Resort
Westside Road, Box 1321
Station A
Kelowna, British Columbia
V1Y 7V8
(604) 769-3511

7. Bicycle Tour Guides

There are a number of Canadian-based bicycle tour operations which annually hire young people to act as guides. These companies run trips both in Canada and abroad. The ability to speak a foreign language, extensive travel experience and top physical condition might well be required of applicants. If you feel up to the challenge of the job, the rewards can be substantial. While the actual salary might not be anything to write home about, the Alpine scenery and fascinating people encountered along the way probably will be.

For those you don't feel quite up to the physical demands of being a bicycle tour leader, why not consider being a bus tour guide. You'll see the same scenery (granted, it'll be through tinted glass, but you'll be in an air-conditioned recliner) and still meet up with lots of interesting people, although perhaps a little older (like over 65), a little less adventurous and toting substantially less cash than the typical cycle tour member.

Organization: Ontario Legislative Assembly
Program: Legislative Page Programme at Queen's Park

Legislative Page Programme
Room B-15
Legislative Building
Queen's Park
Toronto, Ontario
M7A 1A2
(416) 325-7457

Coordinator: Mr. Arthur Birenbaum

Facts at a Glance:

Age: grade 7 or 8

Duration: 4 - 6 weeks

Regional eligibility: Ontario

Salary: small honorarium to assist in covering accommodation and transportation costs incurred during the term of duty.

Getting in: for more detailed information and an application form, send a letter stating why you are interested in the program to the above address.

- must have consent of your principal
- minimum scholastic average of 80%
- must have accommodation in or near Toronto
- very competitive (1000 apply for 120 positions)

Overview: The Legislative Page Programme allows 120 students to work behind the scenes in Queen's Park for a period of four to six weeks. Five groups of 24 students are chosen each year, divided evenly between males and females. Students come from all regions of Ontario and are predominantly very academically motivated and outgoing. It is considered an honour to be chosen to act as a Legislative Page.

Inside View If you consider yourself to be a bright, motivated and adventurous person this program is definitely something you should consider. The chance to spend four to six weeks working and learning with 23 other interesting students may well be the most important benefit you gain. The fact that you'll be working with politicians in

Queen's Park, seeing government in action on a daily basis (becoming more politically interested all the time), and being tutored in the legislative process as well as core subjects makes it a truly unique learning experience. The fact that you'll be living in or around Toronto will round out the program by providing you with perhaps a first taste of semi-independent living.

While you're on duty in the Legislature, tasks you'll perform will include fetching water, passing notes and keeping files updated. You'll wear a black wool suit provided by the program, which, according to past pages, gets quite hot under the spotlights. So, while your actual duties may not be of the most stimulating sort, seeing how government works first hand is sure to prove intriguing.

The entire application process for this program is very important. The initial letter you write when requesting more information and an application form should be neatly typed and thought out. You'll need to have at least an 80% average. When filling in the actual application form make sure you take your time with it and give the questions a lot of thought. One thing you might have to give an extra amount of consideration to is the fact that you'll need to come up with someone to stay with while you're in Toronto. If you don't already live there, don't have any uncles or aunts or cousins and your parents don't have any close friends, don't give up hope. Perhaps a favorite teacher has a contact there you could stay with, or you might want to ask someone involved with your local Rotary or other service club if they know of anyone who might be able to put you up. If all else fails, you could phone the program coordinator, explain your dilemma, and ask for advice. Where there's a will there's always a way!

Organization: Volunteer Ontario
Program: Young Leaders Tomorrow

2 Dunbloor Road
Suite 203
Etobicoke, Ontario
M9A 2E4
(416) 236-0588

Executive Director: Ms Lorraine Street

Facts at a Glance:

Age: 15-24

Duration: 1 year

Regional eligibility: all regions of Canada

Cost: none

Overview: Young Leaders Tomorrow is a unique program in leadership training. Established in 1985 as a pilot project for International Youth Year, it is a two-phase theoretical and practical approach to teaching youth about what it is like to be a "Member of the Board". Through 40 hours of intensive classroom instruction, and with the help of several teaching manuals, participants learn about group dynamics and the decision-making process. Participants are then placed with a community organization. For one year, the student serves as a regular committee or board member. After the year, participants have a good idea of what it is like to be an integral part of the running of a community organization. This program expanded dramatically during its first two years of operation when it was administered by the Ontario Ministry of Citizenship and Culture. At its height, about 1000 students were participating. These days it is up to individual cities to decide if they will adopt the program. Volunteer Ontario holds the copyright to the program and they are currently marketing it to non-profit organizations all across the country. Volunteer Ontario plans to market this program more aggressively during the coming years.

Inside View: Have you ever wondered what it would be like to sit on the Board of Directors of EXXON or General Motors? Until recently, you might have had to wait a few years for the opportunity to find out, but through the Young Leaders Tomorrow Program you can now participate as an active member on a committee or Board of Directors of a community volunteer organization. The program aims to familiarize youth with community organizations and to provide them with practical experience, thus encouraging them to be future community leaders. Over the past eight years the program has benefited both participating students and organizations alike. For the associations involved, interns often provide their boards with fresh ideas and outlooks and remain involved with the organization after their YLT term ends. For the young person, YLT is an excellent learning experience developing valuable management, leadership and communication skills. In addition, you'll acquire insight into a particular organization, practical experience and important contact networking.

YLT made Maureen Sloan, 18, realize how important community volunteers are. For one year she was a voting board member on the Thunder Bay Regional Arts Council. The program taught Maureen about the function of a board, interpersonal relationships, group dynamics, and volunteer community involvement. The YLT program allowed Todd Miller, 18, to sit on the volunteer association board of Old Fort William. The great thing about YLT is that, whatever your interests, there is probably a place for you. Your internship can be served on the boards of libraries, museums, dance companies, conservation organizations, and Native organizations to mention a select few. Also, this program is not limited to students. Whether you are employed, unemployed, a full-time or a part-time student, you are eligible for YLT. This last fact raises another important point. This program is not intended to be selective; it is designed to appeal to any young person. Selection depends on your interests and whether or not you can be matched with an appropriate intern organization. The selection procedure includes a very important interview. The committee will be particularly interested in why you want to be involved in this program. They will also evaluate your attitude and your ability to communicate and interact with others. Above all, the committee will look for high interest and willingness to learn and participate.

Because Young Leaders Tomorrow is a very interesting concept, it is unfortunate that it is not in operation in every community in the country. A few communities have adopted the idea but have yet to put it into action. We have heard that youth in Windsor, Belleville, Sault Ste. Marie and Kingston are likely to find the program in operation. Write to Volunteer Ontario at the above address or give them a call to find out if you can participate in your area or to learn how the program can be started in your city.

Organizations: Provincial Ministries of the Environment and Ministries of Natural Resources
Program: Environmental Youth Corps

Several Provincial Governments have created youth work programs designed to allow young people to participate in the improvement of their environment. These are fabulous programs for young people. Most pay a salary, some allow you to design your own project, and all give you invaluable work experience and a satisfaction that you arc contributing to thc future health of your country. The programs are very similar in scope and aim but vary somewhat in their organization and the way they run.   What follows is a short synopsis of each provincial program and how you can participate.   If you are interested in participating in one of these programs we suggest that you write to the relevant address noted below.   Only the provinces listed below run these programs, but New Brunswick is considering a similar one so you might check to see if anything has come into being.

Newfoundland and Labrador Conservation Corps

Newfoundland and Labrador Conservation Corps
3rd Floor, Beothuck Building
20 Crosbie Place
St. John's, Newfoundland
AIB 3Y8
phone: (709) 738-0199
fax: (709) 738-2469

Project Manager: Mr. Don Quigley

Overview: Green Teams are the NFLD Conservation Corps' youth work force. Green Teams give interested youth, between the ages of 16 and 30, the opportunity to work and gain experience in projects which improve the environment.   Any organization can propose a project. These are paid positions.   Newfoundland also participates on a joint project with Nova Scotia called the Environmental Leadership Program, which sends four local youths from each province to Costa Rica for two months on a program sponsored in part by Canada World Youth. At press time only 4 youths from each province participated but Nova Scotia was hopeful that they would eventually be able to send all of their team leaders on the program. Interested people must apply by March 26 and you must be 21-24 years of age. This is a program unique to these two provinces but it is possible that other provinces will participate in the future.

Nova Scotia Youth Conservation Corps

Nova Scotia Department of the Environment
P.O. Box 2107
Halifax, Nova Scotia
B3J 3B7
phone: (902) 424-4924

Co-ordinator: Mr. William Smith

Overview: Nova Scotia offers a program for 17-24 year olds, designed to conduct community projects. There are positions for 97 youths. Their "Regular Program" has been around for four years and places youth on already identified projects in their home community. These jobs pay minimum wage. In 1993 they began a new program called Youth Environment Challenge which allows youth to propose environmental concerns and a useful projects. You form your own team of four and raise your own operating funds. In this case, accepted projects also receive funding from this department. In 1993, they approved 9 projects in communities across the province ranging from a compost demonstration project to a beach restoration project and a purple loose strife ornamental weed management project. Project proposals must be submitted by March 1.

Prince Edward Island Young Environmentalist Program

P.E.I. Department of Environment
4th Floor, Jones Building
11 Kent Street
P.O. Box 2000
Charlottetown, PEI
C1A 7N8
phone: (902)368-5000
fax: (902) 368 5830

Co-ordinator: Mr. Brent Campbell

Overview: This program operates somewhat like the one in Ontario, but not on the same scale. If you are interested you should write to the above address for detailed information.

Ontario Environmental Youth Corps

Ministry of the Environment
Human Resources Branch
40 St. Clair Avenue West
5th Floor
Toronto, Ontario
M4V 1M2
phone: (416) 314-9300

Co-ordinator: Mr. Greg Matthews

Overview: Ontario has the largest environmental youth corps program and employs 1000 students in a variety of positions. In 1993 all projects ran for 8 weeks. These jobs all relate to environmental projects and most involve physical labour. All pay minimum wage. The program is jointly sponsored by several Ontario Ministries and outside organizations. These outside organizations do their own hiring so you apply directly to them. To find out which organizations are involved, pick up an EYC contact book at your local employment centre or perhaps at your highschool. You could also call the Ontario Government Youth Hotline for more information at 1 (800) 387-0777.

Manitoba Environmental Youth Corps

Bld 3, 139
Tuxedo Avenue
Winnipeg, Manitoba
R3N 0H6
(204) 945-3554

Co-ordinator: Karen Warren

Overview: The Manitoba program is a funding program. If you have a proposal for an environmental project you can apply for a grant. The program is open to youth between the ages of 6 - 24! That's right

Manitoba wants everyone to do their part to improve the environment and no one is too young. Manitoba will give up to $5000 to fund a project, but this is not used for salaries. This youth corps is a volunteer project but you certainly get great work experience. With summer jobs hard to come by these days why not take some initiative and get yourself great job experience if you can't find a paying job.

Saskatchewan Environment Youth Corps

c/o Saskatchewan Environment & Public Safety
Walter Scott Building
3085 Albert STreetRegina, Saskatchewan
S4S 0B1
phone: (306) 787-6061

Past Co-ordinator: Ms Shannon Bellamy

Overview: This program used to provide summer jobs for 70 students. However, as we prepared this third edition we learned that this program had recently been cut due to budget constraints. The person we spoke with was not optimistic about the program being revived in 1994 but if you are interested you may want to give them a call.

Yukon Environment Youth Corps

We were told that the Yukon may also run this sort of program but we were unable to track it down. If you live in the Yukon inquire at the Department of the Environment.

Organization: The Student Conservation Association
Program: Resource Assistant Program

P.O. Box 5n50
Charlestown, New Hampshire
03603 U.S.A.
phone: (603) 826-4301
fax: (603) 826-7755

Facts at a Glance:

Age: 18 years and over

Duration: 12 weeks all year round

Regional eligiblity: all provinces

Salary:
- travel grant to cover least expensive mode of transportation to your program and return
- free housing at the Resource Area
- a stipend for food and basic living expenses
- a uniform allowance

Where can I go?
- all over the United States, including the Virgin Islands, Alaska and Hawaii

Getting in:
- obtain an application formfrom the above address
- apply by march 1 for May (generally 3 months before you want to start)

Overview: This is an American based conservation program but it is open to Canadians. The Student Conservation Association (SCA)is a non-profit, educational American organization based out of New Hampshire. The program is mainly a practical work experience for students specializing in the natural resource field, but is open to anyone over the age of 18. The organization places about 800 people in the field each year in about 230 resource areas in over 35 states. About 75% of these positions are offered in the summer months. Resource Assistants work individually in a professional capacity for

12 weeks completing a variety of resource management duties as an equal member of the resource staff of an agency.

Inside View: We don't normally feature American programs, except if they are particularly interesting and if they provide a unique opportunity for Canadians to apply. We heard about this program through one of our readers. Elske Van Essen of Picture Butte, Alberta wrote to tell us about his experience as a Resource Assistant with SCA the previous summer. He wrote a great letter and described the program as a very interesting and worthwhile volunteer program. We agree that this looks like a perfect program for outdoors lovers. It gives you great work experience where you can make a contribution to the preservation of our earth and it doesn't cost you any money.

Elske wrote, and we quote:

> There are really excellent positions available all over the United States. I ended up working in Dahlgren, Virginia, for the US Navy Department of Natural Resourses, doing projects such as building nature trails, doing wildlife surveys, administering the hunting program and establishing fish habitats. I plan on going fulltime in this line of work, and it was very good practical experienc for me. It is open to Canadians, however the obtaining of a position depends entirely on your employer who receives the applications from the SCA. [Lodging] is provided and a substantial living allowance is sent to the volunteer every two weeks. Travel allowance is also provided based on the least expensive mode of travel. I found that it was sufficient.
> This program not only provides you with an interesting way to spend three months, but it also gives you an opportunity to live in and experience the United States. SCA also runs highschool programs you can write to the above address to find out more about them.

Organization: Ontario Ministry of Natural Resources
Program: Ontario Rangers

Ministry of Natural Resources
Youth Programs Office
P.O. Box 7000
Peterborough, Ontario
K9J 8M5
(705) 740-1208

Special Projects Officer: Ms Sandy White

Facts at a Glance:

Age: 16-year-olds who will be 17 by December 31, and 17-year-olds who will not have turned 18 by July 31

Duration: 8 weeks (July-August)

Regional eligibility: Ontario

Salary:
- $35.55 per day
- room and board
- return travel from home to worksite except for $50 which you must pay

Getting in:
- application forms available from above address
- selection is based on a geographic, random process
- deadline is January 30th

Overview: This program offers high school students eight weeks of outdoor work, learning and recreation in northern Ontario. The aim of the program is to enable students to acquire a knowledge of the management of natural resources through hands-on experience. Over 500 young people participate each summer.

Inside View: If you want to get away from North American commercialism and spend a summer planting trees, canoeing, maintaining parks and roads and clearing nature trails, then this is the opportunity you've been looking for. If you're accepted you'll be in for eight weeks of new experiences, new people and a lot of fun. There are no special skills required; you only have to be physically fit. The work is physically demanding and no job is too big or too small for a Ranger. As one participant recalled, "you name it, we did it." You might find yourself cutting portages, developing new campsites or constructing buildings, to mention just a few possible duties. Along with your work, there will be field trips, lectures, safety training, and a week-long canoe trip.

If you go, don't expect all of the modern conveniences of home. You'll live with thirty kids (sorry, not co-ed) in cabin camps which may or may not have electricity or running water. Don't panic at this thought—conditions are very livable. Although there are cooks, you'll be asked to help out. Your parents will be pleased and surprised to find out that you'll be doing your own laundry all summer, although you may not share their view.

Derek Emond, was a Ranger when he was 17 years old and couldn't be more enthusiastic about the program. Even after six years he sounded like someone was paying him to hype the opportunity. He advises participants to let go and loose contact with the outside world for two months, to experience the true woodsman lifestyle. For Derek, it was a summer of great cooks, a terrific tan, a lot of fun and many challenges.

Alberta runs a Junior Forest Ranger Program for 16-18 year olds. We heard about it from a reader who used to be a crew leader on the program. He wrote that, in his opinion "it is a very good opportunity for "urban" kids to learn something about forestry (and how to cope without running water and electricity!). If you are interested in participating get in touch with the provincial Ministry of Natural Resources.

Organization: Ontario Ministry of Natural Resources
Program: Rangers II

Ministry of Natural Resources
Youth Programs Office
P.O. Box 7000
Peterborough, Ontario
K9J 8M5
(705) 740-1208

Special Projects Officer: Ms Sandy White

Facts at a Glance:

Age: 17 - 24 (up to 29 if disabled)

Duration: 9 weeks (July-August)

Regional eligibility: Ontario

Salary:
- minimum wage
- some partial subsidies for housing are available

Getting in:
- must have previously been an Ontario Ranger
- information available from above address
- apply directly to district in which you would like to work
- flexible deadline is January 30th
- successful candidates are notified June 1st

Overview: This program offers students nine weeks of outdoor work, learning and recreation in northern Ontario. The aim of the program is to enable students who have already acquired some experience through their participation with the Ontario Rangers to expand their knowledge. Over 500 people participate each summer.

Inside View: This program is an extension of Ontario Rangers. It places students who already have a summers worth of experience in more challenging positions. Some jobs you might be eligible for would include being an Assistant Conservation Officer, assisting on fish or wildlife projects or working as an Assistant Naturalist.

Jody Rosenberger told us about his experiences last year. Because he had such a good time as a Ranger at a fire station on Lake Superior last summer, he decided to apply for the Ranger II program. He sent his application directly to 12 districts. He accepted the first position that he was offered. Jody spent the summer in the interior of Algonquin Provincial Park cleaning and clearing backpacking trails and campsites. He would often be flown into an isolated lake where his team would set up camp and then spend the week cleaning and creating campsites. On the weekends, Jody went canoeing, biking and hiking with the other park staff. Many people spend thousands of dollars to spend time at Algonquin Provincial Park, but Jody got to spend the entire summer and also got well paid. The fact that Jody is returning to Algonquin for a second summer with Rangers II is a testament to the fact that despite the hard labour involved in the job, the experience is rewarding and fun!

Organization: Frontiers Foundation
Program: Operation Beaver

2615 Danforth Avenue
Suite 203
Toronto, Ontario
M4C 1L6
(416) 690-3930

Program coordinator: Mr Marco Guzman

Facts at a Glance:

Age: 18 and over

Duration: 3 months minimum (year round)

Regional eligibility: all provinces

Salary:
- room and board
- return travel from home to work site

Where can I go? Ontario, Quebec, Alberta, Northwest Territories (especially northern Canada)

Getting in:
- application forms available from above address
- $25 non-refundable fee required with the application
- emphasis placed on good reference letters
- somewhat selective (400 applicants for 130 spots)

Overview: Operation Beaver, run by the Frontiers Foundation, offers students and non-students the chance to learn valuable manual skills while experiencing life in another part of Canada. That the labour involved here is manual should be stressed—the work you'll be volunteering to do will be hard physical labour. Usually the work involves construction or renovation. In Alberta, only recreation projects are offered. In these jobs, emphasis is placed on organising games and activities in small Native communities for children and young teenagers. For your efforts, you will be rewarded with free room and board. Travel costs from your home to the work site will also be covered. Operation Beaver work teams range in size from two to eight people and are composed of both Canadian and international volunteers.

Inside View: If you think you could handle the hard physical labour and relative isolation of the work site, then Operation Beaver is a program worth considering. Volunteers normally arrive at their work sites with no construction skills and leave after a couple of months quite handy with a hammer. You'll learn skills that will make you competent around the house for the rest of your life. Think also of the travel opportunity that Operation Beaver offers you. Most of the work sites are in the far north and your travel expenses are covered. What a prime opportunity to live in the Northwest Territories for a few months—expense-free! Another reason why Operation Beaver volunteer experiences are so interesting is that the work teams include volunteers from such countries as Japan, Australia, Scotland, and Spain, not to mention that many of the volunteers are Native Canadians. Working with people from such varied backgrounds makes for a unique cross-cultural learning experience.

Sean McDowell, a Queen's University student, spent three months last summer working on two Operation Beaver projects in northern Ontario. Both projects centred on the construction of housing for Native people. Sean reports that work days began at 5:30 A.M. and were often physically challenging. Despite the early rising and long days, Sean liked Operation Beaver for several reasons. First of all, through on the job training he was able to learn a significant amount about construction and renovation. Secondly, Sean was the only Canadian on his particular work site; the rest were volunteers from abroad (mostly from England). Also, the experience opened his eyes to the social and economic diversity which exists in Canada. Living, working, and becoming involved in a community which has no roads, has only one phone, and is plagued by social problems was a real education. It also made the whole experience valuable to know that he was doing something tangible to help.

Organization: Ministere du Loisir, de la Chasse et de la Pêche
Program: Mouvement Québecois Des Chantiers

4545, avenue Pierre-de-Coubertin
C.P. 1000, succursale M
Montréal, Québec
H1V 3R2
(514) 252-3015

Information Agent: Ms Isabelle Lord

Facts at a Glance:

Age:
- 18-25 for Québec chantiers
- 18-25 for chantiers in Europe

Duration: 3-12 weeks

Regional eligibility: priority given to Quebec residents

Salary:
- return travel from home to the work site
- room and board
- those who work on a chantier in Europe are charged between $400 and $800 to defray the cost of airfare

Where can I go? all over Québec, France, Great Britain or Belgium

Language: must be fluent in French

Getting in:
- a catalogue of upcoming work projects and application forms are available from the above address
- apply early, as it's strictly first come, first served
- European program is competitive (250 apply for 75 spots)

Overview: The Mouvement Québecois des Chantiers places volunteers on community work projects in Québec and in Europe. The work is usually physically demanding, as the majority of chantiers involve renovation or construction. Groups of ten to fourteen volunteers live together in accommodations provided for the duration of the project, and work about 30 hours each week. A few of the Québec work projects include international volunteers, and the European projects are composed of international participants.

Inside View: If you've recently finished secondary school and haven't yet decided what to do, this program is particularly suited to you. It is fairly easy to get accepted to work on a Québec chantier, where you'd live with about a dozen other volunteers for the duration of the project. Although you wouldn't earn any money, all of your expenses would be paid and you'd be providing a valuable community service, learning new skills and making some good friends. Stephan Coté, a 19-year-old from Thetford Mines, Québec, is taking a year off from school and has already been on two chantiers in the province. On his first, the group lived at a camp for the deaf and helped coordinate activities. On the second, a few of the volunteers were from France and the group lived in a firehall! Stephan has applied to go on a third chantier and would also like to take advantage of the M.Q.C.'s programs in France. To get accepted on an overseas chantier, it helps to have already had experience working with a group. Whether you want to work in Québec or France, it is essential that you speak fluent French.

Organization: Royal Canadian Mint
Program: Summer Guide

320 Sussex Drive
Ottawa, Ontario
KIA 0G8
(613) 993-8990

520 Lagimodière
Winnipeg, Manitoba
R2J 3E7
(204) 983-6400

Responsible Manager: Mr. J. Collin

Facts at a Glance:

Age: usually university students, since most jobs begin in May

Duration: 4 months (summer only)

Regional eligibility: all provinces

Salary: approximately $10 per hour

Language: some positions require candidates to be fluently bilingual

Getting in:
- apply directly to the Mint in early January
- quite competitive (number of students hired varies from year to year— as few as 20 or as many as 50)

Overview: The Royal Canadian Mint is an industrial manufacturer which specializes in precious metals, collector coins and the refining of gold. They market their goods and services throughout Canada and to over 60 countries worldwide. Each summer the Mint hires a number of students to work in the plant, in the head office and as tour guides. The Royal Canadian Mint is an equal opportunity employer.

Inside View: Although the number of jobs available varies from year to year, if you do land one of the much sought after spots you'll likely have a really interesting summer. Each year several tour guide positions become available. To qualify, you must be bilingual, be able to think well on your feet and have very strong communication skills. Guides take groups of twenty visitors on a tour on the catwalk above the Ottawa plant and explain each stage of the production process. Other students work as assembly line workers in the plant and do whatever is necessary. You might assist in shipping one day and the next day work in the rolling room, where the metals are rolled to the correct thickness. Other possible duties include staffing the purchasing, communications or human resources departments.

Organization: Ontario Science Centre
Program: Host Position

770 Don Mills Road
Don Mills, Ontario
M3C 1T3
(416) 429-4100
Manager of Program: Mr. Vishnu Ramcharan

Facts at a Glance:

Age: 16-30

Duration:
- part-time positions available year round
- full time positions during the summer
-

Regional eligibility: all provinces (must have Toronto accommodation)

Salary: up to $14.00 per hour

Getting in:
- apply anytime to above address
- two interviews
- very competitive (1000 apply for 12 positions)

Overview: The position of host at the Science Centre involves giving demonstrations, explaining scientific principles and wandering around the display rooms answering questions. The Centre keeps a staff of 27 part-time hosts year round. Hosts are able to plan their own hours according to a flexible schedule. In the summer, full-time positions are also available. Turnover of hosts is fairly regular; consequently, positions become available quite frequently. However, a large number of students apply for these spots, and the Centre can afford to be quite selective. Science North in Sudbury also has similar volunteer positions.

Inside View: The position of host is ideal for those Toronto-area students who are interested in science. Your hours are flexible, which makes it easy to keep this job while studying full-time. And with hourly wages of up to $14 an hour it is quite lucrative. If you expect to have a chance of being hired, you should possess good communication skills, an ability to work with others, a willingness to learn and an interest in science. Being bilingual is a definite asset. Practical training or a degree in science is not required.

Organization: Royal Tyrrell Museum of Palaeontology
Program: Volunteer Fossil Hunter

Royal Tyrrell Museum of Palaeontology
Volunteer Coordinator
Box 7500
Drumheller, Alberta T0J 0Y0
phone(403) 823-7707, fax (403) 823-7131

Facts at a Glance:

Age: 18 years and older

Duration: 3 weeks during the summer months

Regional eligibility: all provinces

Salary: room and board

Getting in: about 100 applicants apply for 30 spots; apply in January or February

Overview: Every summer volunteers from around the world come to the badlands of Alberta to work on excavation sites. The Royal Tyrrell Museum has one of the world's best collections of dinosaur fossils and many of them were unearthed by volunteers sponsored by the museum. Most of the digging takes place in Dinosaur Provincial Park which UNESCO has placed on its World Heritage List. Volunteers are responsible for their own travel expenses to the work site. Once there, they live in campers or tents in campgrounds and are provided with meals.

Inside View: This program works the way a volunteer program should work. You show up and work and they provide you with food and a place to stay. Each summer about 30 people are chosen from about 100 applications they receive from around the world. About half of those chosen are Canadians. The main criteria for selection is a sincere interest in archaeology. What you actually do at the work site is help to unearth bones and fossils which have already been located by scientists. On your own time you are free to go exploring wherever you think you smell a fossil. You also help to wash and catalogue finds. This is a great opportunity and it is unfortunate that, due to government cuts the program was not offered during the summer of 1993. For the summer of 1994 staff at the museum are hopeful that the program will be resurrected. It will likely work the way it always has, except that there might be a nominal charge for room and board. Write to them and find out what's going on - persistence goes a long way toward landing a good position.

Organization: The House of Commons
Program: The Page Program

P.O. Box 1111
House of Commons
Ottawa, Ontario
K1A 0A6
(613) 996-0897

Coordinator of Recruitment: Miss Annette Leger

Facts at a Glance:

Age: entering 1st year university

Duration: 1 year (August-August)

Regional eligibility: all provinces

Salary:
- $9,250
- return travel from home to Ottawa

Language: good comprehension of both official languages

Getting in:
- application forms available at all Canadian high schools
- all applicants write a general-knowledge test
- those who score well are interviewed
- deadline is end of October
- extremely competitive (500 applicants for 42 spots)

Overview: The Page Programme allows 42 Canadian students the opportunity to study in Ottawa for one year while seeing Parliament in action. The students are chosen from all provinces. Their selection is based on their academic averages (at least 80%), results of a general-knowledge test, and a lengthy interview. Applicants must be able to function in both official languages. Those chosen enter their first year of university at either the University of Ottawa or Carleton University and spend 15 hours each week working in the House of Commons. After one year in the Page Programme, it is up to participants whether or not they'll continue their education in Ottawa. Participants in this program very rarely experience any difficulty in transferring their credits to other universities.

Inside View: This is a very well-organized, unique program and if you can manage to get yourself accepted you'll be in for a once-in-a-lifetime experience. Not many people make it onto the floor of the House of Commons, and despite the fact that most of your time there will be spent delivering notes and fetching "the almighty glass of water," you will learn an incredible amount about Canadian politics. The government contacts you are likely to make could certainly prove quite useful too. Even more important than those political connections will be the lasting friendships you'll develop with the 41 other pages. The program tries to ensure that the pages are housed close to each other in either the Ottawa or Carleton residences. Furthermore, because all past and current pages share the same experience, they have formed a nationwide resource network for each other.

Annette Leger, who has been with the program since its inception, is dedicated to easing difficulties and making the pages' Ottawa experience as memorable as possible. She also spends a lot of time ensuring that the students who are best qualified are the ones who are chosen. A real interest in the workings of government, an ability to perform diplomatically under stressful conditions and the ability to work with others would probably stand you in good stead. Miss Leger takes pride in the fact that many of her pages have come "full circle"—that is to say that after the Page Programme, they were hired by some government agency. Witness Tranquillo Marrocco, who was a page a few years ago, and now works as a procedural clerk at the House of Commons while finishing a second degree.

Note: early applications are appreciated; your guidance office should have the forms by November.

Organization: Senate of Canada
Program: East Block Heritage Program

Senate Communications
Victoria Building
Room 300
140 Wellington Street
Ottawa, Ontario
K1A 0A4
(613) 992-1149

Toll free: 1 (800) 267-7362
Coordinator: Mr. Gord Lovelace

Facts at a Glance:

Age: must be full-time undergraduate university student

Duration: 1 year (full-time June-August; 1 weekend per month during the rest of the year)

Regional eligibility: anyone able to be in Ottawa as the work schedule demands

Salary: $10.00 per hour

Language: must be fluent in French and English

Getting in:
- applications available from above address
- knowledge test and interview required

Overview: Each year approximately 12 bilingual university students serve as guides in the East Block on Parliament Hill. Each guide conducts historical tours which take visitors through a series of rooms restored to the 1870s period, when Sir John A. Macdonald occupied the Prime Minister's office. Tours are conducted in groups of 10 in both French and English. Whereas the Centre Block tour has a stronger current affairs component to it, the East Block tour is historical in focus.

Inside View: For all you political buffs who aspire to life on Parliament Hill, this could be your first step to realizing your life-long dreams. Seriously, if you are interested in history and politics, enjoy interacting with the public, are bilingual, and have strong public speaking skills this is great summer job. You work 40 hours per week, conducting about twelve half-hour tours per day. Shifts are eight hours long and you can expect to work most weekends. Since you'll be guiding visitors day in and day out for two solid months, it will take some effort on your part to keep the tours fresh. You must be able to adapt to the interests of your visitors and be able to tackle the many questions that they will be asking (from the serious and probing to the ridiculous and trivial). You must be flexible and dynamic and think well on your feet.

The application procedure is similar to that of the Centre Block Guide Service, but because this program is not nearly as well advertised, there are fewer applications (sometimes as few as 25 for the 20 positions offered). The written portion of the application's knowledge quiz really tests your familiarity with Canadian history and politics. Expect questions about the House of Commons, the Senate, current Senators and topical issues. If selected for an interview you will be tested further on your historical knowledge, asked various "what if" situational questions and asked to recite a tour in both official languages. You can hold the position for two years and even a third if you apply for the position of team captain. Most students elect to stay on for the second year; thus there may be anywhere from 3 to 6 positions available each year.

Chris Kent, a 22-year-old law student at McGill University, spent two years as a Senate guide. It doesn't seem possible to be more enthusiastic about the experience than Chris was when he spoke about it. He described it as an incredible cultural experience through which you are guaranteed to meet people with whom you wouldn't normally interact with, but with whom you have much in common. For Chris, the people are the best part of the job. He said that the guides do everything together and that the social life after hours is fantastic! Guides come from a very wide range of backgrounds, which helps each of them develop a good idea of what makes Canada tick. Co-workers are your friends long after the work term is up. Chris advises all interested applicants to prepare thoroughly for the written exam and interview. In his mind it is not possible to be overly prepared.

Organization: Government of Canada, House of Commons
Program: The Parliamentary Guide Program

Parliamentary Guide Program
P.O. Box 1111
House of Commons
Ottawa, Ontario
K1A 0A6
(613) 992-7033

Coordinator of Recruitment: Miss Annette Leger

Facts at a Glance:

Age: must be a full-time university student

Duration:
- 4 months (first Monday of May through Labour Day)
- some guides choose to work part-time during the academic year

Regional eligibility: all provinces

Salary:
- $11.00 per hour
- round trip travel expenses from your home to Ottawa

Language: must be fluent in French and English

Getting in:
- applications available from above address or from Student Placement Centres at Canadian Universities
- general knowledge test, personal interview
- deadline is late October

Overview: The Parliamentary Guide Service operates through the Public Information Office and since 1981 has provided millions of visitors with non-partisan information on the role and activities of the House of Commons. Guides lead tours through the Centre Block, the largest of the three Parliament Hill buildings. They provide information about the construction of the buildings as well as explain the role of the House of Commons and the Senate.

Inside View: If you are a dynamic and articulate bilingual university student with an interest in current affairs, politics and history, then why not consider spending a summer in Ottawa leading tours on Parliament Hill. Besides earning a good salary and refining your interpersonal skills, you'll have a chance to work and socialize with other young adults from all across Canada, not to mention the opportunity to meet visitors from around the world.

Guides conduct groups of around 30 on half-hour tours which include the Library of Parliament, the Hall of Honour, and the foyers and chambers of the House of Commons and the Senate. They work 35 hours per week. Since hours are offered seven days a week (tours leave every 10 minutes in the summer), don't expect weekends off—this luxury will occur once every three weeks or so—you'll be very busy.

The selection process is quite involved and consists of a preliminary application form followed by a written examination administered at universities across the country. The test is designed to assess your knowledge of current affairs, history and geography of Canada, and history of the Parliament Buildings. You are responsible for preparing for this test, which is very challenging. There are some 30 students hired each summer (this job you can hold for only one summer) and in any given year there can be upwards of 500 applications for these spots. Since 1988, the Program has pursued a vigorous nationwide recruitment program so that they will have guides from as many of the provinces as possible. All new guides participate in a compulsory two-week training program before starting work. Briefings are given by MPs and House of Commons officials. However, as the Program itself asserts, "No amount of training can prepare guides for some of the questions people ask." A couple of prime examples include the following queer queries, "How much do all the books in the library weigh?" and "Wasn't Lincoln the first Prime Minister?" A sense of humour and the ability to think quickly are undeniably assets for the parliamentary guide.

While in Ottawa, if you're unable to secure your own accommodation, the Program will assist you in obtaining a room in one of the university residences. The guides spend a lot of time together socializing as well as working—and all leave the program having gained a broader understanding of Canada.

Organization: Management Board Secretariat
Program: Ontario/Québec Summer Student Job Exchange Program

Management Board Secretariat
Ontario/Québec Summer Student Job Exchange
595 Bay Street
Suite 303
Toronto, Ontario
M7A 1Y7
(416) 325-0263

Program Assistant: Ms. France Menard

Facts at a Glance:

Age: enrolled in full-time undergraduate or graduate program

Duration: 13 weeks (May-August)

Regional eligibility: Ontario and Québec residents only

Salary:
* approximately $225 to $350 per week depending on academic level
* return travel from home to job

Language: some knowledge of your second official language

Where can I go?
* most positions in Ontario are in Toronto
* most positions in Québec are in Montréal or Québec City

Getting in:
* apply at your school placement office or to above address
* deadline is early January
* quite competitive (1,000 applicants for 300 spots)
* interviews take place in February and March

Overview: This program allows 100 Québec university students to spend a summer in an Ontario Government Ministry office and 100 Ontario university students to work for the government of Québec. Participants have an opportunity to improve their knowledge and understanding of the other province and usually improve their second language tremendously. The most important aspect of the program is the cultural experience and therefore the jobs are not necessarily career-oriented.

Inside View: The Ontario/Québec Summer Job Exchange is a great way to live and work in another province for a summer while improving your second language. You'll be placed in a job in a government office where your duties might range from research projects to acting as a guide. In some cases, jobs are career-oriented, but you should be prepared to accept a position that is not directly related to your field of study.

The interview is crucial, so be prepared. You will be asked about your background, and aspirations, as well as your knowledge of the political process and Ontario-Québec relations. In Ontario the interview will be conducted in French, to get a sense of your ability in that language. Don't worry if you are far from fluently bilingual, questions will also be asked in English if you are having difficulty. While you must have some ability in French, people of many different proficiency levels are accepted. Above all, they are looking for students who are very interested in living in a new culture and who want to continue working towards strong Ontario-Québec relations. If you can show that you are highly motivated and eager to learn, you'll be in good shape. If accepted, you'll be responsible for your own accommodations for the summer.

Martine Bourgault, 21, of the Université de Québec, found the experience rewarding both professionally and personally. The internship-like position gave her first-hand exposure to a lot of inside information and she felt that the experience gained was worth far more to her than the pay.

Note: The same type of interprovincial exchange agreement also exists among Alberta, Manitoba, Saskatchewan and Québec. The programs are not as large as the Ontario-Québec exchange, with Alberta annually sending 45 students to Quebec and Manitoba and Saskatchewan sending only 10 each. All the programs are reciprocal in nature. The addresses for the these three programs follow:

Alberta Career Development and Employment
Program Director: Mr. Don Green
10155 - 102nd Street
8th floor, City Centre
Edmonton, Alberta
T5J 4L5
(403) 422-1184

Manitoba Employment Services and Economic Security
Program Director: Mr Lemma Mekonnen
114 Garry Street
Winnipeg, Manitoba
R3C 1G1
(204) 945-3676

Saskatchewan Public Service Commission Employment Services
Coordinator 2103 - 11th Avenue
Regina, Saskatchewan
S4P 3X9
(306) 787-7657

Saskatewan did not participate in the program in 1993, so call to see if
the program will be revived.

Placement Étudiant de Québec
Coordinator: Anne-Michelle Bergevin
2700 Blvd. Laurier, 3e étage
Ste. Foy, Québec
G1V 2L8
(418) 646-2460
1 (800) 463-2355

Organization: Council of Ministers of Education Canada and the Office of the Secretary of State, Canada
Program: Official-languages Monitor Program

National Coordinator
Official-Languages Monitor Program
Council of Ministers of Education
252 Bloor Street West, Room 5-200
Toronto, Ontario
M5S 1V5
phone: (416) 964-2551, fax (416) 964-2296

Facts at a Glance:

Age:
- must have completed at least 1 year of post-secondary education

Duration:
- part-time: 8 months
- full-time: 10 months

Regional eligibility: all provinces and territories

Salary:
- part-time: $3,500
- full-time: $11,400
- monitors are reimbursed for some of their expenses

Language: fluency in French and English is required

Getting in:
- brochures and application forms are available from universities and colleges and from the regional offices of the Secretary of State and the provincial/territorial coordinators of the program, as well as from the above address
- deadline is mid-February
- an interview is an important part of the selection process

Overview: The part-time program is for bilingual post-secondary students who are attending university or college where their mother tongue is the second language. While there, they act as teaching monitors of French or English as a second language. The full-time program is for post-secondary students who want to take a year away from studies to work as a language monitor in a rural or semi-rural community where their mother tongue is the second language.

Part-time monitors spend eight hours a week helping out in schools, universities, and colleges. Full-time monitors work five hours per day.

Inside View: Monitors work with small conversation groups helping students improve their second-language skills. They also acquaint their students with the culture associated with the language. Applicants are chosen on the basis of their academic background, language ability, and personality. All else being equal, preference is given to students who plan a career teaching English or French as a second language. Anyone thinking about this job should be aware of two other important pieces of information. The first is that while the job is very well paying, depending on what kind of school you are at (elementary, highschool, CEGEP or university) you may really earn every dollar if your school has you speaking, one on one, with thirty kids in one day! Secondly, it is entirely possible that your teaching school will require an hour and a half commute, and you won't be paid for this time.

Organization: Federal Government
Programs: Career Oriented Summer
Employment Program (cosep)
Geological Survey Assistants Program

Senior Staffing Advisor
Geological Survey Student Assistant Program
Energy Mines and Resources Canada
601 Booth Street, Room 237
Ottawa, Ontario
K1A 0E8
(613) 995-4171

Facts at a Glance

Age:

- For COSEP: full-time student at a post secondary institution
- For Geological Assistants Program: 17-25 and a full-time post-secondary Earth Sciences student returning to studies in the fall

Duration: 4 - 6 months

regional eligibility: all provinces

Salary: varies according to education

Where can I go? all over Canada

Getting in:

- applications available at student employment centres or from above address.

- deadline for all COSEP applications is late February, but it is recommended that you apply before December.

Overview This program offers summer jobs in the federal public service that may be relevant to your future career.

Inside View This is an annual program which allows students to gain valuable study-related experience during the summer. To apply, you must complete a COSEP application form, which asks questions about your academic background, including specific courses taken. The program forwards your application to a suitable office and the prospective employer interviews selected candidates. Often an employer will re-hire a student in subsequent summers. The geological program is particularly aimed at students majoring in geology, geophysics, geochemistry and physical geography.

Organization: Natural Science and Engineering Research Council
Program: Undergraduate Student Research Awards

Research Manpower Directorate
NSERC
200 Kent St.
Ottawa, Ontario
KIA IH5
(613) 996-2009

Program officer: Ms Linda Mealing

Facts at a Glance:

Age:
- full-time undergraduate student within 4 terms of graduation
- some positions for first year university women

Duration:
- up to 4 months
- usually May-August, but you can go during the fall and spring

Salary:
- NSERC contributes $900 per month
- return travel from home to the job

Where can I go? anywhere in Canada

Getting in:
- application forms available from science and engineering department heads at all universities or from the NSERC
- deadline dates vary depending on the university or industry

Overview: This program allows students to get valuable first-hand research experience while working in a university or industrial laboratory. Each year 1,850 university and 500 industry positions are made available. Through travel grants, NSERC encourages students to work in an other part of the country. Also, since 1991, NSERC has offered a number of research awards exclusively to female students studying physical sciences or engineering.

Inside View: Competition for these job awards varies depending on where you wish to work. A quota of awards exists at each university and competition for the awards occurs within each institution. Many universities actively advertise their available positions, and while some may choose from internal applicants, quite a few will only consider external applicants. To obtain a position in an industry, a student must first find a job with a company. That company will then forward the application to the NSERC. A list of participating companies is available from the above address.

The major strength of the program is the opportunity to work with a professor or an industrial scientist on his or her research projects. Occasionally it does happen that a student is given only very menial tasks, but for most the work performed is both interesting and challenging. Selection is based on academic performance and letters of reference. It is very important that your application be endorsed by a professor who knows you well, as this is really the selection committee's only basis for decision.

Lenly Adams, a 20-year-old from Moncton, New Brunswick, spent a summer working in bio-chemistry research at Guelph University. He recommends the program as a great way to see how another university operates and especially encourages second-year students interested in summer research to apply. He advises applicants to investigate the work of the professors with whom they might be working to ensure that they will be working with someone whose research is consistent with their own interests.

Organization: Canadian Youth Foundation
Program: Intern Program

55 Parkdale
Ottawa, Ontario
KIY IE5
(613) 761-9206

Executive Director: Ms. Lucie Bohac Konrad

Facts at a Glance:

Age: 18-24

Duration: 1 year (usually May-May, but this is flexible)

Regional eligibility: all provinces

Salary: $18,000

Language: bilingualism an asset but not required

Getting in: apply directly to the above address at any time

Overview: The Canadian Youth Foundation is a non-partisan, non-profit institute established in 1986. The Foundation researches, analyses and monitors the impact of public policies and programs on Canadian youth. Each year, five interns are hired to staff the foundation. This one-year internship on public policy, lobbying and volunteering provides practical experience which develops research, reporting and organizational skills.

Inside View: If you think and express yourself clearly, can show that you have initiative and are an independent worker, this internship might be an ideal vehicle for you. It is a dynamic job involving research, presentations to Senate and other committees, monitoring proceedings such as the CRTC hearings, and writing reports. Emphasis during selection is on your abilities, interests and suitability regardless of your formal education. And, most important, the foundation looks for a real interest in public policy.

Lucie Boileau, a 22-year-old graduate of the University of Ottawa, spent a year as an intern. She was involved in monitoring CRTC hearings, researching for Employment and Immigration Canada, and participated on a cross-country fact-finding tour. She found the position to be a great learning experience, as well as an excellent way to make contacts. Anyone considering applying for an internship should note that this organization may have moved its office by the time our book is out. At the time that we went to press, they were unsure about their future address. So, be sure to phone them before you write for information.

Organization: Canadian Political Science Association
Program: Parliamentary Internship Programme

One Stewart Stret, Suite 205
Ottawa, Ontario
KIN 6H7
phone: (613) 564-7550, fax: (613) 230-2746

Director: Professor Francois Houle

Facts at a Glance

Age: must hold a university degree

Duration: 10 months (September-June)

Regional eligibility: all provinces

Salary:
- $15,500 dollars
- return travel from home to Ottawa

Getting in:
- applications available from above address
- deadline is January 5
- interview in March for selected applicants
- very competitive (250 apply for 10 spots)

Overview: Each year this program provides 10 outstanding young Canadians with a chance to work within the core of the parliamentary process. Interns are assigned to a government backbencher for half of the term and to an opposition backbencher for the other half. Study visits to the Québec and Ontario Legislatures, the U.S. Congress and the British Parliament are integral parts of the program.

Inside View: This is an extremely competitive program, but for those who have what it takes to get accepted it is an outstanding opportunity to gain insight into the everyday work of a Member of Parliament. The interns work alongside their assigned members and perform a multitude of tasks. The exact nature of the work depends largely on the preoccupations of the Member for whom they are working. Participants also undertake a major academic research project as part of their internship. The program is a neutral, non-partisan one which aims to improve understanding between the private and public sectors.

Successful candidates come from all fields and each possesses outstanding educational qualifications and a thorough theoretical knowledge of Parliament. The selection committee also considers the candidate's letters of recommendation, community involvement, and interpersonal skills, as well as his or her potential contribution to the program.

Organization: Canadian Political Science Association and the Legislature of Ontario
Program: Legislative Intern Program

Legislative Intern Program
c/o Mr Doug Arnott
Ontario Legislature
Toronto, Ontario
M7A 1A2
(416) 325-3506

Facts at a Glance:

Age: recent university graduates (average age is 26)

Duration: September to June

Regional eligibility: all provinces

Salary: $16,000 (under review)

Getting in:
- application forms available from above address
- must be a graduate of a Canadian university
- deadline is late January
- interview for short listed candidates
- quite competitive (up to 150 apply for 8 or 9 spots)

Overview: Each year up to nine highly qualified recent university graduates are selected to provide backbenchers in the Ontario Legislature with intelligent, keen assistants. These interns participate in a unique educational experience that gives them first-hand knowledge of the workings of government. Participants spend five months working for a government backbencher and five months working for an opposition backbencher.

Inside View: Organizing a task force tour, answering constituency mail, writing Question Period questions for an MPP, attending meetings, visiting a members constituency and participating in seminars could all be part of your experience as a Legislative Intern at Queen's Park. If this sounds exciting, why not apply. It's a great opportunity to get an up-close view of the workings of a provincial legislature. You can expect to work long hours attending to matters from the mundane to the fascinating. But you can also come out of the entire experience with a great intuitive understanding of how the democratic system works. This program is very similar to the federal one, but some students feel that participants receive more interesting jobs and gain wider experience in the provincial program, since Members usually have more time to spend with the interns and interns have more of an opportunity to shadow their Member.

The program looks for self-motivated people who have a lot of initiative. You must be able to show a strong interest and knowledge of Ontario and of the general political scene. It is also important to be adaptable. Sometimes you can be under-utilized by the Member, but since you choose whom you want to work for, by doing some homework you should be able to pick someone who'll use your services as much as possible. The idea is that you will learn a lot while contributing valuable assistance.

Olga Szkabarnicki, is currently participating in the program. She highly recommends the program but stressed that you really have to want to do it. Often the Members are too busy to get work for you—so the experience is what you make of it. Olga described the internship as an excellent educational work experience and said anyone with the opportunity to participate should jump at the chance. One of the most positive aspects of the year was the amount of respect that she gained for the politicians and the political process. If you participate, don't expect to spend all of your time in Toronto. All interns go on a group visit to governments in Halifax, Québec City, Boston, and Yellowknife .

Note: There are several other intern programs across the country. Below is a brief glance at how they operate.

British Columbia Legislative Intern Program

Speaker's Office
Room 207
Parliament Buildings
Victoria, British Columbia
V8V 1X4
(604) 387-3952

Coordinators: Dr Paul Tennant; Ms Sandy Wharf

- 8 positions
- 6 month position (January 1 - June 30)
- must hold a degree from a B.C. university
- application deadline February 15

- $1,500 stipend per month
- approximately 130 applicants each year
- two-week intensive orientation program followed by six-week assignment with a ministry Policy Department, usually working with an Assistant Deputy Minister of an Executive Director, then placed with a caucus and usually assigned to work with a particular Member

Alberta Legislative Intern Program

Alberta used to offer a legislative intern experience for four recent university graduates. But due to recent budget cuts, this program has been cut. Interested students might want to inquire into whether the program may be resuscitated for 1994-95 by writing to the address below.

Legislative Assembly Office
801 Legislative Annex
Edmonton, Alberta
T5K 1E4
(403) 427-2580

Manitoba Legislative Intern Program

Clerk's Office, Room 237, Legislative Building,
450 Broadway,
Winnipeg, Manitoba,
R3C 0V8
(204) 945-3636

Coordinator: Dr Cathy Brock, Dr Barry Ferguson

- 6 positions
- September through August
- recent university graduates who are Manitoba residents
- application deadline is late February
- $1,200 monthly stipend
- interns placed with a caucus office

Québec Legislative Intern Program

Fondation Jean Charles Bonenfant
AF Richard Breton
National Assembly
Québec, PQ
(418) 528-1589

Coordinator: Mme Maide Legoffe

- 4 positions
- September through June
- must be a graduate of a Quebec university in political science, history, economics, law, journalism or communications
- application deadline is late April
- $15,000 stipend
- interns work for one Member for the entire period

Nova Scotia Legislative Intern Program

c/o Professor Adamson
Acadia University
Political Science Department
Wolfville, Nova Scotia
B0P 1X0
(902) 424-5707

Coordinator: Professor Agar Adamson

- 3 positions
- September through June
- residents of Nova Scotia who are recent university graduates or recent graduates of any Nova Scotia university
- application deadline April 1
- $1,400 per month stipend
- interns are placed with a Minister's office or Deputy Minister's office for half the program and then work for a caucus member where they work on research projects

Organization: United Nations Secretariat
Program: Graduate Student Intern Programme

United Nations Secretariat
United Nations
New York, New York
10017 USA
(212) 963-1234

Program Coordinator: Mr. Adnan Issa

Facts at a Glance:

Age:
- In theory Graduate students, this includes law students, in a few cases non-graduate students are accepted
- average age about 26 years old
- you cannot already hold a graduate degree

Duration: 6 weeks - 3 months depending on the job

Regional eligibility: all provinces

Salary: no salary - volunteer position

Languages:
- must speak 2 languages
- it's an advantage if you speak an uncommon laguage i.e. Russian, Japanese, etc

Where can I go? New York and Geneva, Switzerland

Getting In:
- application forms available from the above address
- application deadline is 6 months before you wish to go (ie apply in November for June)
- there are no interviews so your application is crucial

Overview: There are internships of various durations available with the United Nations in both New York and Geneva. There is a formal Internship administered within the United Nations Secretariat as well as intership positions with individual United Nation agencies such as the World Health Organization, UNICEF, the International Labour Organization to name just a few. These positions are designed to give young people from around the world the opportunity to see the United Nations from the inside and to expose them to a broader understanding of what the United Nations is all about.

Inside View: Imagine working with 80 other young people at the world's chief diplomatic mission - hobnobbing with Delegation Chiefs, sitting in on sessions of the Security Council and meeting people from around the world. If this appeals to you, an internship at the United Nations is just what you may be looking for. Students from around the world find internships each year and although few Canadian tend to apply, Canadians are very well liked and stand an excellent chance of being selected. There are also positions available with the various United Nations agencies and if you have a particular specialization (for example in health sciences) you stand a good chance of finding a position with one of those agencies.

Jennifer Woolcombe, a 27 year old law student at McGill University, was an intern in the Department of Public Information in New York during the summer of 1992. She was involved in preparations for the World Conference on Human Rights and the International Year for World Indigenous People. Jennifer did everything from writing articles for press kits to researching and attending organizational meetings. As a result of her summer at the United Nations she got a great inside look at the workings of the organization. She was fortunate to have been encouraged to talk to any Delegates she desired, to sit in on committee meetings and to have been given interesting work.

Jennifer told us that how interesting your work is will depend on who you end up working for so it's a bit of a crap shoot. But she reinforced that whatever your interest, you'll find something to your taste because the United Nations does such varied work - everything from peacekeeping to health services. Jennifer met a lot a neat people and made good friends from Columbia, Japan, Germany and Switzerland and recommends the experience very highly. The only downside is that you don't get paid and you have to arrange your own accomodations in New York and Geneva. However, you might see if you can arrange a stipend or research grant from your university or a professor to help you support yourself.

Organization: Junior Achievement of Canada

One Westside Drive
Toronto, Ontario
M9C 1B2
phone: (416) 622-4602, fax: (416) 622-6861

Program Director: Mr Jim Billing

Overview: Junior Achievement is an international, non-profit organization which offers high school students the opportunity to discover at first hand the real workings of the business world. Supported by business and industry, the organization is dedicated to teaching young people about the free-enterprise system. Each year 8,100 young people, assisted by 1,775 advisors in over 125 cities and towns across Canada, form their own board of directors, work force and sales staff. Achievers meet with, listen to and get assistance from professionals from the over 350 Canadian businesses that are an integral part of J.A. Many students also earn the opportunity to attend provincial and national conferences and are eligible for scholarships and other rewards.

Inside View: If the world of business, balance sheets and shareholders' reports interests you, J.A. can provide practical, learning-by-doing experience starting and managing a company. Chapters exist from St. John's to Victoria. Each fall, J.A. companies composed of 12 to 20 students are formed. They elect officers—a president, vice presidents, etc.—and decide upon a company name and a product. Capital is raised by selling shares to relatives, friends and the general public.

Anyone can join J.A., and, as we learned from 17-year-old Josée Oulette from St. Bruno, Québec, you get every type of kid at the local level. Some students are naturally highly motivated, while others are shy at first but soon become actively involved. Still others decide that the business world is not their calling. For those of you who think that J.A. is full of dreadful bores, 19-year-old Craig Flint from Midland, Ontario, will tell you that his J.A. chapter had this reputation for several years. This has changed, however, as the result of the efforts of a small group of students who publicized the value of J.A. experience and promoted the organization to their friends.

Based on marketability, feasibility and production costs, companies make products ranging from breadboards to clocks, T-shirts to recipe books, and first-aid kits to money boxes. The Board of Directors plans and executes the promotion and sale of the product through door-to-door sales, exhibitions, and wholesale distribution. J.A. companies pay all applicable provincial and federal taxes. Company members must also keep financial records, prepare financial and management reports, and work on production lines. Every April, J.A. companies are liquidated; shareholders in profitable companies have their share redeemed and receive dividends. In every respect J.A. companies operate like "real" companies. The company meets for two and a half hours one night a week to take care of business.

Andrea Sorensen, 17, from St. John's, Newfoundland, joined J.A. the first year it came into her region. She stresses that what you get out of J.A. depends on what you put into it, and she strongly recommends J.A. as a means of learning about the real business world, as well as a way of helping you make career decisions. Loren Lailey, 17, from Calgary, Alberta, adds that J.A. also allows students to develop self confidence, leadership, interpersonal and entrepreneurial skills. It allowed Craig Flint to discover leadership abilities and to become more outgoing. Once too shy to talk to anyone, Craig is now frequently asked to speak at conferences and Rotary Club meetings. According to Mike Brun, 18, of St. John, New Brunswick, J.A. teaches a sense of responsibility, teamwork and respect for employee-manager relations.

We spoke with several students who admitted that at first they disliked J.A. but the more involved they became, the more they understood and enjoyed what they were doing.

You should also know that throughout the year achievers are constantly evaluated. There are regional and provincial conferences where students meet to hear leading business figures speak and to participate in workshops. At the end of the year a banquet is held where students are given awards for their performance (top salesperson, company of the year, etc.). Also annually, one student from each club is chosen to attend CANJAC (a national conference for cream-of-the-crop achievers). Selection is based on a set of exams and interviews. CANJAC is held at in a different Canadian city each year and is the most enjoyable part of J.A. It is a week of lectures, workshops, and people-meeting. Past speakers have included Sonja Bata, Director of Bata Ltd.; the President of General Motors; and vice-presidents of Defasco, Westinghouse Canada, Stelco and McDonald's.

Many students also found that J.A. experience led to summer job offers. At 17 years of age Josée Oulette was recruited for a high paying job with C.N. When trying to find a job, or when applying to a university or for a scholarship, all the students with whom we spoke felt that J.A. gave them an edge.

GETTING IN: If you are interested in joining J.A., check the white pages of the phone book or contact the national office at the address above.

Organization: Ontario Ministry of Industry, Trade and Technology
Program: Youth And Student Venture Capital Program

Ontario Ministry of Industry Trade and Technology
Youth Start-up Capital
625 Church Street, 1st floor
Toronto, Ontario
M4Y 2E8
(416) 326-5820

Program coordinator: Ms Lynne Allen

Facts at a Glance:

Age:

- student program: 15 to 29 and returning to high school, college or university in the fall
- youth program: 18 to 24 and not attending school full-time, 25 to 29 with a recent post-secondary degree

Regional eligibility:

- Ontario residents only
- similar programs exist in most other provinces

Salary:

- student program—interest-free loans of up to $3,000 (must repay loan on or before October 1 of the year received)
- youth program—interest-free loans of up to $7,500 (repayments begin in the 13th month)

Getting in:

- applications available from the Royal Bank, school guidance offices, or from the above address
- very thorough application process
- applications are submitted to your Chamber of Commerce for the student program
- applications for student program are accepted until early June
- no deadline for youth program

Overview: These programs allow young entrepreneurs to (a) set up their own summer business or (b) set up their own full-time business, both with the help of interest-free loans. They also provide professional guidance, advice and assistance throughout the entire process. In 1992, over 700 businesses were approved. To apply, you need only have a good idea, a sound business plan and the desire and commitment to make your venture a success.

Inside View: As the old saying goes, "There is nothing like being in business for yourself." For many, the idea of starting their own business is intriguing, but the limitations appear to be staggering. The students we spoke with have without exception found working for themselves to be a great opportunity. All admit that it is a lot of work, but the financial and personal rewards and skills acquired are well worth it. Student Venture Capital can assist you with one major stumbling block by providing interest-free loans. Contrary to what you might think, you don't have to be the next Donald (or Ivana) Trump to start your own business. The businesses individuals start range from basic lawn-cutting firms to t-shirt design shops, to sophisticated high-tech endeavors. The majority of projects are service-oriented.

If you have an idea, pick up an application form. Filling out this detailed form forces you to carefully think out your plans. The subsequent interview is also grueling to ensure that you are really on top of your proposal. Your success is monitored over the summer and advice on tax-planning, marketing and legal advice is always available. There is risk involved, but the program is designed to ensure that this risk is a calculated one.

David Fear, an 18-year-old from Toronto, started Coolies Clothing Co. with the help of an interest-free loan. This allowed him to set his own hours and be his own boss. However, he soon found out that those hours were usually 7am-9pm, seven days a week! Like many students on the program, David will continue his business into the school year. Caroline de Gorter and Julie Greenwood, both music students at Queen's University, have financed their Young Musical Theatre in Stratford, Ontario, with Student Venture loans. Both have learned a lot about business and improved their organizational skills while working in their field of interest. They encourage anyone with an idea to go for it, but stress that you must be sure of your market.

One other businessman we spoke with was 19-year-old Michael Bleeher, from the University of Western Ontario. Michael used technical and sales knowledge he had picked up co-editing his high school newspaper to put together a calendar which he marketed to Guelph University. Once Michael had sold the university on the idea of providing freshmen with weekly organizer calendars, he went about the task of selling advertising space to campus-life and student oriented companies. Selling the advertising space more than covered the cost of producing the calendar and the profits rolled in when the university purchased a large quantity. Next summer Michael plans to expand his operation to cater to a few more universities.

STUDENT PROFILE

Name: Jennifer McGowan
Age: 22
Home: Mississauga, Ontario

The Business of Clowning Around

In just two summers, Jennifer McGowan turned her recreational pastimes of unicycling and juggling into a full-time summer business. In an attempt to find summer employment that offered more than "the traditional summer job," Jennifer started her own business, Rent-A-Clown, in 1986. She was 17 years old at the time. By 1988, she employed 20 students.

Jennifer was interested in getting a job that involved performing unicycle and juggling tricks, but knew that the Student Employment Centre was not overflowing with such listings. Through the Ontario Student Venture Capital program (page 55), Jennifer obtained a $1,200 interest free loan that allowed her to start up her own clown rental service. She saw a market for clowns as a means of publicity for stores and hoped that she could get businesses to hire her to hand out flyers and promote specials.

Even though she thoroughly planned her business and attended the professionally led seminar workshops offered by the Student Venture Program, she soon discovered that stores were not her market: in fact, business was downright rotten. Where others might have quit, however, Jennifer persevered. She started performing at birthday parties and managed to pay off her loan. But her business did not end here. She realized that by marketing herself for hire at private birthday parties, she might be able to create a very successful business. So throughout the fall and winter she continued to run her business on a small scale. In the spring she put up interview notices in schools and student employment centres looking for students interested in being a clown for the summer. Again she applied for and received a Student Venture Loan, this time for $3,000.

In her second summer of operation, she had 20 part-time and two full-time clowns working for her. She advertises her company widely, hiring her clowns to perform at birthday parties. In the summer of 1987 she also negotiated a contract with The Bay and Simpsons to have her clowns do face painting. The Bay hired her to set up face painting booths at each of their 12 stores in the area. And she formed a partnership with the owner of a Mississauga Teen Club. They began to co-host birthday parties in the fall of '87.

Although initially Jennifer often performed as a clown herself, now she rarely finds time to accept assignments. Rent-A-Clown became so successful that she devoted more and more of her time to the business side of the operation. In fact, Rent-A-Clown rapidly evolved into a placement agency for clown performers. In general, Rent-A-Clown was very successful in its second summer.

Jennifer's entrepreneurial spirit resulted in a lot of personal, business and financial satisfaction. She acquired a lot of business experience, and some very important skills at a young age. These will definitely stand her in good position in the future. Although it was rough going at first, Jennifer stuck with it and is the first person to tell anyone involved in such an activity to keep going. "With hard work it will eventually work out," she advises.

Depending where your interests lie, you might consider starting your own business one summer. If you have an idea, look into a Student Venture Capital Program. Most provinces administer a program similar to the one in which Jennifer was involved. For more information inquire at your provincial Department of Development, Ministry of Labour, Ministry of Industry and Small Business Development or Opportunity Company (Alberta only).

Work Overseas

Au Pair Survival

Working as an "au pair", (or "mother's helper", as they are more commonly known in North America) has long been a popular way for a young person to live, work and travel abroad. In many cases, it allows the au pair to learn or improve a second language while living in a far-off place. If you've been thinking you might like to be an au pair there are some things you should know.

The usual arrangement is that you'll do light housework and take care of the children in exchange for your room, all of your meals and a small salary. Your position will probably last for either a summer or a school year.

In some cases, the au pair is treated like a new member of the family: he or she is taken along on vacations, expected to eat meals with the family and given reasonable amounts of free time. In Canada, families often hire mother's helpers for the summer months while at their cottages. If your family doesn't happen to own a sumptuous country place, that doesn't mean you can't spend your summer living at one! Make no mistake—it won't be a relaxing vacation for you. You'll be expected to work at least five or six hours almost every day. Most of that time will be spent entertaining the little kids, taking them to the beach, dishing them up ice cream, or even changing their diapers. Let's face it: if you don't love little kids you might as well forget the au pair thing right now. In fact, some agencies won't place you unless you have some experience working with children.

While many people get placed with excellent families who provide comfortable living quarters, hearty meals, and fair work hours, there are also those who get stuck in less than ideal households. It does happen that students are hired as cheap labour and worked like slaves. In this situation, the relationship that exists between the family and the au pair is one of master and hired hand. Remember that people's idea of what constitutes "light housework" can greatly vary. Finding yourself in what you consider an unfair arrangement can be particularly hard if you're in a foreign country. That is why it is very important that before accepting an au pair position you do your homework.

There are many au pair placement agencies in Canada, the U.S. and Europe, of varying reputation and credibility. When dealing with a placement agency, be sure to investigate their status with the Better Business Bureau. It is also a good idea to ask the agency for the names of a few people whom they have placed, and call these people. In this case word of mouth is the best way to learn whether you can trust a particular agency.

You may also be able to obtain an au pair position without the help of a third party. Advertisements are often placed in The Globe and Mail or your local newspaper by families across Canada and abroad who are looking for help. Of course, the ideal way to find a position is through family members or friends: this way you'll probably earn a higher wage and you can be sure of the family's reputation.

However you decide to search for your au pair position, be sure to find out exactly what your duties, obligations and privileges will be. If you do this, your experience should be terrific!

Listed below are just a few established au pair agencies you might like to contact for more information. We stress that we cannot comment on the credibility of any of these private agencies.

Agencé M.F.M.

18 Westminster Avenue North
Room 108
Montréal, Québec
H4X 1Y9
(514) 485-3604

Director: Mme. M.F. Deslauriers

- places females only
- ages 19 to 25
- placements in France and England
- minimum one-year placements
- good references required

Cultural Homestay International

103 Redwood Court
Sherwood Park, Alberta
T8A 1L2
(800) 463-1061

Program Manager: Ms Vivian L. Hart

- ages 18 to 25 (females only)
- placements in France and perhaps England and Germany by 1994

C.H.I. places high school graduates in French homes to act as au pairs. The cost to be placed is about $2000. This will pay for your round trip air travel, insurance, work permits and the services of a C.H.I. representative in France. You will work in a home a certain number of hours per week and in exchange you get room and board and about $350 per month. You have to make a committment of at least six months up to one year. If you're a highschool graduate with some baby sitting experience and enough French to communicate they should be able to place you.

Carnaby Bureau

36 Marshall Street
London W1A 4QE
U.K.

- placements in Germany, Italy, Japan, Greece and France

Work Permits

Getting a job overseas may sound like great fun, but you must be aware that each country has laws regulating foreign workers. In most countries you will need a work visa in order to legally accept employment. Some students accept under-the-table short-term jobs when abroad, but this is illegal and potentially risky.

If you are interested in short-term, part-time work abroad, you may be able to obtain what is called a Working Holiday Visa. Canadians are able to get these permits for Japan, Australia and the U.K. The visa allows you to travel in the country and accept short-term jobs whenever you wish. However, you are often limited to working a maximum number of hours a week. While you probably won't get great job experience, this is a fantastic way to finance your trip. Applications are available at the embassies and consulates of participating countries.

To accept a full-time job abroad, most countries require that you have a confirmed job offer before you can be issued a work permit. Even then, some insist that you be sponsored through a joint government agreement. If you are thinking of working abroad, we suggest that you contact the relevant country's Canadian Embassy or Consulate. They will be able to provide you with information regarding work visa requirements. They should also be able to inform you of government agreements that may assist you in gaining entry to work in their country.

You may also want to refer to *The Directory of Overseas Summer Jobs* (Vacation Work, 1993), which has a section at the back entitled "Visa, Residence and Work Regulations". It has information on work and visa regulations for 25 countries and, while intended for U.K. readers, the information is also useful to Canadians. *Work, Study, Travel Abroad: The Whole World Handbook*, by Marjorie Cohen, is an other source of information on obtaining work visas.

As a final note, embassies are in general very helpful in providing you with answers to any questions you may have about their country. They are a source of information that you should definitely take advantage of.

Organization: Canada World Youth

Canada World Youth
386 Bloor Street West
Toronto, Ontario M5S 1X4
(514) 922-0776

Canadian Director: Mr Paul Shay

Facts at a Glance:

Age: 17-20

Duration: 7 months

Regional eligibility: all provinces

Cost:
- $500 (gathered through fundraising)
- $200 participation fee (many scholarships available based on financial need)

That covers:
- return travel from home to overseas site
- room and board
- modest weekly allowance

Where can I go? one of 40 Third World countries

Getting in:
- application forms available from your regional CWY office
- thorough application process
- deadline is mid - January
- very competitive (4,000 applicants for 450 spots)

Overview: Canada World Youth provides young Canadians with the opportunity to work and live in both a new region of Canada and a developing nation. The program matches each successful applicant with a foreign counterpart. Participants and their twins, along with a group of other volunteers, live and work in a Canadian community where they are billeted with families for 14 weeks. Participants then travel to their counterpart's country where they live for the next 14 weeks. While in the host country, they are required to make personal appearances and present cultural shows.

Inside View: Canada World Youth is not the program for everyone, but everyone who applies stands approximately the same chance of being accepted. When building their work teams, CWY directors attempt to create a microcosm of Canada, selecting participants of all religions, languages, occupations, backgrounds and from every physical region of Canada. Through this program you can expect to learn as much about your Third World exchange country and its people as you will about Canada, its people and yourself. You will probably learn another language, be exposed to several new lifestyles and learn about the similarities between peoples. The experience is an informal education in geography, politics, history and diplomacy.

To apply, you fill out an application form which primarily asks about your socio-demographic background and your views on international development. The initial selection process is a random selection based on obtaining a good mix of Canadians. If chosen you will participate in an intensive day-long evaluation session to assess your ability to work with others under stressful conditions. If you make the grade, you will be assigned a Third World counterpart and told where you'll be posted in Canada.

All the CWY people we spoke with felt privileged to have been involved with the program, describing it as an exciting and unique challenge. They unanimously stressed that the program, while eye-opening and fun, was also a lot of work. If you plan to sit around soaking up the sun and scenery, forget it—this is definitely not a tourist operation. Caroline Meehen, a 21-year-old University of Toronto student, went on a Canada World Youth exchange after her second year of university. She worked on an organic vegetable farm in Courtney, B.C., and then spent three months in Ecuador where she taught in a girl's school. She also helped paint the school and run a potato farm. Both Caroline and Ann Mauchline, a 22-year-old Ryerson student who went to B.C. and Indonesia with CWY, stressed that you have to work at getting along with your counterpart and your group. There are often age and maturity discrepancies in the twinning, so you must be flexible.

Organization: National Air and Space Museum at the Smithsonian Institute
Program: Internship Program

Intern Coordinator, Education Division
National Air and Space Museum
Smithsonian Institute
Washington, D.C. 20056
(202) 786-2106

Program director: Ms Myra Banks

Facts at a Glance:

Age: university undergraduates and first year graduate students

Duration: 13 weeks (January - April)

Regional eligibility: all provinces

Salary: varies depending on the position, alot are volunteer

Where Can I go? Washington, D.C.

Getting in:
- application forms available from above address
- essay, transcript (G.P.A. of 2.8 required) and letters of recommendation
- deadline is November 15

Overview: Every year a number of internships are offered at the National Air and Space Museum at the Smithsonian Institution in Washington, D.C. These positions offer a unique behind the scenes experience at one of the world's most visited museums. Responsibilities of some recent positions have included guiding tours, raising funds, developing a hands-on exhibition called "How Things Fly", and working in a photo lab. Various amounts of experience are required for the different internships. Although these positions are targeted to American students (i.e. advertised on campus bulletin boards), Canadians are welcome and encouraged to apply. The details of the program vary each year so it is best for you to write to the above address for current information.

Organization: Youth Challenge International
Program: Overseas Volunteer Program

11 Soho Street
Toronto, Ontario
M5T 1Z6
(416) 971-9846

International director: Mr Grant Hogg

Facts at a Glance:

Age: 18 to 25

Duration: 3 months

Regional eligibility: all provinces

Cost: $3,300 (raised through fund raising)

That covers:
- airfare
- accommodations and meals
- materials and incidental expenses

Where can I go? South America or the Arctic (in 1994)

Getting in:
- application forms available from above address (enclose a self-addressed stamped envelope)
- applications accepted year round
- must speak English and be able to swim 500 metres
- selection "experience weekends" held in fall and spring

Overview: Building upon the successes of Operation Raleigh, a new Canadian-based initiative—Youth Challenge International—combines community service and environmental research in adventurous projects conducted by young volunteers. During 1993, Youth Challenge coordinated dynamic projects in Guyana, Costa Rica and the Solomon Islands which provided over 100 Canadians with the opportunity to live and work with youth from the these and other countries. Similar projects are undertaken each year. "Challengers" make important personal contributions towards scientific endeavors, community development and the environment. In the process, they acquire new skills, and learn the value of teamwork and international cooperation. Regardless of the program, Youth Challenge is sure to provide an unforgettable experience which will have a profound effect upon the lives of all who participate.

Inside View: Youth Challenge is a non-profit organization created by past participants of the Operation Raleigh Canada Foundation. To give you an idea of what this program is all about let us tell you about a past project they have undertaken. In 1990, 65 young Canadians worked in Guyana and the U.S.S.R. on research and community service projects. The following is a lengthy quote about the experience of ten lucky Canadians.

> On May 25, 1990, ten Canadian and ten Soviet youth, aged 19 to 25 will travel to their base camp at the foot of the Northern Ural Mountains. Gathering environmental data along their route, the team will hike across the Ural Range from Europe to Asia, descend into Western Siberia in rafts along the Voykar and Ob Rivers, to eventually reach a remote Nantzy village, where a school house will be constructed. At the completion of the project, the group will travel to northwest Siberia to join Soviet scientists in a study of the environmentally sensitive Yamal Peninsula.
> In late July, the crew will be flown to Canada, where extensive training will prepare team members for the rigours of Canada's high Arctic. Following transport to the remote Inuit community of Arctic Bay on the northeast coast of Baffin Island, Venturers will then set out in kayaks to conduct wildlife surveys along sections of both the Borden and Steensby peninsulas. Across ancient river valleys and open tundra, the team will monitor migrating caribou herds, bear populations and breeding birds. The group will then traverse the Arctic waters of Admiralty Inlet, reaching base camp at Arctic Bay, where they will work with Inuit villagers on the final community project.

If this kind of experience sounds fascinating to you, why not give Youth Challenge a call and find out what they have planned for the future? The application process is somewhat involved and includes filling out a four-page questionnaire, having someone write a reference letter and later participating in a "selection weekend". During this weekend outdoors, stressful situations are simulated and the committee will look for people who work well in groups and have a sense of humour and initiative. If you're chosen (it's fairly competitive because so few spaces exist), you'll then enter a stage of fundraising and training. For example, those chosen for the Guyana project needed to (a) learn how to repair mountain bikes and generators,

(b) earn a ham radio license, (c) earn a bronze cross in swimming, and (d) take an advanced first aid course, before heading to the project.

Ken Tong, a 22 year old Ontario university student, went to Guyana in the fall of 1992. Ken told us that the selection weekend itself left him with a mental high and that being accepted for the actual program was a sort of bonus. He spent the three months working on a study of the rain forests, building a school in an Amerindian village accessible only by canoe and doing research in the capital city of Georgetown. His accomodation during the projects ranged from a hammock suspended under a tarp to a church. Ken was wowed by this program - it really made a difference in his life.

Applications are accepted all year long and the selection weekends are held in the spring and fall. Because of the commitment required to raise funds, learn new skills and then participate on the project, it's next to impossible to be a student at the same time. For an experience such as this it is worthwhile to take a term or a year away from your studies. Of course, this makes Youth Challenge an ideal opportunity for you if you're no longer in school. There are no academic requirements at all and they look for a broad range of personalities and backgrounds.

Organization: Canadian Federation of Students
Program: Student Work Abroad Program (SWAP)

Canadian Federation of Students Services
243 College Street, 5th Floor
Toronto, Ontario
M5T 2Y1
Phone: (416) 977-3703

Director: Mr David Smith

Facts at a Glance:

See chart on page 78 for details on the many options now offered

Getting in:
- applications available from your local Travel Cuts office
- cover letter explaining why you are interested in SWAP
- competition varies according to the country

Overview: SWAP offers young Canadians the chance to work over-seas while on vacation by providing them with a working-holiday visa. The purpose of the program is to allow students a chance to extend their visits abroad by supplementing their money with short-term jobs. Along with the work permit, SWAP provides participants with a two-day orientation upon arrival in the host country. They also suggest background reading material before leaving Canada and pro-vide a job-finding service once in the host country. Furthermore, because SWAP is administered by Travel Cuts and all air fares must be booked through this agency, discount rates are available.

Inside View: If you're planning to do some extended touring around Europe or the South Pacific, why not extend your vacation with the extra money you can earn by working at short-term jobs?

Whether you'd like to work for a couple of months in a London bookshop, or for a full year at an Australian resort, SWAP can save you the hassle of getting the necessary work permits. They also book your flights (you have no choice in this matter), and give you a two-day orientation upon arrival in the host country.

Over the past couple of years the SWAP program has expanded considerably. The doors to Germany, Czechoslovakia, Hungary and Poland have now been opened to Canadian students looking for a working holiday out of the country. Because these four countries are new to the system, it is probably safe to assume that SWAP's job-finding networks there will not be as complete and efficient as they are in Britain or Japan.

According to Rachael Clark, a 20-year-old from Berwick, Nova Scotia, the orientation she and her group received in Sydney was interesting, but not very helpful. She wrote to a friend, "At the end of the first two days I was left with the feeling of, 'Is that it?'" She added that although it was a rocky start, she had no trouble finding work on her own. It is important to keep in mind that SWAP does not pretend to do everything for you. What they offer is more like a bit of advice and the security of knowing that someone's there in case you really run into disaster. Rachael spent a full year living and working all over Australia, managing to catch some of the America's Cup while she was at it. That's the beauty of SWAP: the jobs you are likely to find are temporary and so you can easily divide your time between flaking out on a beach and waiting tables. It's not a bad trade-off. After her SWAP experience, Rachael ended up saying, "I've never been more content, confident and sure about where I'm going. Knowledge like that couldn't have come from years studying at university."

Brian Uhl, a Brock University student who also went to Australia with SWAP, had nothing but praise for the program. He too found many jobs, including waiting tables, acting as a courier and tutoring French. Previous experience in service industry jobs helped him to both get accepted to the program and more readily find work in Australia. Brian managed to save enough money from his various jobs to finance stopovers in New Zealand, Fiji and Hawaii on his way home.

SWAP at a glance:

COUNTRY	BRITAIN	IRELAND	FINLAND	FRANCE	GERMANY	EASTERN EUROPE	AUSTRALIA	NEW ZEALAND	JAPAN	U.S.A.
ELIGIBILITY AND AGE LIMITS	FULL AND PART TIME STUDENTS AND '93 GRADS. AGES 18 TO 27	FULL AND PART TIME STUDENTS AND '93 GRADS AGES 18 TO 30	FULL AND PART TIME STUDENTS AND '93 GRADS AGES 18 TO 30 INCLUSIVE FOR TRAINEES AND 18 TO 23 INCLUSIVE FOR FAMILY PROG.	FULL TIME STUDENTS AND '93 GRADS MINIMUM AGE 18. NO MAXIMUM AGE LIMIT.	FULL TIME STUDENTS AND '93 GRADS MINIMUM AGE 18. NO MAXIMUM AGE LIMIT	FULL TIME STUDENTS AND '93 GRADS 18 TO 30 INCLUSIVE.	NO STUDENT STATUS REQUIRED 18 TO 30 INCLUSIVE.	FULL TIME STUDENTS AND '93 GRADS 18 TO 30 INCLUSIVE	NO STUDENT STATUS REQUIRED 18 TO 30 INCLUSIVE.	FULL TIME STUDENTS AND '93 GRADS MINIMUM AGE 18. NO MAXIMUM AGE LIMIT
APPLICATION DEADLINES	YEAR ROUND DEPARTURES. APPLY AT LEAST 8 WEEKS PRIOR TO DEPARTURE DATE.	YEAR ROUND DEPARTURES. APPLY AT LEAST 6 WEEKS PRIOR TO DEPARTURE DATE.	JANUARY 15, 1993 FOR EARLY JUNE DEPARTURES	MARCH 1, 1993 FOR MAY/JUNE/JULY DEPARTURES JUNE 1, 1993 FOR SEPT DEPARTURES	MARCH 1, 1993 FOR MAY/JUNE DEPARTURES	MARCH 1, 1993 NO DEPARTURES PRIOR TO MAY 1, 1993	MARCH 1, 1993 FOR MAY DEPARTURES. JUNE 1, 1993 FOR SEPTEMBER DEPARTURES	MARCH 1, 1993 FOR MAY DEPARTURES, JUNE 1, 1993 FOR AUGUST DEPARTURES	YEAR ROUND DEPARTURES. APPLY AT LEAST 8 WEEKS PRIOR TO DEPARTURE DATE.	MARCH 1, 1993 NO DEPARTURES BEFORE JUNE 1, 1993.
REGISTRATION FEE (INCLUDES GST)	$215	$160	$215	$215	$215	$215	$250	$225	$225	$150
SUPPORT FUNDS	$1000	$1000	TRAINEE $700 FAMILY $500	$1000	$1000	$1500	$2000	$1000	$2000	$400 WITH JOB OR SPONSOR, $750 WITH TENTATIVE JOB OFFER
VISA	ANY PERIOD UP TO ...	ANY 4 MONTH PERIOD ...	JUNE, JULY AND AUGUST	ANY 3 MONTH PERIOD COMMENCING	ANY 3 MONTH PERIOD COMMENCING	ANY 4 MONTH PERIOD COMMENCING	UP TO 1 YEAR	FROM ARRIVAL UNTIL OCTOBER ...	ANY PERIOD UP TO ONE YEAR	ANY PERIOD FROM JUNE 1/93 TO OCT 1993

Teaching in Asia

Asia—the new frontier of the 1990s. As more and more North American businesses begin doing business with countries such as Japan, Taiwan, and Thailand and as the Hong Kong people prepare for 1997, young people in Canada are studying Japanese and Chinese in increasing numbers. At the same time, Asians from many countries are scrambling to learn English by the millions. The number of private language schools boggles the mind—the only thing more surprising is the amount of money Asians are willing to pay to take English conversation classes. Whether you're interested in travelling and picking up short-term work, spending a year or two working in one city, or studying a new language and working to pay the bills, there is an opportunity out there for you. While it is possible to make a fair bit of cash teaching in a country such as Japan, these jobs shouldn't be looked on as "a get-rich-quick scheme". Those who go over just "for the money" don't usually last very long and often don't enjoy the experience.

To live in Asia takes an adaptable personality, someone who is flexible and doesn't expect life to be like in Canada. This is very much a cultural and educational experience for the Westerner. The customs are strange. You must get used to how Asians think and there will be many obstacles and frustrations that occur due to language barriers. Living in Asia is a great lesson in diplomacy and patience. In countries such as China, expect things to happen very slowly—be prepared to deal with a lot of red tape and annoyances. In Japan you'll have to adapt to the formality and "super-politeness" that characterize business in Japan. Leave your bad temper, strong words, and impatience back in Canada—they will get you nowhere in the land of Sony, kimonos and sushi. In Thailand, if you stay in Bangkok, you'll have to adjust to horrible crowds, incredible traffic congestion, and outrageous noise and air pollution. But if you do your homework—read a lot about the culture and customs, learn some of the local language and go over expecting things to be different, you can have the experience of a lifetime. With your eyes wide open and a willingness to be open to new ideas and ways of doing things, you can see and do many new and exciting things. You'll find out that you learn just as much about Canada as about whatever new country you happen to be in, since you can't help making comparisons and considering the strengths and weaknesses of each culture. There may be many things you won't like about your Asian home. Because you've done your background reading, you may understand why certain situations occur or why people act in certain ways, but in many situations it won't make it any easier to accept.

Two common teaching situations

With A Private Language School: Commonly involves a year-long contract or at the very least a six-month commitment. This type of arrangement is secure and the school sometimes houses you and provides meals. You might teach young children basic grammar and vocabulary in the morning and hold a conversational class in the afternoon with a group of professionals. Some schools offer to pay your airfare if you sign a contract of a certain length.

Freelance: This type of work is best found by answering the many ads to be found in newspapers and employment centres or by placing an ad yourself. This arrangement is ideal for someone who desires flexibility and freedom—work as much or as little as suits you. Giving private lessons enables you to charge more per hour and thus, if you put in full days, working freelance can be very profitable. A fringe benefit to freelance is the fact that your lunches and dinners (that's when most businessmen have time for a little bit of paid English conversation) will often be paid for on top of your hourly rate.

China

Many universities in China hire native English speakers to teach in their classrooms. The best way to find these jobs is to write directly to the English Department enclosing a resumé and letters of recommendation. Don't expect a prompt response—nothing happens quickly in China and you may well wait six months before hearing from anyone. You can expect to make somewhere around $150 per month as well as having room and board provided on the university campus. The salary is very low, but so is the price of food and travel in the country. So, while you won't be able to save much, if anything, the money you earn while there will be enough to cover necessities. Foreigners usually live in separate areas, away from Chinese students and teachers. Your dining room would also likely be separate. You can expect to work up to 18 hours per week and the course curriculum is usually provided for you. Chances are, you'll be the centre of attention in China, so be prepared to draw a crowd of curious onlookers if you stand still too long! In addition, you can expect a steady stream of eager young Chinese hoping to practice their English and learn more about the West.

The situation in China has changed somewhat since June of 1989. For a while it was dangerous for local Chinese to be seen speaking with foreigners, but as time goes on, there is less tension and many exchanges that had been suspended have now been resumed. To find out more about teaching opportunities in China, try writing to the following addresses:

Public Information Office
AFS International
125 East 65th Street
New York, New York
10010 U.S.A.
(212) 744-8181

China Institute of America
International Programs
A-313 East 43rd Street
New York, New York
10017 U.S.A.
(212) 949-4242

Chinese American
Educational Exchange
Room A - 323
College of Staten Island
715 Ocean Terrace
Staten Island, New York
10301 U.S.A.
(212) 390-7654

CET
1110 Washington Street
Lower Mills
Boston, Massachusetts
02124 U.S.A.
(617) 296-0270

Japan

Despite the worldwide recession, there are still literally thousands of jobs for English teachers in Japan. As a Canadian, you have the ability to get a working-holiday visa which allows you to work (legally) up to 25 hours per week. Drop yourself in the middle of Tokyo and you should have a choice of jobs within a couple of days. However, for the first time in history, there is now unemployment in Japan. Japan is not as rich as it once was and consequently the demand for English teachers has peaked and fallen off somewhat. Having said this, there are still lots of opporunities to work in Japan — not necessarily accompanied by the outrageous salaries of the 1980s. (When you first arrive, you might want to stay at the hostel, but you must reserve ahead as it is always 100% booked.) Your first task upon arrival should probably be to find a place to live. Because jobs are plentiful, by finding housing first, you can then concentrate on jobs located relatively near to you. Long commutes are common and anything you can do to limit them is wise. By picking up a copy of the Japan Times you'll have your fingers on countless want ads from schools all seemingly wanting English teachers and hostesses (to work in bars). The Monday issue is particularly full of ads. Although jobs are plentiful year round, they peak in availability in April, September and January, the beginning of the school terms. While most foreigners tend to stay in Tokyo, doing so means that your living costs will be extremely high and your commuting time will be hard to keep under an hour. Commutes of over two hours each way are quite common. If this sounds outrageous, after a few months in Japan you'll realize that almost everyone does it!

If you go to Osaka or even smaller centres, the job opportunities will be fewer but the pace of life will be more relaxed. Jobs outside of Tokyo also appear in the Japan Times. Job choices range from private language schools for adults, to teaching employees of large companies, to cram schools for kids. Of course, the freelance option always exists. Why not organize a conversation group with a group of doctors or lawyers once a week, or with a couple of university students at a cafe? Use your imagination and you'll quickly be making anywhere from $20 to $50 per hour. And you'll need it. Accommodation is small and expensive and you'll likely have to pay a large deposit if you do get an apartment. For more information on jobs in Japan you might refer to this book although it is somewhat outdated:

Jobs in Japan: The Complete Guide to Living and Working in the Land of Rising Opportunities by John Wharton (Global Press, 1986).

Taiwan

Taiwan is the latest hot spot for English teaching opportunities. It's hard to get a work visa (although more schools are now willing to sponsor teachers), but you can easily enter Taiwan on a visitor's or student visa and find work teaching. Everyone does it and since there is such a demand for English speakers, the authorities turn a blind eye to the practice. There are jobs for the person wishing to stay three weeks as well as for the person wishing to stay a year or two. Canadians are very popular and you can expect to find a job immediately. English clubs, private schools, and universities are all good sources for employment. There is also a lot of work in hostessing positions, with tour services and in hotel reception (although some knowledge of Mandarin would likely be required for these positions). To look for jobs, read ads in English-language papers and on bulletin boards. You'll likely earn between $15 and $20 per hour and can teach as much or as little as you desire. Food will cost between $7 and $10 per day and housing is very expensive and hard to find. Many foreigners find rooms in the homes of Taiwanese families at a reasonable rate. When in Taiwan try not to limit yourself to Taipei. Jobs in the south are less plentiful, but the fantastic scenery and lack of pollution make up for this.

Thailand

There are a lot of job opportunities in the Thai cities of Bangkok, Chiang Mai, and Hat Yai for English teaching at all levels. Ads in the Bangkok Post will direct you towards available opportunities and are particularly plentiful at the start of each semester—June and November. Almost anyone, speaking any kind of English, can find work as a language tutor. Often degrees are not required. You can expect to make a minimum of $10 per hour or about $700 per month. It is possible to live comfortably on very little money in Thailand. Banks, industrial companies and hotels are useful places to visit since they are often eager to give their employees opportunities to improve their English. If you can establish a network of foreign and Thai friends, you could make a very comfortable living tutoring. It is difficult to get a work permit to stay in Thailand, so most people use a tourist visa, which must be renewed every three months. You must leave the country and then return in order to renew the visa. This can be done easily by going by train down the peninsula to Malaysia—a very cheap trip given transportation costs in the region. If you lack teaching experience, don't worry as it's not necessary. It is also easy to get by without speaking any Thai. Compared to prices in other Asian countries, food and housing are bargains in Thailand.

Korea

Despite the shortage of qualified English teachers in Korea, it is still difficult to get legal teaching positions in this country. You will more than likely need at least a bachelor's degree. It will facilitate matters if you take transcripts, resumes, a copy of your diploma and letters of reference with you, as well as records of teaching experience you might have. You can enter Korea on a 90-day tourist visa. It will take a week or two to find a job and your best bets for finding them will be Seoul and Pusan. Pay schemes include hourly salaries, which average $15 per hour, or taking a cut of the total tuition for a class. The percentage scheme is often more profitable, especially if you teach company classes. Most employers will want you to work for a year. Once you've found your job, you'll have to leave the country to apply for a teaching visa (you'll have to be sponsored by your new-found employer). Many people go to Hong Kong or Taiwan to wait out the processing (which often takes between 10 and 30 days).

As in Japan and Taiwan, the job of English teacher carries a certain amount of prestige in Korea. You'll have an opportunity to come into contact with an exciting cross section of the local population. Not only will your students learn from you, but you can also learn a great deal from them. Don't try teaching under the table, since the government is very strict about enforcing its laws, even in regard to English teachers. Teaching an unauthorized class can definitely get you thrown out of the country. Take the time to find a legal job and you will be able to live comfortably on your earnings. It is even possible to save up to 70% of your salary.

Teaching in Eastern Europe

With the opening of the former socialist states, there are a weath of oppurtunities to teach English. People in Hungary, Czechoslovakia, Poland, Bulgaria, Romania, and the countries with made up the former U.S.S.R. all offer new work opportunities. There are jobs to be found at both private and state run schools. It is the right time to be a part of the painful changes that are being undertaken in this part of the world. You'll meet people eager to learn the language of world commerce. The downside of such work is the pay. The money you will earn there will be pretty good by local standards but a real shock to the western mindset. What makes the salary even more marginal is the oput of control inflation characterizing these slowly emerging capitalist economies. So most teachers are doing well to break even. If you do manage to save some of the money you earn, in Csechoslovakia and Hungary you still can't convert their currency into hard currency - so you have to spend it all there. The need for english teachers is most pentiful in Hungary and Czechoslvakia since they first headed off en masse in 1989. The need for teachers is steadily increasing in Poland.

In most cases, if you are thinking of heading overseas to teach English you won't need a teaching degree to find employment. However, in most countries you will stand a better chance of finding a variety of potential work possiblities if you have some sort of English as a Second Language degree (ESL) or a Teaching English as a Second Language certification (TESL). Courses of varying durations are offered by community colleges and universities across Canada.

As part of your research into various teaching opportunities around the world, you should definitely invest in a book in the popular British Vacation Work series called *Teaching English Abroad: Talk Your Way Around the World*, Susan Griffith, 1991. This book gives lots of practical advice as to how to go about finding work in over 50 countries on all countinents. Readers are also provided with addresses of schools and organizations who employ foreign language teachers.

Organization: Government of Japan, Ministry of Education
Program: Japanese Exchange and Teaching Program (JET)

Embassy of Japan
255 Sussex Drive
Ottawa, Ontario
KIN 9E6
(613) 236-8541

Program Coordinator: Mr. Jeremy W. Melhuish

Facts at a Glance:

Age: university graduates (up to age 35)

Duration: 12 months (August 1 - July 31)

Regional eligibility: all provinces

Salary:
- approximately $2,500 per month
- return airfare from Canada to Japan

Getting in:
- application forms available from any Japanese embassy or consulate
- application deadline is early December; short list selected for interviews

Overview: Each year a selected number of Canadians, Americans, Australians, and Europeans are chosen to work as Assistant Language Teachers (ALTs), and as Community and International Relations Officers (CIRs) in Japan through a Japanese Ministry of Education-sponsored program. Canadians have been part of the JET program for three years now and the program has become increasingly popular and well known. AETs teach English conversation in high schools or junior high schools throughout Japan, and the CIRs work in prefectural governmental offices on special international projects. The positions provide an excellent opportunity to gain first-hand experience into the language, culture and customs of the Japanese people. It also serves to familiarize the Japanese people, especially the teenagers, with Westerners and attempts to integrate a strong conversational component into the English teaching curriculum. Teaching experience is not required, but would obviously be an asset.

Inside View: This is another program that greatly facilitates the transition involved in moving to the Orient—in this case, Japan. If you're selected, all of your travel arrangements, orientation, job details, and in most cases your accommodations are taken care of for you. If you speak no Japanese, AET is the position you would apply for, and once on the program you would spend your days teaching English conversation to young Japanese students. While this might seem easy enough, you'll be in for some surprises. Living and working in Japan involves a lot of adjustment. The Japanese think in entirely different ways from Westerners—their customs are complex and learning and adapting to them is crucial to a pleasant stay in the country. JET gives you a headstart in adjusting to the East by supplying you with many orientation materials prior to your departure. They also give you Japanese-language tapes. Learning Japanese is a challenging task—and after a year some return having learned very little, while others come back quite fluent. What you learn depends on what you put into studying and with whom you spend your free time. You must make an effort to practice your Japanese—it is easy to conduct your daily life completely in English, since everyone is so eager to practice English with you. Some AET spend the year at a base school, whereas others pay visits to 20 or more schools over the course of their contract.

When interviewing, JET looks for flexible, people-oriented personalities. They also look for a curiosity about Japanese culture or business and someone with a broad range of interests. The idea is for the Canadians to act as ambassadors who will share information on Western ways. It obviously will help greatly if you enjoy chatting and meeting people, because you will be doing a lot of both. They are also looking for a strong sense of diplomacy (necessary for survival in Japan). During the interview your diplomacy will be tested through a series of situational questions. Overall they want people who will benefit from living in Japan; make outgoing, motivated teachers; and be able to handle the ups and downs of being a "gaijin" (foreigner) in Japan.

The pros of the program include a very good salary and a structured format. On the down side, you must remember that you are in a system where you aren't really wanted. 80% of the Japanese teachers you meet will be nervous around you because their English won't be very good. The Ministry wants you to teach English conversation, but the teachers are on a strict schedule, following a rigid formula to prepare students for their crucial university entrance exams. It would be an eye-opening year, but one in which PATIENCE would be the operative word.

Julie Chiba, an occupational therapy graduate of the University of Toronto, spent a year in Rumoi, on the northern Island of Hokkaido. She found her job tiring occasionally and sometimes felt that she wasn't making an impact on the students. She felt that her students were learning more about Canadian culture than about the English language. But this, she believes, was in itself achieving a lot. She highly recommends the experience, but warns others to be patient, and not to bring expectations of effecting dramatic changes in the classroom. She also suggests reading everything you can about Japan before going.

Organization: Education for Democracy
Program: English For Democracy

425 Adelaide Street West, 5th floor
Toronto, Ontario
M5V 3CI
phone: (416) 463-3745 Fax: (416) 392-1085

Facts at a Glance:

Age: minimum of 20

Duration: 2 to 6 months; can be extended

Regional eligibility: all provinces

Salary: subsistence level stipend

Language: English

Where can I go?: Czechoslovakia

Getting in:
- application forms available from above address
- apply at least 2 months prior to planned departure
- chapters in most major centres across the country

Overview: Education for Democracy was founded on January 5, 1990, in Toronto. The aim of the non-profit organization is to help the newly liberated countries of Eastern Europe adjust to democracy. Teaching the people to speak English, the international language of science, business, and technology, is seen as the first step in this process. To date, over 300 Canadians have entered Czechoslovakia on six-month visas to teach primary and conversational English to university students who are interested in learning or upgrading their language skills. The interest level is high in both Canada and Eastern Europe.

Inside View: As Jonathan Shime, a McGill University student, said in 1990, "I can't imagine a better place to be than in Prague right now." Jonathan was one of the first group of teachers to go to Czechoslovakia with Education for Democracy. Because of the high demand for English teachers in Eastern Europe, your chances of being accepted to the program are very good. If you are enthusiastic, motivated and have any teaching experience whatsoever, you'll likely be accepted. At this early stage of the program, it is largely up to the accepted teachers to put together their own teaching plans. You'll also be expected to take along flashcards, a dictionary, pictures, information about Canada, magazines and other classroom supplies. They even recommend bringing your own chalk!

If accepted, you are responsible for paying for your own airfare, although the organization can aid in finding discounted flights. Once in Czechoslovakia you will be met at the airport and taken for an orientation session in one of ten universities. Teachers work approximately 20 hours per week. Food and accommodation are provided free of charge: you'll live in the student residence or with a family, eat at the cafeteria and live very much like a student. The small monthly salary you'll receive (approximately $70) will go surprisingly far owing to the startlingly low cost of living. For instance, a substantial lunch at a very fine restaurant in Prague will cost only about $3, a litre of beer will run about 30 cents and a metro ticket is roughly one cent. Because the average national monthly income is only $100, you should be able to live sufficiently with what you're earning.

In the next decade Eastern Europe will continue to undergo rapid changes politically, economically and socially. It will be an exciting time to be there and also a time when Canadians will be much needed. Whether you can go for a summer or for a year, any time you spend in the newly liberated countries of Europe is sure to be very rewarding.

NOTE: The future of this great program is in question. The organization is currently very shorts on funds and it is not certain that they will be able to continue operation into 1994. At press time, Education for Democracy was still sending people overseas and we have included them in the hopes that they will find the funding they desperately need to stay alive. If you are interested in this program write to the above address but be sure to include a self-addressed stamped envelope to ensure a reply.

STUDENT PROFILE

Name: Warren Cooney
Age: 25
Home: Montréal, Québec

Teaching at The American School in Switzerland

Imagine living in Switzerland for two years, spending your weekends travelling through France, Italy and Austria and getting paid for it all. This is precisely how Warren Cooney spent his first two years after graduating from Hamilton College. During his final year of university, he applied for a position as teaching intern at The American School in Switzerland (TASIS). A teaching degree was not necessary, although Warren had spent several years as an instructor at hockey camps and as a tutor. TASIS seeks flexible people who can teach academic subjects as well as coach a sport or two. While at TASIS, Warren taught economics and history and coached soccer, cycling, and tennis. His high school experience at a U.S. boarding school also helped prepare him for the responsibilities and challenges of being a don at TASIS. The school provided him with teaching materials, guidance and a thorough orientation session. The first year he was there he taught three classes and also served as the student weekend activity organizer. This involved planning various excursions to neighboring countries. During the second year he was a member of the teaching staff and taught a full load of five classes.

For Warren, these two years were a wonderful opportunity to have a go at teaching and live in Europe at the same time. As he explained, TASIS is a fascinating school with students from over 35 countries. Many are accustomed to moving around a lot as their parents are diplomats or professionals with international careers. Although some come from money (you might get the feeling that TASIS is an elitist institution), others come from very poor developing countries and are at TASIS because their parents' employer pays for the opportunity.

TASIS operates sister schools in London and Athens. Your best bet is to write to the address below in the fall expressing an interest in a position with one of the schools. Each year before Christmas the principal of the school takes an inventory of who is returning and finds out how many new interns are required. The turn-over is very high. Interviews are usually held in New York City or Boston. As a part of the application form you'll be asked how you feel your background qualifies you to teach at TASIS and you'll also be asked to write an essay discussing your philosophy of education. The job pays $1,100 per month, but there are many fringe benefits (mostly in the form of travel). You are also provided with a furnished apartment as part of the package, and TASIS will provide you with money towards your airfare.

Other private schools in Canada, the U.S., and internationally hire recent graduates as teachers and interns. Very often a degree in teaching is not a prerequisite.

For further information on TASIS and its sister schools write to:

The American School in Switzerland
CM 6926
Montagnola Lugano
Switzerland

(91) 546471 or (212) 570-1066
(the New York representative is David Damico)

Organization: Association Québec-France
Program: Summer Work Exchange

Maison Fornel
9 Place Royale
Québec City, Québec
GIK 4G2
phone: (418) 643-1616, toll-free: (800) 661-9965 fax: (418) 643-3053

Director: Ms Jocelyne Renaud

Facts at a Glance:

Age: 15-30 (35 for grape harvesting)

Duration: 2 weeks - 1 year

Regional eligibility: Québec residents only

Cost:
- $35

some positions require a medical exam in France which will cost you $100

That covers: administration fee

Salary:
- approximately $850 per month

Language: must speak fluent French

Getting in:
- application forms available from above address
- deadline varies depending on the program
- moderately selective (500 apply for 400 spots)

Overview: The Association Québec-France have expanded their offerings to include a number of work and holiday options for Quebec residents from 15 to 35. The majority of jobs are at summer camps, but other positions can be found at pools, parks, libraries and public buildings. Those chosen to work in France are responsible for all travel expenses. Most jobs are available in the summer, yet the Association Québec-France can arrange three-month work permits any time of the year.

Inside View: Because France very rarely issues work permits to foreigners, this program provides quite a useful service. If you're chosen, they'll place you in a government job and provide you with all the necessary legal documents. About 80% of the jobs are at summer camps, where workers receive their room and board and a salary of about $800 per month. Otherwise, you'll live with a family or in a youth hostel (where you'll be expected to contribute money for rent and food) and work at a manual job such as grounds maintenance. Salary for these jobs is about $1,200 per month—more than enough to cover all of your expenses.

Along with the summer job program, the Association Québec-France annually sends about 200 people to France to help with the fall grape harvest. Practically anyone who applies can go and earn $500 for two weeks of picking grapes. As with the other programs, participants are responsible for their own air fare. People purchase an open-return ticket, which allows them to remain in France for up to a year. It is fairly easy to find jobs in the fall, when students are back in school. The Association can renew your work permit for another three months. Canadians rarely have any difficulty finding short-term jobs in restaurants, on farms or at campgrounds. If you're between the ages of 15 and 17 you should be aware of two week long summer trips offered by the Association Quebec-France. Write to them for details, they are flexible and helpful.

Organization: International Voluntary Workcamps
Program: Summer Volunteer Program

Cotravaux
11 rue de Clichy
75009 Paris, France
phone: 33 1 48 74 79 20, fax: 33 1 48 74 14 01

Facts at a Glance:

Age: 18 - 30

Duration: average of 2 or 3 weeks

Regional eligibility: all provinces

Cost: $50 - $200

What does that cover? room and board, basic activities

Language: must be fluent in French

Getting in:
- applications available from above address
- not particularly selective

Overview:

Cotravaux is a large French agency which places volunteers on temporary work projects all over France. They offer a service similar to what is offered by Association Quebec-France the difference being that Cotravaux does not require that you be a resident of Quebec. All that is required is that you speak French well. They also offer work and other camps for kids age 12 to 17 which are somewhat more expensive. We have not spoken to anyone who has been placed by this organization so are unable to give you any inside information. You should write to them to request more information.

Program: Agence Québec / Wallonie-bruxelles Pour La Jeunesse

500 Sherbrooke West
Bureau 210
Montréal, Quebec
H3A 3C6
(514) 873-4355 (collect calls accepted)
Director: M. Benoit LaLiberte

Facts at a Glance:

Age: 18-30

Duration: 1 week - 1 year

Regional eligibility: Québec residents only

Cost: $250 - $425

That covers:
- return travel from Canada to Belgium
- daily allowance of about $40

Getting in:
- application forms available from above address
- deadlines vary according to the program
- somewhat selective (400 proposals—300 accepted)

Overview: The goals of this agency include fostering international cooperation and understanding and helping young Québec residents gain business connections in Belgium. To this end, the agency arranges short trips to Belgium for Québec youth. Participants are sent so that they can investigate some aspect of Belgian business, technology, tourism or society. The hope is that, having returned to Canada, participants can put what they learned in Belgium to practical use. Applicants must submit a specific proposal concerning the type of business they'd like to research while in Belgium.

Inside View: For Québec residents, this program offers a very inexpensive way to travel to Belgium. To be chosen, it really helps to have a business contact in Belgium who'll write a letter stating that you'd be welcome to come over and view his or her operation. If you don't have any Belgian contacts at the moment, don't despair—if you write to several Belgian companies explaining your situation, there's an excellent chance you'll receive a positive reply.

Stephan Archambault, a 23-year-old Montréal resident, draws cartoon strips for a hobby and was looking into getting them published somewhere. At a book fair, he learned the names of several Belgian editors. He wrote to them, explaining that he would like to come to Europe to show them his work; they agreed to take a look. When Stephan made his proposal to Agence Québec/Wallonie-Bruxelles, it was readily accepted. He spent two weeks meeting with editors and making important contacts, and then stayed an extra week to travel. Stephen was asked to contribute $400 before he went to Belgium; however, because he received a daily allowance of about $45 per day, the trip ended up costing nothing! If you think you could justify a trip to Belgium, then this program is for you!

This agency has initiated a number of new programs in the past two years. They include group exchanges, twinning programs, visits of various lengths of time, and a fund which provides for Belgian contacts to fly to cultural or business events in Québec.

Organization: Office Franco-Québecois pour la jeunesse
Program: Work Terms In France

1441, boulevard Rene Levesque Ouest
Montréal, Québec
Phone: (514) 873-4255

Program Director: Mme Madeleine Bourgeois

Facts at a Glance

Age: 18-35

Duration: 1 week to 6 months

Regional eligibility: Québec residents only

Cost: $300

This covers:
- return airfare
- orientation in Paris which includes a one night hotel stay
- health insurance

Language: must speak French

Where can I go?: France

Getting in:
- application forms available from above address
- enroll 6 months before your planned departure (selection takes place in February and October)
- Somewhat selective (2,600 apply for 1,300 spots)

Overview The Office Franco-Québec pour la jeunesse (OFQJ) aims to provide young Québec residents with a chance to experience various aspects of life in France. To this end the OFQJ each year sends about 1,200 people to France for stays ranging from two weeks to one year. OFQJ offers a number of different programs which enable participants to either study French culture, work at a short term job or research a business opportunity.

Inside View This office provides services similar to those provided by the Agence Québec/Wallonie-Bruxelles. As with the AQWB programs, your chance of being accepted will be much higher if you already have a contact in France. When you present an application proposal, you should, if possible, include a letter from your French business contact stating that you'd be welcome to view their operation. Participants pay a fee of $300 for their trip, which covers return airfare and a two-day orientation in Paris. This office offers a number of other programs as well, including a homestay fortnight and a group exchange. All the programs cost between $300 and $350. On most programs you will be responsible for paying your own room and board.

Organization: Israel Antiquities Authority
Program: Archaeological Excavations

Israel Antiquities Authority
P.O. Box 586
91004 Jerusalem, Israel
Fax: 972 2 292 628

Director: Ms Harriet Menahem

Overview: If you are physically fit and can find your way to Israel then you can probably find work on an archaeological dig. You have to be in good shape because the work is demanding - especially in the sweltering heat. On these digs not only do you put in a solid days work, but you pay about $30 per day for the experience. In exchange for what you give, you get room and board. This is one of the few non-Canadian based programs which we feature in the book. We do not know much about them, but wanted to include their address because they do offer a unique service at a moderate cost - good characteristics in a student program.

Organization: Veterans Affairs Canada
Program: Vimy Battlefield Memorial Guide Program

Veterans Affairs
66 Slater Street
Ottawa, Ontario
K1A 0P4
(613) 996-6250

Coordinator: Mr Réal Charest

Facts at a Glance:

Age: must be a full-time post-secondary student

Duration: 2 - 3 months (April - November)

Regional eligibility: all provinces

Salary: $11 per hour plus $16 per diem post allowance

Language: must be fluently bilingual

Getting in:
- thorough application requiring essay and reference letter
- telephone interview
- deadline is December 10, the year prior to departure
- very competitive (140 apply for 14 spots)

Overview: Every summer the Department of Veterans Affairs is responsible for staffing the Vimy Battlefield Memorial in France with Canadian guides. These guides give walking tours of the battlefield in both French and English. Guides are responsible for their own transportation to and from France, and also for their room and board once there. They are, however, provided with a list of inexpensive accommodations and the local people are usually very willing to help Canadians.

Inside View: This program offers both a fantastic work experience and a way to finance a European vacation. When you apply, you indicate which months you would like to work. You might choose to spend May and June working at Vimy, and then spend July and August exploring Europe on your earnings. After spending two months guiding thousands of tourists through the park, chances are you'll meet at least a few who'll be willing to put you up for a couple of nights while you're passing through their town.

Denis Couture, a 26-year-old student at the Université de Québec à Montréal, has been a guide at Vimy for the past two summers. As well as meeting people from all over Europe during his first summer, Denis also met a lot of people from the nearby village of Arras. His second summer he lived with friends he met there. Both summers, Denis travelled after his assignment at Vimy. He said that because the pay is quite good and local rents are not high (a small apartment costs about $200 per month) he was able to save enough money to pay for his air fare and all his travels. Guides work five days in a row followed by two days off. This makes Paris, Rouen and Lille easy weekend destinations. If you want to improve your chances of being chosen, Denis suggests taking a hard-working approach to your application—do a thorough job and show them you're serious about the job. Your chance of being selected will vastly improve if you stress any previous guiding experience you might have and if the essay you write is both factual and original. Overall appearance of your application as well as early submission will also help you get your foot in the door.

Organization: Association International des Étudiants en Science, Economique et Commerciale (AIESEC)
Program: International Trainee Exchange Program

1450 City Councilors
Suite 540
Montréal, Québec
H3A 2E5
phone: (514) 987-1325, fax: (514) 987-1329

Vice President: Mr Russ Erickson

Facts at a Glance:

Age: undergraduate or graduate student

Duration: 2-18 months

Regional eligibility: all provinces

Cost: $160 administration fee

Salary: usually just enough to cover all living expenses and most travel

Where can I go? 74 countries (every continent)

Getting in:
- application forms available from local AIESEC offices
- limited to members of AIESEC
- competition for placements varies according to the district

Overview: AIESEC (pronounced EYE-sek) is an international, student-run organization committed to developing international business relations. To this end, AIESEC annually places a few hundred Canadians in business positions around the world, taking care of arrangements such as work permits and accommodation for participants. The jobs found for trainees usually relate to their field of study (most commonly accounting, finance, management, or computer science) and are often with large multi-national corporations. While living in the host country, trainees are responsible for their own room, board and travel expenses. They must also cover the cost of return travel from Canada to their overseas posting. However, trainees are paid a good salary which will normally cover all costs.

Inside View: This program is a fantastic chance to combine first-rate business experience with international living—a great combination! If you're not already a member of AIESEC, and you'd like to go overseas with their exchange, don't be discouraged—AIESEC has local offices at 38 universities across the country. One student we spoke with, Deidre Fo of the University of Toronto, joined AIESEC looking to gain work experience abroad. Just four months later she was placed with IBM in Iceland. She spent the summer working at a variety of jobs and living on a farm with three other trainees. She told us that she met with a warm reception upon arrival in Iceland, and that every weekend she and other trainees were escorted around the island and hosted at dinners. Deidre was so impressed with AIESEC that she has become very active in her local office and is currently planning to go on another exchange—this time to France!

Organization: International Association for Exchange Students in Technical Engineering (IAESTE)
Program: International Trainee Exchange

IAESTE
P.O. Box 1473
Kingston, Ontario
K7L 5C7
(613) 549-2243

Chairman: Dr C.N. Kerr

Facts at a Glance:

Age: university students

Duration: 2-12 months (mostly during the summer)

Regional eligibility: all provinces

Cost: $155 administration fee

Salary: usually just enough to cover all living expenses

Where can I go?: 59 countries world-wide

Language: some countries require ability in their language

Getting in:

• applications available from the above address
• must be a current student of science, engineering or applied arts and technologies
• deadline is December 3
• quite competitive (800 apply for 200 spots)

Overview: The major aim of IAESTE is to promote international understanding and cooperation among scientists, technologists and those involved in industry. As a means to this, IAESTE Canada annually places about 200 qualified students in short-term, career-related work assignments around the world. The program allows participants to broaden their outlook, make important contacts and possibly learn another language.

Inside View: IAESTE offers the same services as AIESEC, except that they place students of science and technology rather than business students. Unless you get lucky and are placed with a very generous company, you probably won't make much money—but you'll certainly make enough to pay for your room and board. Although financially you'll probably just break even the contacts you'll make could be very valuable, not to mention the new skills you'll pick up. IAESTE placed Bob Neville, a 23-year-old Queen's University engineering student, in Copenhagen for a one-year stint at the Building Sciences Institute. The research he did there was almost exclusively in English, yet he was able to learn Danish over the course of the year. Bob told us that those students who really want to take advantage of the program should have a good academic record and should make their enthusiasm known to the placement committee. He also said it wasn't all work in Copenhagen. About 100 AIESTE trainees from all over the world were working in the city and they got together frequently to investigate the night life.

Organization: Canadian Association of University Teachers of German (CAUTG)
Program: Student Summer Work Program

CAUTG
Department of Germanic and Slavic Studies
Brock University
St. Catharines, Ontario
L2S 3A1
(416) 688-5550 ext. 3314

Contact: Professor McRae

Facts at a Glance:

Age: 18-30

Duration: up to 3 months

Regional eligibility: all provinces

Cost:
- must pay own return travel to Germany (subsidies of up to 70% available from German government)
- must pay own room and board (sometimes provided by employer)

Salary: varies according to the job

Language: must have a working knowledge of German

Getting in:
- application forms available from university German departments
- applications are accepted until late November
- fairly competitive (450 apply for 100 spots)

Overview: The Canadian Association of German Teachers, together with the German government, arranges for approximately 100 Canadian university students to work in Germany each summer. The program allows students studying German at university to immerse themselves in the German culture and improve their German language skill for a period of up to three months. Traditionally, students get jobs in hotels, restaurants, banks or factories and make enough money to cover their expenses. In some cases, students even manage to save money. Many students travel for a few weeks after they finish work, possibly on the money they saved.

Inside View: As we've mentioned in other sections of this book, it is sometimes very difficult to obtain a work permit for foreign countries. Established programs which cut through the red tape can make it easier to work overseas. This CAUTG program does just that if you are interested in working in Germany for a few months. In co-operation with the German government, CAUTG provides summer jobs for some 100 Canadian students each year. Most jobs are in the hotel or restaurant industry, but positions are also secured in banks, city parks and factories. Generally, you shouldn't expect to obtain career-related experience; however, the language and educational benefits can more than make up for this. If you are male, you are admittedly at a disadvantage, as many more positions are found for women. The program coordinator told us that they don't get enough jobs for men. The more German you speak, the better your chances of acceptance will be, but at a minimum you're required to have studied the language for at least one post-secondary year. An attempt is made to give at least one seat to every university in the country and a set number of positions are allotted for CEGEPs in Québec. Most jobs are found in the Black Forest and Southern Alps of Germany, but a few are available in Berlin. The pay you can expect varies depending on the location and nature of the job.

Michael Emrich, 21, from Peterborough, Ontario, spent three months working in a Berlin paper factory through CAUTG. He highly recommends the experience and said that his vocabulary improved tremendously. Although fluent in German before he went, he said it was an invaluable opportunity to use the language every day in a wide range of situations. As was the case with most students, the work he did was not stimulating and he wasn't delegated much authority, but that was unimportant when considering the entire experience. He advises, however, that if you have a lot of doubts about going, you shouldn't go. You must be flexible and willing to try new things.

Unlike some of the other work programs available, this one leaves you no guess work. Your job, flights and accommodation are all arranged. You are not left hanging at all, which makes settling in much easier. However, once over there you are on your own (usually with other students nearby), so don't make the mistake of thinking that you'll be supervised.

Organization: Union des Producteurs Agricoles
Program: Agriculture Students Exchange

555 boulevard Roland Therrien
Longueuil, Québec
J4H 3Y9
(514) 679-0530

Program Director: Mlle Helene Varavessos

Facts at a Glance:

Age: 18-30

Duration: 3-6 months

Regional eligibility: Quebec residents

Cost:
- $550 for France or Belgium

That covers:
- administration fee
- return travel from Canada to Europe
- insurance

Salary:
- room and board

Language: must speak fluent French

Getting in:
- application forms available from the above address
- one year of farming experience or agricultural training required
- deadline is December 1 for April departures
- deadline is May 1 for September departures
- somewhat selective (100 apply for 50 spots)

Overview: The Union des Producteurs Agricoles provides opportunities for young, French-speaking Canadians to work on a European farm. Participants live with a family on a farm where they receive free room and board and a small allowance. Positions are available for either three or six months.

Inside View: This program offers a very good opportunity to spend time in either France or Belgium. Through various government agreements, participants who travel to either of these countries pay only $550 for their return air fare! Whichever country you decide you'd rather work in, once you arrive you receive room and board in exchange for the work you do on the family farm.

Organization: International Agricultural Exchange Association (IAEA)

1501 - 17th Avenue S.W.
Suite 206
Calgary, Alberta
T2T OE2
(403) 244-1814

Consultant: Ms Debbie Klegzel

Facts at a Glance:

Age: 18-30

Duration: 6-12 months

Regional eligibility: all provinces

Cost: $2,200 - $7,000

That covers:
- return travel from Canada to overseas site
- on the longer programs, stopovers (hotel, meals, etc.) totalling approximately 10 days in Hawaii, Singapore, and Fiji
- complete insurance

Salary:
- approximately $500 per month
- room and board

Where can I go?: Australia, Britain, Denmark, Germany, Ireland, Holland, New Zealand, Norway, Sweden, Switzerland, Japan

Getting in:
- application forms available from above address
- informal interview
- agricultural training or practical experience required
- deadline for all programs is 2 months before departure

Overview: Every year the IAEA arranges for over 100 young Canadians to do agricultural work in a number of interesting and exotic locations. Young Canadians are sent overseas to learn new agricultural techniques and gain an understanding of another culture. The exchange is available to students of agriculture as well as to those who possess practical farming skills.

Inside View: If you grew up on a farm or are studying agriculture and haven't travelled much, this program might be an ideal way to get a first taste of living and working abroad. It's of particular interest to inexperienced travellers because the arrangements are taken care of for you. You will be matched to a suitable host family and given a work permit, your flights will be booked and you will participate in a thorough orientation seminar when you arrive in your host country.

Janna Pickett, a 20-year-old accounting student from Bassano, Alberta, had never travelled before she went to New Zealand through the IAEA. She spent eight months living and working on a family farm. Because Janna grew up on a farm, and knew how to drive a tractor, she was very useful to the farm. At the same time, she learned a great deal about the farming practices of New Zealand. She was also paid a modest salary and allowed five weeks of vacation time.

This program is very well established and offers a good international support network to exchangees. The exchanges run smoothly and are headache-free for participants. However, you pay a fairly high price for their services. You may be able to gain similar agricultural experience by booking your own flight to a country and applying for a working-holiday visa. This will require a bit of research and planning on your part, but would definitely save you money.

Organization: External Affairs Canada
Programs:

Canada-Switzerland Young Trainee Exchange Program
Canada-France Young Workers Exchange Program
Canada-Germany Young Workers Program
Working Holiday Programs

International Youth Exchange Programs
Lester B. Pearson Building
125 Sussex Drive
Ottawa, Ontario
K1A 0G2
(613) 992-6142

Programs Manager: Ms Janine Godin

Facts at a Glance:

Age: 18-30 years

Duration: 3-12 months

Regional eligibility: all provinces

Cost:
- you pay for your own travel, room and board
- in a very few cases the employer may cover travel costs

Salary: you are paid by the local employer

Where can I go?: Australia, Japan, United Kingdom, Finland, Germany, Ireland, Sweden, France, and the Netherlands

Getting in:
- application forms are available from the above address
- applications accepted year round

Language:
- you need a working knowledge of the language of the country you wish to work in

Overview: The Department of External Affairs administers work exchange programs with four foreign countries. They are designed for Canadians holding a post-secondary degree or diploma, who wish to obtain career-related work experience abroad. Although the program does assist you in finding employment, for most countries it is recommended that you do your own job search in order to improve your chances of finding a position.

Inside View: The major strength of these External Affairs programs is that they assist you with the red tape that is normally involved in finding work abroad. In fact, many countries will not give you a work permit unless you are sponsored under a program-agreement between the two countries involved. This is especially true for Switzerland. France also insists that you participate on this External Affairs program. The conditions for admission and details of each program are similar, but a few notable differences do exist.

The Switzerland Exchange is the most competitive, receiving 1,500 applications each year for 150 positions. Of those accepted, 100 had made job contacts on their own. To be considered, you must have a minimum one year of degree-related work experience. Most positions are in the hotel, restaurant, health services, or banking fields. The program is aimed at those wishing to gain professional expertise in their field of training.

Graduates in the fields of industry, commerce, or science and technology are eligible to participate on the France and Germany programs. Once again, one year of working experience directly related to your training is required. In France, most jobs are found in agriculture or business. Each year 1,000 Canadians apply for each of the programs, and 200 are successfully placed in jobs.

Your chance of acceptance to either is conditional on there being a suitable and available job in the exchange country. Your application is sent to the foreign government and they undertake a job search on your behalf. The specific opportunities available vary from year to year.

The Student Working Holiday Program differs significantly from the other External Affairs programs. It provides university and college students with an opportunity to live and work in several countries for up to three months during the summer (renewable in some cases). For Australia, Japan, and the United Kingdom you can apply for the visa directly at the embassy of the country or at one of their consulates in Canada. As work is incidental to the holiday, you can find your own work while in the host country. For Finland, Germany, Ireland, Sweden, and the Netherlands, you must have a written offer of employment. Once you have a written job offer, you must communicate the details with the foreign embassy or a consulate in Canada. It normally takes up to three months to obtain a work permit.

Organization: Canadian Bureaus of International Education
Program: International Workcamps

85 Albert, suite 1400
Ottawa, Ontario
KIP 6A4
(613) 237-4820

Facts at a Glance:

Age:
- 18 years of age or over

Duration:
- 2 to 4 weeks
- 4 to 12 weeks in Québec
- camps are held mainly in July and August

Regional eligibility: all provinces

Cost: $125

That covers:
- administration fee
- room and board

Where can I go?: one of 12 countries in North America and Europe

Language:
- must speak reasonably fluent French for France and Québec
- English is spoken on the rest of the camps

Getting in:
- application forms available from above address
- cheque or money order for $125 must accompany application
- deadline for application is April 1st

Overview: The Canadian Bureau for International Education offers young people the opportunity to participate on an international workcamp with volunteers from other parts of the world. Workcamps normally involve from 10 to 20 volunteers and last three or four weeks. Examples of the type of work done on the camps include building a playground, clearing hiking trails, restoring a castle, going on holiday with mentally handicapped adults, collecting tools for the Third World, or setting up a festival for peace. Most projects are manual labour and volunteers will work about 30 or 40 hours per week. Room and board is provided at the workcamp. It will be simple—probably in a church basement, youth centre, or other community building. Members of the group take turns cooking and cleaning up. At most workcamps, participants will get a chance to talk about subjects related to the work, whether it's ecology, modern social problems, or prehistory. There are also work-study camps which include formal study of a theme through discussion, excursions and so on. Volunteers are responsible for transportation to and from the workcamp.

Organization: Up With People

1 International Court
Broomfield, Colorado
80021, U.S.A.
phone: (303) 460-7100, fax: (303) 438-7300

Facts at a Glance:

Age: 18 - 26

Duration: 11 months

Regional eligibility: all provinces

Cost: $11,500 U.S.

That covers:
- 5 week training camp in Denver, Colorado
- all travel after the training camp
- accommodation and meals

Where can I go?: varies, but typically all over the United States and Europe

Getting in:
- applications and performance schedules available from above address
- selection is based on a personal interview which takes place immediately following performances (i.e. you must attend a show)
- very competitive (8,000 apply for 650 spots)

Overview: Up With People, founded in 1968, is a unique organization which provides young men and women with year-long opportunities for cross-cultural education, diverse community service, on-stage musical performance experience and extensive world travel. Each year 650 young people are selected and broken into five touring troupes. Within each troupe, up to 20 countries may be represented. During the one year of involvement, the group travels to 80 or 90 cities in several countries, performing a two-hour musical production at each stop. While travelling, performers stay in the homes of host families. As well as putting on shows, each member of Up With People puts in many hours of community service in hospitals, elementary schools, prisons, or senior citizens' homes while on tour.

Inside View: If you've ever fantasized about running away with the circus, here's a program which might satisfy your dream. Up With People allows you to travel around the world with a group of 129 young energetic students, performing musical shows as you go. Possessing musical talent, obviously, will better the odds of your being accepted. However, selections are made after personal interviews and not auditions. What they're looking for above all are mature, motivated people with a genuine interest in community service and multicultural understanding.

The application process for Up With People is sort of convoluted. First send away for an application form and performance schedule. You'll have to hope the troupe will be somewhere in your neighborhood in the near future, because that's the only way you can get an interview with them. You have to attend a performance and they do all of their interviewing right after the show. If they're not passing directly through your town you'll have to get yourself to their closest show. Once you've been interviewed, if they like you, you'll be sent music sheets and asked to tape yourself playing an instrument or singing. After they've heard your tape they make final selections and all those they pick head to Tucson for a five-week training camp. You're responsible for getting yourself there. At the camp you'll learn the song and dance routines and be assigned to a troupe. Immediately following the training you'll be off on tour—typically criss-crossing the United States and Canada for the first six months and then to Europe. Some lucky troupes have been sent to Moscow, Beijing, and Brisbane—it all depends on where shows are booked.

The cost of being a part of Up With People seems a little steep, but if a career in the entertainment industry interests you, it has to be a fantastic learning experience. To help defray your costs the organization will send you ideas about fund-raising prior to your stint.

STUDENT PROFILE

Name: Tim Pitt
Home: Toronto, Ontario

OUT TO AFRICA

Tim Pitt was about to enter his fourth year of university at St. Francis Xavier when he made a choice which altered the direction of his life. He had always wanted to explore Africa and decided that the time was right for a break in formal education. So, never having been to Africa, off he went, alone, to the Dark Continent. He spent a full year there, sometimes travelling with people he met along the way. During his time there he managed to visit a large portion of the continent. After his adventurous and unstructured year, Tim returned to Canada and graduated from university.

Almost immediately after graduation Tim was back in Africa again. This time he was in Botswana on the WUSC summer seminar (see p.123). Normally WUSC prefers to choose people who have never been to Africa before. They also like people who are returning to university the next fall. The selection committee must have sensed Tim's special committment and interest. During the seminar, Tim studied the apartheid issue, among other things. After the summer in Botswana Tim came back to Canada — but not for long.

Shortly after his return to Canada Tim boarded a plane and headed back across the Atlantic — this time to France. Now that Tim's interest in Africa was really solidifying, he decided that it would be a good idea for him to improve his French language skills. At the same time that Tim was studying language he began volunteering for an international organization called Medecins Sans Frontiers. MSF is a group of doctors, health and development workers who toil in war torn areas of the world - often under very dangerous conditions. What Tim did, for the most part was research and writing for doctors who were presenting papers.

One day Tim received a call from MSFs Spain office. They were in need of someone to run operations, a logistician, for their medical relief efforts in Somalia. They wanted Tim for the job. Just four days later Tim left for Somalia with a paid position and a position which carried with it a lot of responsibility. He is in charge of organizing movements of the staff, ordering supplies, scheduling and security for the whole Spanish MSF Somalia operation! Recently, when the political situation got too hot for even MSF to handle, Tim made the decision to evacuate the group into the safety of neighbouring Kenya.

The events which have transpired in Tim's life over the past few years exemplify our suggested approach to maximizing your success and contentment. Tim took the initiative to explore his interests through travel, study and volunteer positions and it has led to a very rare and important job. It looks like the start of a wonderful career.

Hmmmm, I wonder what Tim would be doing now if he'd gone straight on to fourth year university? Luckily the world and particularly Africa will never know.

Organization: Canadian Crossroads International
Program: Overseas Programs

31 Madison Avenue
Toronto, Ontario
M5R 2S2
(416) 967-9078
Director of External Relations: Mr Michael Cooke

Facts at a Glance:

Age: 19 and older

Duration:

- Overseas Program: 4-12 months (starts September, December or May)
- Group Program: 2 months
- Agriculture Program: 6 weeks

Regional eligibility: all provinces

Cost: $2,100 which is raised through community fund raising

That covers:
- return travel from Canada to work site
- room and board
- small allowance

Where can I go?: 36 Third World countries

Getting in:
- apply to your local Crossroads Committee or write to above address for forms
- thorough application process with essays and interviews
- very competitive (approximately 10% of applicants are chosen)

Overview: Canadian Crossroads has been sending Canadian volunteers to Third World countries since 1958. Through their three programs, Canadians travel to Asia, Africa, the South Pacific, the Caribbean, or South and Central America to work on "self help" educational, health, agriculture, and community development projects. The aim is to educate Canadians about international development and to promote cross-cultural awareness. Each year, about 250 people live and work in developing countries through Canadian Crossroads International.

Inside View: Crossroads is a great way to experience a culture and way of life which completely differs from your own. Volunteers are matched to development projects in developing countries and spend four to six months working on such things as building roads, teaching, working in clinics or harvesting crops. Crossroads' largest program is the individual placement, which matches volunteers to development projects. You are eligible to apply if you have not participated in a similar program and you have not previously spent time in a developing country. The selection process is very thorough, requiring completion of a comprehensive application form followed by an interview. You must show evidence of sensitivity, emotional stability, adaptability and maturity. Previous volunteer experience is also a great asset. There are no educational requirements, but in the past the majority of participants have been university educated.

Competition for selection takes place first regionally and then locally. Regional quotas exist to allow participation from all across Canada. You can state a preference for your country assignment, but there is no guarantee that you will be placed there. Upon your return to Canada, you are required to do 200 hours of volunteer work for Crossroads over the following two years.

The group program allows Québec francophones to work in West Africa for two months every summer. Each year, 400 applications are received for the 40 positions available. Again, you are responsible for raising some money for the trip and must attend a series of orientation meetings. On the Agriculture Exchange, Canadians spend six weeks on a Caribbean farm and then host a Caribbean youth on their farm in Canada. Selection occurs through local farm organizations.

Organization: Canada World Youth

Ontario Regional Office
386 Bloor Street West
2nd floor
Toronto, Ontario
M5S 1X4
phone: (416) 992-0776
fax: (416) 992-3721

Program Officer: Ms Anne Game

Facts at a Glance:

Age: university graduate

Duration: 10 - 24 months

Regional eligibility: all provinces

Salary:
- coordinators — $2,017 per month
- group leaders — $1,285 per month

Where can I go?: One of 40 participating Third World countries

Getting in:
- applications available from above address
- suitable applicants are invited to an evaluation day
- most qualified are then interviewed by committee
- quite competitive

Overview: Canada World Youth is a non-profit organization which offers young people a non-formal education program based on community and international development. The organization is looking for people to plan and supervise its activities. They are looking for bilingual applicants with experience in budget planning, work experience in a developing country, the ability to plan and operationalize an educational program, and a degree in social sciences. The job involves initial training in Montréal and a three-month placement in a community in Canada followed by a three-month stay in a developing country. If you have participated on CWY, the WUSC summer seminar, or have experience in a Third World country, this might be an ideal position for you.

Organization: World University Service of Canada (WUSC)
Program: Volunteer Programme

1404 Scott Street P.O. Box 3000, Station C
Ottawa, Ontario
KIY 4M8
phone: (613) 798-7477, fax: (613) 798-0990

Programme Officer: Ms Joanne Sunsrum Menard

Facts at a Glance:

Age: no limit

Duration: normally 2 years

Regional eligibility: all provinces

Benefits:
- return travel from Canada to overseas project site
- local-level salary
- housing
- settling in and resettlement allowance
- medical insurance coverage

Overview: WUSC is a non-governmental organization involved in international development. The volunteer programme was established in 1977 and recruits Canadians for overseas positions in Benin, Botswana, Lesotho, Malawi, Mali and Swaziland on a continual basis.Close to 130 WUSC-recruited Canadians, the majority of whom are volunteers in a variety of disciplines, work on technical assistance projects in developing countries. These professionals work in education, health, agriculture, business administration, management and training, community development, environment, vocational trades and population and human settlements. WUSC is also the Canadian co-operating agency for the United Nations Volunteers Programme, Geneva and recruits qualified Canadians for positions world-wide.

Inside View: In order to serve as a WUSC volunteer, you must have a post-secondary degree or diploma. Work experience in the field of expertise is required and overseas experience is an asset. Candidates must meet the health standards and personal qualifications required by the employing agency/ministry and WUSC. If you're just graduating from university, it can't hurt to apply, as approximately 30% of volunteers who are sent overseas are recent graduates.

Ann Witteveen, of Woodbridge, Ontario, a graudate of Guelph University, teaches English and science at Ntjanini High School in Swaziland. She was only at her posting for two weeks when she acquired some company to share "my cavernous three-bedroom house" -a young high school student and her litter sister, still in primary school. Ann writes, "I'm sure some of my best Swaziland memories will be made from the universal joys of just being around children. Certainly there aren't many greater pleasures than sitting with a six-year-old on your knee listening as she sounds out the syllables in her grade reader, watching her wrinkled brow in deep concentration turn to a wide-eyed grin as she forms her first words. Most time, communication isn't about talking."

Organization: Plenty Canada
Program: Cooperant Program

R.R. 3
Lanark, Ontario
K0G 1K0
phone: (613) 278-2215, fax (613) 278-2416

Cooperant Coordinator: Ms Nancy McDermott

Facts at a Glance:

Age: university graduate

Duration: 1 to 2 years

Regional eligibility: all provinces

Salary:
- subsistence-level salary
- return travel from Canada to overseas posting
- health and life insurance
- resettlement allowance

Getting in:
- application forms available from above address
- thorough evaluation of all applicants
- apply anytime

Overview: Plenty Canada, a small organization involved in international development projects, seeks qualified staff to work overseas for one and two year postings. The projects are at a grass-roots level. Most projects involve work with agriculture, forestry, or gravity fed water systems.

Inside View: Working on projects in a Third World country can teach you much about others and yourself. With Plenty, you spend two years working with local people on community development projects. Although you are there to provide technological expertise, you are also there to organize and coordinate. Above all, your attitude will determine whether you are a suitable candidate. You must be socially and culturally flexible and be someone who wants to learn as well as teach. And you must be committed to development. Your technical and educational background is as important as your character.

Organization: CUSO

135 Rideau Street, 3rd floor
Ottawa, Ontario
KIN 9K7
(613) 563-1264

Communications officer: Mr Chris Neal

Facts at a Glance:

Age: university/college graduates or people with sufficient trade/work experience

Duration: 2 years

Regional eligibility: all provinces

Salary:
- subsistence-level salary
- return travel from Canada to overseas work site
- all insurance and health care
- $9,200 resettlement allowance

Where can I go? developing countries in Africa, Asia, the South Pacific, Latin America, and the Caribbean

Getting in:
- application forms available from above address
- pre-screening interview
- 6-12 month waiting period

Overview: CUSO sends qualified Canadians overseas to work in the poorest sectors of developing nations. They do not, under any circumstances, recruit students who are still in university. However, a good number of those sent overseas are recent graduates. Students coming out of a co-op program stand a better chance of being placed because they possess practical work experience. This is important, as many CUSO volunteers have already spent many years in the workforce. Along with co-op graduates, those with training in agriculture or the health sciences are always easier to place overseas. Spending two years working in a developing nation might not be of much professional benefit—personal growth is the main asset to the volunteer.

Organization: Canadian International Development Agency (CIDA)

Human Resources Directorate
CIDA
200 Promenade du Portage
Hull, Québec
KIA 0G4
(819) 994-6206

Head of Trainees and Awards: Mr Andre Champagne

Facts at a Glance:

Age: university graduate with 3 years of work experience

Duration: varies widely (2 months - 2 years)

Regional eligibility: all provinces

Salary:
- equivalent to a Canadian salary
- all travel expenses
- resettlement allowance

Getting in: apply to above address

Overview: CIDA selects university graduates with a few years of work experience for placement in developing countries. Those with technical skills, health-care experience, or agricultural training are particularly easy to place. Past experience in community work is an asset. Although you may not now have the necessary qualifications to go overseas with CIDA, you might want to keep them in mind for a few years down the line.

STUDENT PROFILE

Name: David Zemans
Age: 24
Home: Toronto, Ontario

Charting an International Career Path

David Zemans, at 24 years of age, has already managed to live and work in South America, Europe, Africa, and several places in North America; not an unimpressive feat for someone who is still a student at Dalhousie University Law School. David's resume reads more like an exotic travel itinerary than a chronological list of jobs held. David has made the most of his summers and early university years. Brought up in Toronto, he was encouraged to explore and see first hand what the world had to offer. After high school, he participated in Canada World Youth. He spent half of the program working on projects in Bolivia and the other half in a small Nova Scotia community. It was his first experience of living in Eastern Canada and this first taste would later help him decide to study law in Halifax. As fate would have it, half way through the Canada World Youth program the group was in need of a new leader and David was selected for the job. This experience proved to be invaluable when he later applied to be a cycling guide for Butterfield and Robinson. For two summers he took groups of students and adults on luxury tours through Europe. His previous travel experience in Europe and ability to speak Spanish as well as some French helped him secure the position.

After his first year of university, David sought to discover first hand whether or not a foreign service career would be to his liking. He enquired about summer jobs at Canadian consulates in New York and Boston as well as the embassy in Washington. The consulates wrote back indicating that all jobs were filled (often by family members of the staff), and while the Washington embassy didn't have any internships, they wrote back suggesting other possibilities. David phoned them up and by the end had managed to set up his own internship. The only catch—he was to be a volunteer. David was lucky that he was in a position to spend a summer this way—but it would pay off in many ways down the road. He lived in residence at George Washington University and spent two months working in every different area of the Embassy. As staff took summer holidays, he would fill in for them. Over the course of the summer he worked on the Dome Stadium Promotion Project, helped organize press conferences, did writing and research, and assisted with events surrounding a White Paper being delivered by Perrin Beatty. Embassy staff recognized that he was interested and they made sure that the job was a learning experience for him. Whenever something interesting was going on he was encouraged to go and observe or assist with it. The summer made him cognizant of the pros and cons of working in the foreign service. Another way in which David profited from the job was by receiving university credit for an independent research paper he did which focused on his experience.

The following summer David's embassy experience helped him to get a six-week job working for the Economic Summit which was held in Toronto. He was put in charge of hotels for several delegations, motorcades, security, and various logistical problems which had to be taken care of. It was another fascinating and well-paying experience during which he was given a significant degree of responsibility.

Now in law school, David is continuing to use his initiative to arrange interesting work experiences in far-off lands. Most recently he has combined a summer job with a large corporate firm with a seven-week placement working at three different legal clinics in South Africa! He's made no definite career plans for the future, but there is little doubt that all of his past experience will stand him in good stead for whatever he decides to do.

If you have an interest in the foreign service, why not see if other Canadian embassies would consider hiring a summer intern. The Canadian Embassy in Washington now employs two or three each summer. Don't be afraid to inquire into unusual opportunities. If you present them with an interesting and well-thought-out proposal, you might find that the company or organization might create something for you!

CHARTING AN INTERNATIONAL CAREER PATH

Today, more and more students are aspiring to an exotic lifestyle that includes international travel as part of their work or even a career that would allow them to live as an expatriate in some far-off land. As more and more students study foreign languages, spend a "year abroad" in Europe or further afield, and major in international politics, development or economics, they are not only broadening their outlook on life, but are trying to prepare themselves for a job on the international career track. But many, upon graduation, find that they are not sure where to begin looking for that entry-level position in the international market place. Some also find that they don't have the skills they need for these positions. Others simply expect that plum job in India to land in their lap. There are thousands (at least) of opportunities out there, but you are not likely to find them advertised in the want ads of your local newspaper. It's up to you to go looking for them. Searching for that prize job will take time and a great deal of energy. It will mean a lot of research, letter writing, and networking, but in the end, you will likely feel that the effort has been well worth it. In this next section we will discuss some approaches you might take to establish an international career, as well as highlight some of the skills you should develop in order to make yourself marketable. We will also review two seminars which could assist you in realizing your goals.

Foreign Service Examination and Career Counselling

FSECC
404 Laurier East
Suite 104
Ottawa, Ontario
KIN 6R2
phone: (613) 567-9229, fax: (613) 567-9098

The prospect of serving as part of Canada's diplomatic corps, as a representative in some far-flung corner of the world prompts several thousand young Canadians to write the annual entrance examination for the position of Foreign Service Officers with the Department of External Affairs and International Trade. These exams are held each fall at university campuses across the country. Those who pass it, and not very many do, are then invited for an interview. The entire selection process is extremely competitive.

Barry Yeates, President of FSECC, runs a two-day seminar designed to prepare you for the exam. He provides you with strategies and guidelines for each stage of the selection process. The course includes sample tests and drills using Foreign Service-type multiple-choice questions, special techniques for analyzing questions, advice for the written portion of the test, and a briefing on what to expect from the interview day (assuming you make it that far). Mr Yeates was himself a Foreign Service Officer and served in the Press Office in Ottawa, as well as in Washington as Executive Assistant to Canada's Ambassador. He now works as a private consultant for industry and government in Canada and abroad.

The examination tests your knowledge about international affairs, domestic politics and culture, and government policies and institutions. You can expect to be asked specific questions which relate to the trade, immigration, geopolitical, and macroeconomic responsibilities of External Affairs. To help you tackle these questions, you'll receive a study kit prepared by Barry Yeates. It includes sample questions, key statistical summaries, a concentrated bibliography, and essential publications and articles chosen to focus your reading and save you time. Literature includes the Annual Reports of CIDA and External Affairs, Canadian foreign policy statements and speeches, and newspaper clippings and press releases—among other materials. For a fee of $75, this kit is available from FSECC even if you don't take the course. However, the course shows you how to use these materials in a manner that will improve your exam performance.

Mr. Yeates' classes allow for personal attention, and his use of lectures, slides, and discussions ensure that the seminar is not only useful, but also stimulating and enjoyable. Mr. Yeates himself is extremely personable and helpful and is eager to speak with students and answer any questions they may have.

The seminars are offered at university campuses across Canada. They are sometimes sponsored by Student councils or other student organizations. The cost of the two-day seminar with kit is approximately $160. If you get in touch with Mr. Yeates he will be able to provide you with information on upcoming seminar dates and locations. By the way, the seminar has proven to be very helpful to students who have taken the exam. Attendees have a documented success rate that is more than three times that of the general test-taking group. If you're serious about wanting to give the Foreign Service Exam your best shot, this seminar is likely to be an invaluable investment.

Mr. Yeates also offers a career-oriented seminar which he introduced in response to the floods of questions from university students interested in entering the international job market. Since many people are not successful in their attempts to get into the Foreign Service Officer Program, they look for other opportunities. But, as Mr. Yeates was aware, there is very little information available to guide young people towards these international openings. In today's world of increasing global interdependence there is, among graduates, an increased interest in international jobs and there is an ever-increasing demand for Canada's graduates to work internationally.

This seminar is designed to prepare today's youth for these international career opportunities. Barry Yeates says that the course "surveys the sectors and types of positions which exist, the qualifications required, the competition encountered, and reviews the many avenues open to individuals to gain experience and improve their chances for obtaining work in the international arena."

All participants receive a comprehensive bibliography and address list of reference books and organizations to use as a starting point for job hunts. The formal part of the seminar, composed of lecture and visual segments, usually lasts an hour. After that Mr. Yeates makes himself available to answer specific questions and to give participants a chance to browse through the materials recommended in the bibliography. Mr. Yeates has presented his seminar at the invitation of many organizations, including the University of Toronto, AIESEC, the UN Association International Conference, and the Faculty of Management of McGill University, to name a few. As Mr. Yeates explains in his seminar, you don't need an Ivy League degree and connections with international "movers and shakers" to land overseas jobs with business or government. But, on the other hand, you're making a big mistake if you think that "a B.A. and a good head will land you work" with an international development agency, the UN or a Canadian Embassy. Recruiters seek people with language skills, technical knowledge, and advanced academic degrees. Experience is often an additional requirement, along with evidence that you'll be able to adjust to the stresses of an international posting. Mr. Yeates provides many ideas as to how you can work in a foreign land and develop the experience needed to land the top-flight jobs. If you're eager to attend this seminar, just give Mr. Yeates a call, or drop him a note, and he will let you know of a seminar being offered near you. If you are a student leader, why not get one of your campus organizations to sponsor this event and provide an excellent service to your fellow students?

Preparing Yourself for an International Career

Even if you are years away from applying for a full-time job, it's never too soon to start developing skills that will help to make you marketable on the international (or domestic) job market. Besides looking for a university education, many companies and agencies, when recruiting for overseas positions, look for people who have foreign language skills, experience working with other cultures and living abroad, and experience that shows you are adaptable, flexible, and able to deal with the challenges of living abroad. There are hundreds of opportunities that you can begin to take advantage of at a very early age, that will allow you to start developing some of these skills and qualities.

French and other language immersion classes help you to develop valuable language skills. Summer language study sessions in Canada and abroad allow you to perfect these skills, and year-long exchange programs round out the cultural experience. Specific opportunities can be found in the study section of the book. Programs such as Canada World Youth (p. 70), can help you develop work skills while learning and living in a developing country. Joining debating clubs, science fairs, and model UN groups will allow you to meet other Canadians and, in some cases, young people from around the world, increase your confidence and public speaking skills and possibly allow for some travel.

Your university years can be enriched by spending a study year abroad. Joining organizations such as AIESEC, WUSC, or participating on programs such as SWAP in order to spend a few months working in a foreign country are all worthwhile endeavors. You might also try volunteering your services part-time during the school year or the summer in order to gain experience in a hard-to-break-into field (for example, an international agency, embassy, or non-governmental organization). You might even consider taking a year off from school to work abroad on a program such as JET.(p. 85)

Becoming involved in organizations that are consistent with your interests will help you to meet people in the field. Why not try to do a few informational interviews? Simply make an appointment to speak with someone in a particular organization or agency that you are interested in working with in the future and find out what it takes to get your foot in the door. If you are professional, have done your homework, and can come across as articulate and intelligent, you'll likely get an opportunity to speak with someone who'll be more than happy to answer your questions and give you some advice and guidance. On the following pages you'll find the names of some organizations through which you may be able to start looking for jobs. Some have specific jobs available, while others may be good resources for general information. Don't just fire off letters to these places. First, find out all you can about what they are involved in and then plan a strategy. Decide what information you want to learn from the group, identify who in the organization might be best able to assist you and then send a well-written and presentable letter. Follow it up with a telephone call and ask for a meeting if it seems appropriate. Be sure to consider both Canadian and international public sector organizations, non-governmental organizations and associations, private-sector companies, foundations and academic opportunities through schools, scholarships and exchanges.

Canadian Human Rights Commission
90 Sparks Street
Suite 400
Ottawa, Ontario
KIA IEI
(613) 996-0026

Canadian Institute for International Peace and Security
360 Albert Street
Suite 900
Ottawa, Ontario
KIR 7X7
(613) 990-1593

Canadian Security Intelligence Service
P.O. Box 9732
Ottawa Postal Terminal
Ottawa, Ontario
KIG 4G4
(613) 954-2382

CIDA/BMC Project
c/o Mr. A. Millington, Associate Director
International Development Support Centre
Bureau of Management Consulting
Supply and Services Canada
8th floor, Journal Tower South
365 Laurier Avenue West
Ottawa, Ontario
KIA 0S5
(613) 995-7465

Export Development Corporation — Head Office
Place Export Canada
151 O'Connor Street
P.O. Box 655
Ottawa, Ontario
KIP 5T9
(613) 598-2500 (many regional offices across the country)

Foreign Service Recruitment
c/o Mr. George Rejhon, Senior Advisor International Appointments
Personnel Operations Bureau (APD)

Department of External Affairs
Lester B. Pearson Building (D-4)
125 Sussex Drive
Ottawa, Ontario
K1A 0G2

International Centre for Ocean Development (ICOD)
5670 Spring Garden Road, 9th floor
Halifax, Nova Scotia
B3J 1H6
(902) 426-1512

International Development Research Centre (IDRC)
250 Albert Street
P.O. Box 8500
Ottawa, Ontario
K1G 3H9
(613) 598-0543

Investment Canada
240 Sparks Street, 5th floor West
P.O. Box 2800, Station D
Ottawa, Ontario
K1P 6A5
(613) 995-9639

Petro-Canada International Assistance Corporation (PCIAC)
1601 - 360 Albert Street
Ottawa, Ontario
K1R 7X7
(613) 990-6000

Youth Initiatives Program
c/o Ms. Lucie Bohac, Coordinator
Canadian International Development Agency
Place du Centre
200 Promenade du Portage
Hull, Québec
K1A 0G4
(613) 997-5456

Asia Pacific Foundation of Canada
999 Canada Place
Suite 666
Vancouver, British Columbia

V6V IN4
(604) 684-5986

The Canadian Chamber of Commerce
Ottawa Office
55 Metcalfe Street
Ottawa, Ontario
(613) 238-4000 (regional offices in Montreal and Toronto)

Canadian Institute of International Affairs
15 King's College Circle
Toronto, Ontario
M5S 2V9
(416) 979-1851

Commonwealth Youth Programme: Headquarters Commonwealth Secretariat
Marlborough House, Pall Mall
London, England SW1Y 5HX
01-839-3411

Overseas Development Associates Program (ODAP)
c/o Ms. Yannick Portebois, Coordinator
Institute for International Development and Corporation
University of Ottawa
Ottawa, Ontario
KIN 6N5
(613) 564-5779

United Nations Association in Canada
63 Sparks Street
Suite 808
Ottawa, Ontario
KIP 5A6
(613) 232-5751

Asian Development Bank — Young Professionals Program
Personnel Division, Young Professionals Program
Asian Development Bank
P.O. Box 789, Manila
The Philippines
(63-2) 711-3851

Special Opportunities with Religious Organizations

Often valuable exchange and work opportunities exist within organizations with whom you may already be actively involved. You need only enquire to find out what may be available. This is especially the case with religious organizations. Many denominations run exchange programs in developing countries and others operate work or service programs. Below are addresses for a few organizations whose work programs overseas are widely publicized. To participate in these programs, a firm religious commitment is normally expected. Further information about the programs offered can be obtained directly from the organization.

Mennonite Central Committee
134 Plaza Drive
Winnipeg, Manitoba
R3T 5K9
(204) 261-6381

Canadian Baptist Overseas
Mission
217 St. George Street
Toronto, Ontario
M5R 2M2
(416) 922-5163

Canadian Jesuit Missions
661 Greenwood Avenue
Toronto, Ontario
M4J 4B3
(416) 466-1195

Africa Inland Mission
1641 Victoria Park
Toronto, Ontario,
M1R 1P8
(416) 751-6077

Volunteer International
Christian Service
2475 Queen Street East
Toronto, Ontario
M4E 1H8
(416) 691-3022

Volunteering Your Services

Making money, money and more money. That is what working is all about. Right?

Well...yes, often that is why people work. But how much money you can make shouldn't always be the main criterion for choosing a job, particularly when you are young, probably living at home, and can perhaps afford to take a job for the experience rather than for the salary. If you are lucky enough to be able to do without the extra income of a part-time job, you should consider volunteering your time.

Volunteer work can go beyond the traditional helping out in a hospital or doing community service. These are excellent and rewarding experiences, but students often want to develop skills that future employers may look for. A student might want to acquire these skills within a business or government. Most students would never consider approaching a company or organization to offer to work for them on a volunteer basis. But this is a great way to gain valuable work experience in a field that interests you. You can also make valuable contacts and work with people who might provide references for you at a later date. Chances are, the experience gained will improve your employment prospects when you are applying for a paying job. It may even get you a job at that company as a salaried employee.

If you are considering volunteering your services during the summer or school year, there are a few things you should keep in mind. First of all, employers receive very few requests of this kind. For this reason, some will jump at the opportunity to meet with you, while others will suspect ulterior motives and wonder, "What's this kid's angle?" Still others may not give you the time of day. But don't despair. Unless you try, you won't know what the reaction will be. Besides, if they turn down your offer, it will be their loss and someone else's gain. More often than not, if your approach is right, you will probably find people very receptive to your proposal.

And here is the second point to remember. When approaching someone for whom you wish to volunteer, be professional. This doesn't mean that you must go out and buy a Brooks Brothers, find a briefcase and assume your most convincing Alex P. Keaton imitation. It does mean that you must treat this situation as you would any job for which you might apply. Write to the company you're interested in and explain what you'd like to do. Tell them why you are interested in their firm and be sure to mention how much time you are prepared to give and when you would be available. Ideally, you should suggest a regular schedule (one day per week, Monday/Wednesday/Friday 3pm-5pm, or whatever the case may be), so that you are sure to treat this opportunity as you would any job. After all, this *is* a job, with the only difference that you do not expect to be paid for your time. When you write to the company, include a copy of your resumé and give them an idea of what type of work you can do. If an employer finds your proposal interesting, he or she will probably invite you for an interview.

Once you have succeeded in securing your position, the ball is in your court. At first you will probably be given repetitive and minor tasks. However, if you show that you can follow instructions, are interested and are willing to learn, you may soon find yourself exposed to all kinds of new situations. Remember, you won't become president overnight; just being in this professional working environment is a valuable learning opportunity. You can pick up a great deal through observation, listening and asking questions.

We spoke with several students who spent summers, as well as time during the school year, volunteering for an organization. A student from Florenceville, New Brunswick, volunteered at a Toronto advertising firm one summer. By living with friends, she was able to gain interesting experience in a hard-to-break-into field without worrying about not making any money. A 20-year-old McGill student who was interested in a career in publishing did volunteer work for a small publisher. He had a conventional summer job to earn money for school, but volunteered his days off at the company. The students in these cases, like most students, had no family connections to help them gain experience in their field of interest. What set them apart was their refusal to let this be a stumbling block. All found the work experience extremely interesting and eye-opening. They spoke very highly of this method as a means of beating the vicious circle of "I can't get a job because I have no experience, and I can't get experience because I can't get a job."

If you want to get some hands-on experience and knowledge of a certain field, choose a firm and volunteer your services. The long term-benefits could be invaluable.

There are also numerous organizations, societies and agencies who are always looking for eager volunteers. Most community service agencies, museums, hospitals, retirement homes, and clubs offer interesting volunteer positions. This is a rewarding way to spend a few hours of your time. It can show you new situations and help you acquire skills. *The Directory of Volunteer Opportunities* is an excellent guide in finding the specific volunteer position you seek. This directory is listed in the book review section at the end of this chapter.

STUDENT PROFILE

Name: Lisa Yarmoshuk
Home: St. Catharines, Ontario

From Volunteer To Political Employee

For me what started as part-time volunteer work at the age of 16, in a Member of Parliament's constituency office led to a full-time summer job with the Treasurer of Ontario. Wanting to learn about politics and gain work experience, I wrote to all my area MPs and MPPs, volunteering my services for the summer.

Like most people, I had no personal or family political connections; nevertheless, I felt that I had nothing to lose by trying to get involved. Still in high school, I was living at home and didn't need to earn a lot of money. The value of the experience compensated for the fact that I didn't get paid.

Although only one MP responded to my letter, this was enough. Gilbert Parent, then the MP for Welland, arranged an interview. Our meeting led Mr Parent to offer me a volunteer position in his office for the summer, three days a week. I observed politics at the grassroots: I answered correspondence, assisted constituents, and helped to deal with day-to-day problems. At the end of the summer, I was pleasantly surprised when Mr Parent asked me to continue working for him part-time during the school year—this time as a well-paid employee! I was further shocked when I was paid in full for every hour I had volunteered that summer! My case, although unusual in that I was reimbursed for the time I volunteered, illustrates some of the benefits to be gained from taking a risk and volunteering your services. Employers are bound to respect your enterprising spirit, and even if they don't hire you, they will, at the very least, provide valuable references in the future. Also, you will develop many skills and gain practical work experience.

Depending on your interests, you might try a similar approach in the arts, big business or education. Your novel approach will probably not soon be forgotten.

BOOK REVIEWS

Our book is designed to provide information on opportunities available from Canadian organizations. It does not attempt to provide complete information on opportunities offered by foreign organizations and is not intended to be the last word in information sources. If you are looking for work opportunities abroad, there are a number of very useful guides available. Most of these are American or British publications, but they are usually relevant to Canadian youth. These guides advise on the where, when and how of finding jobs around the world. You will probably find that all of these books provide helpful advice and guidance on a particular topic; to get answers to all of your questions you may well have to look at two or three different publications.

The Canadian Guide to Working and Living Overseas
by Jean-Marc Hachey (Ottawa, Canada: Intercultural Systems/Systemes interculturels, 1992)

The author spent the last five years researching this excellent guide and many years before that learning his topic inside-out by working overseas with various organizations. It is aimed at readers from university age to professionals well into their careers. The 500 page book is full of useful information about international agencies, private firms abroad, exchange programs, career strategies, letter writing techniques etc. If you are thinking about a career abroad, this guide would be an invaluable resource. The cost of the guide is $35 and you will find it in resource centers and book stored across the country

---

Work Your Way Around the World, 16th Edition
by Susan Griffith (London, England: Vacation Work, 1993).

This is a well-written and thorough guide to finding a variety of jobs around the world. Country by country, it tells what sort of work is available and how to find it. In addition, young travellers comment on the jobs they did get and discuss the highs and lows of their experiences. It is updated regularly so you should be able to find a current edition.

Work, Study, Travel Abroad: The Whole World Handbook; by Marjorie Cohen (New York, New York: Council on International Educational Exchange, 1991).

This guide gives details on short-term work and volunteer positions and offers lots of useful hints for planning a working holiday. It is organized by country and gives information about work, study and travel on every continent. It is useful to both teenagers and young adults.

The Teenager's Guide to Study, Travel and Adventure Abroad (New York, New York: Council on International Educational Exchanges, 1991).

This guide has been written specifically for 12-18 year olds. It provides information on independent travel opportunities, exotic summer camps, homestays, foreign language study, and work experiences. The book is written for American teenagers, but many of the programs are open to Canadians. The book also gives helpful suggestions on what to look for when choosing a program. In their most recent edition, the authors interview students who have participated on various programs. We were able to pick this book up at Coles for $0.99! So keep your eyes open.

Working Holidays
by Hilary Sewell (London, England: Central Bureau for Educational Visits and Exchanges, 1993).

This 320 page book can be purchased for $19.95 and details job opportunities on five continents, with an emphasis on Europe. It is updated annually and, while it is written for British travellers, there are opportunities for Canadians as well. There is a special chapter for North American readers which details the process of applying for work permits and visas.

Directory of Overseas Summer Jobs - 1993, 24th Edition by David Woodworth (Oxford, England: Vacation Work).

Published yearly, this book boasts information on over 50,000 overseas paid and volunteer positions. The nature of the work, wage and application procedure is included for each employer. Most positions are in European countries. Written for a British audience, there are lots of opportunities for Canadians.

Summer Jobs in Britain 1993 by Susan Griffith (Oxford, England: Vacation Work).

Another annual publication in the extensive Vacation Work series, this guide tells of short-term job opportunities by region in each of England, Scotland, and Wales.

What in the World is Going On? (Canadian Bureau for International Education, 1991; 85 Albert Street, Suite 1400; Ottawa, Ontario K1P 6A4) (613) 237- 4820.

This recently updated CBIE directory describes hundreds of options for working, studying or volunteering in developing countries. It is full of specific program information, as well as contact addresses and telephone numbers. Its focus is government and non-governmental development organizations. It is available directly from CBIE.

Directory of Canadian Non-governmental Organizations engaged in International Development
(Canadian Council for International Cooperation; 450 Rideau Street; Ottawa, Ontario. K1N 5Z4)

This directory provides further information about opportunities to work in developing countries. However, most of the opportunities are intended for university graduates and individuals with work experience.

Employment Resources
(United Nations Association in Canada; 63 Sparks Street; Ottawa, Ontario. K1P 5A6)

This fact sheet, prepared by the UN, describes how to apply for jobs with the UN and its agencies or field projects. It can be obtained by writing to the above address.

The International Directory of Voluntary Work;
by R. Brown & D. Woodworth (Oxford, England: Vacation Work: 1993).

This is a useful guide to finding volunteer work opportunities worldwide. As with all the Vacation Work books, it is aimed at U.K. readers, but is also of use to interested Canadians. In most cases you pay your own travel, but room and board is provided. Like most of the Vacation Work series, it is published annually.

The Directory of Jobs & Careers Abroad
by Andre de Vries (Oxford, England: Vacation Work 1993).

This directory provides information on many foreign job opportunities on a country by country basis. However, 90% of the positions require specific skills and previous work experience.

Invest Yourself
(The Commission on Voluntary Service and Action; P.O. Box 117; New York, New York. 10009).

This book gives more information about volunteer work through U.S. agencies. Many of the opportunities listed are available to Canadians.

Sojourns
(Canadian Bureau for International Education).

Sojourns is a computer database containing detailed information on a vast array of programs for work and study in other countries available to Canadians. Included are both short and long-term employment, volunteer work, study programs, exchanges, and scholarships. The program is new and is available to members of the CBIE for $250 and to non-members for $350. Sojourns will be available in many university and college guidance offices. For more information contact Ronald Clement at CBIE, (613) 237-4820.

The Directory of Work & Study in Developing Countries
by David Leppard (Oxford, England: Vacation Work)

This is another useful guide for individuals interested in finding work in the Third World. It lists opportunities in the fields of health and education as well as many others. Most positions require specific skills and previous work experience.

Directory of Volunteer Opportunities
(Career Resource Centre; Needles Hall, University of Waterloo; Waterloo, Ontario N2L 3G1).

Want to do volunteer work in your community but don't know what's available or where to begin looking? This is a first rate guide to over a hundred community, regional, and national volunteer opportunities available in Canada. Whatever your interests, there is an organization looking for your help. This directory has been recently updated and can be ordered for a cost of $10.00

The Overseas List
by David M. Beckman and Elizabeth Anne Donnely (Augsburg Publishing House).

This guide focuses on Christian service and is aimed at providing information to those interested in living and working in developing countries. It provides many leads in its sections on business, study teaching, and journalism.

Kibbutz Volunteer
by John Bedford (Oxford, England: Vacation-Work).

A very revealing guide to what Kibbutz living is all about. There are many job opportunity listings, as well as interesting information on Israel.

The Au Pair and Nanny's Guide to Working Abroad
by Susan Griffith and Sharon Legg (Oxford, England: Vacation-Work 1989). This is

One of the best books we can across for anyone wanting to work as an au pair anywhere in the world. The authors discuss all sorts of background information you might want - including how to find a job, what is expected of you, what you should consider when selecting a job and much, much more.

Transitions
(18 Hulst Road; Box 344; Amhurst, Massachusetts; U.S.A. 01004; (413) 256-0373).

A subscription to this quarterly magazine gives you a wealth of useful and up-to-date work, travel, and study information at your fingertips. It informs you of off-beat work opportunities, familiarizes you with many unique study institutions, and whets your appetite for adventurous travel experiences. It is a well worth the price of subscription.

HOT 100: A Quick Guide to Federal Programs and Services for Youth (Minister of State for Youth; Government of Canada).

As the title indicates, this handy book offers information on more than 100 work, travel and study programs, services, and resources financed by the Canadian government. It is well organized, informative, and thoroughly updated every year. The guide was widely distributed across Canada to schools, universities, colleges, libraries, and Canada Employment Centres. Considering that 150,000 copies were printed, you shouldn't have any trouble finding one to look through.

Jobs in Paradise
by Jeffrey Maltzman (Harper Perennial, New York 1993)

This book may help you find your dream job on a tropical, exotic island in the carribean, south pacific or elsewhere.

Teaching English Abroad: Talk Your Way Around the World
by Susan Griffith (Oxford, Vacation-Work, 1991).

This book gives lots of practical advice for how to go about finding work as teacher in over 50 countries on all countinents. Readers are also provided with addresses of schools and organizations who employ foreign language teachers.

International Jobs: Where They Are — How to Get Them (1984)
(Don Mills, Ontario: Addison-Wesley Publishing; (416) 447-5101).

Making it Abroad: The International Job Hunting Guide (1988);
by Howard Schuman (Toronto, Ontario: John Wiley and Sons; (416) 675-3580).

Careers in International Affairs (1982) (Georgetown University of Foreign Service; Washington, D.C. 20057; (202) 625-4216).

"Chainletter" (Career Information Resource Advisory Group (CIRAG); c/o Kathy Harris, Editor; Career Planning and Placement; Queen's University; Kingston, Ontario; K7L 3N6; (613) 545-2992).

Guide to Careers in World Affairs (1987) (Foreign Policy Association; 205 Lexington Avenue; New York, N.Y. 10016; (212) 481-8450).

Travel

Introduction

There is no better time to travel than the present. Lack of money and lack of experience, which you might see as obstacles to travel, are surprisingly easy to overcome. As a student, there's one thing you do have that other people usually don't have: the time to travel. Lengthy summer vacations, as well as numerous school year breaks and relatively flexible term scheduling, provide perfect opportunities to explore the world. As a student (high school, college or university) you can take advantage of discount fares offered by all sectors of the travel industry. With proof of your age and student status you can expect to fly, dine, enter museums and find accommodation at drastically reduced prices. You'll never again be able to travel so inexpensively (perhaps until you reach 65). Not only will you save money on straight discounts but, because you're young and adventurous, you'll cut down on expenses in ways that your parents probably wouldn't dream of. For instance, while in Paris, instead of taking your evening meal at La Tour d'Argent, if you're money conscious you'll more likely pick up a baguette, cheese, and a tartine from the tiny shops which line virtually every street in Paris and enjoy your repast on a park bench. When it's time to go to bed, for around $15 you can stay at a clean, well-kept hostel. If you're still under the misconception that you can't afford to travel, in this chapter you'll read about programs which offer travel absolutely free!

The benefits of travel are endless—learning a new language, meeting interesting people, and seeing incredible scenery are some of the obvious ones. Perhaps most important, travelling broadens your perception of the world. The more you see on your travels, the more doors you'll open for yourself and your future.

The following pages tell you about the many different ways in which you can travel in Canada and abroad. Whether you want to take a trip for one week or one year, or travel alone or with a group, you will find all sorts of suggestions on how to bring your ideas to reality. In one section we tell you about programs that allow you to attend seminars in Ottawa and Africa and conferences in Whitehorse and New York. In another section you can learn about numerous travel opportunities available through several unique youth organizations. Students who have benefited from these experiences tell you what to expect and how to get involved. Under the headings of "Overview" and "Inside View" you can read about the goals of the programs as well as get inside information on the program. In other sections you'll find descriptions of unusual travel agencies which arrange tours combining the excitement of adventure with a more structured program. For the independent spirit who wishes to plan his or her own trip across Canada or to points further afield, we have provided a section of advice and suggestions on how realize your plans.

Throughout these sections, we suggest both ways of spending a fortune on your trip and ways of surviving successfully on the smallest of budgets. In the "Student Profiles" you can read how students managed to make extensive travel part of their high school and university years. At the end of this section we recommend several specialized travel books that can assist you in your preparations.

Whether you decide to venture to Ottawa by bus, to Beijing by train, or to Sydney by plane, this chapter will help you get there. Above all, we wish you BON VOYAGE!

Seminars

Seminars, whether for one week or six weeks, in Canada or abroad, are a great way to meet new people, encounter new ideas and travel to new places. All the programs listed in this section draw students from every corner of Canada. They all involve at least a bit of travel and they cost very little—sometimes nothing at all. So why wait and miss a terrific opportunity to broaden your horizons—take a close look at what's available.

Organization: Council for Canadian Unity
Program: Encounters With Canada

The Terry Fox Canadian Youth Centre
P.O. Box 7279
Ottawa, Ontario
K1L 8E3
(613) 744-1290

Program Director: M Francis Dumont-Frenette

Facts at a Glance:

Age: 15-17

Duration: 1 week (September - May)

Regional eligibility: all provinces

Cost:
$495
often paid by your school, board of education, or a local charitable association)

That covers:

- travel from your home to Ottawa (through grants from the Secretary of State)
- room and board
- materials, tours, etc.

Getting in:

- application forms available from your high school or from above address
- apply at least 2 months before you'd like to participate

Overview: The Encounters with Canada program offers young Canadians the chance to get to know their country, their fellow Canadians and their capital city for one week. It also gives students from all over Canada a chance to meet and get to know each other. Every week from September to May (except for the few weeks around Christmas), roughly 140 students representing every province arrive in Ottawa to stay at the Terry Fox Canadian Youth Centre. When they apply, students are asked to choose one of the following thematic programs: Arts and Culture, Science and Technology, Law, Journalism and Communications, Canadian Experience, or Business and Entrepreneurship. Organizers try to place participants in the program of their choice. Activities during the week include seminars, guest lectures, tours of Parliament and museums, group discussions, and conferences.

Inside View: Encounters with Canada is probably the most social of the five week-long Ottawa seminars featured in this section. Although you're bound to learn a lot about Canadian institutions, the emphasis is on activities which encourage students to get to know each other. You and 139 of your soon-to-be roommates will be housed at the Terry Fox Canadian Youth Centre. You'll eat your meals as a group (in a cafeteria) and sleep in two huge rooms full of bunk beds (men on one floor, women on another).

Your days will be packed with planned activities, including presentations by MPs and senators, and visits to Question Period at the House of Commons and to the Governor General's residence. Except for planned group excursions, you won't be allowed to leave the Centre without special permission (for instance, if your grandmother from Ottawa wanted to pick you up and take you out for dinner, it could probably be arranged). Of course the use of alcohol and illegal drugs is strictly forbidden. The Centre very rarely has problems with students because all participants have been recommended by their high schools. When a problem does arise, students are sent home immediately at their own expense.

If you live far from Ottawa, this program should be of particular interest because all travel expenses are covered by the Secretary of State. It is also important to know that if you live away from Ottawa, (especially in B.C. or Newfoundland), you should apply very early because travel grants are limited.

Organization: Rotary International
Program: Adventures in Citizenship

Contact your local Rotary Club
Chairman: Mr Bob Gammon (Ottawa Rotary Club)

Facts at a Glance:

Age: 17-18

Duration: 4 days (in May)

Regional eligibility: all provinces

Cost: no cost (students are sponsored by local Rotary clubs)

That covers:
* return travel from your home to Ottawa
* room and board

Getting in:
* contact your local Rotary club for application information
* each branch uses different selection criteria
* inquire as early as possible

Overview: Each year, the Ottawa Rotary Club organizes this intro-
duction to Canada, its government, and capital. Representing Rotary
clubs from across the country, 250 students meet in Ottawa to learn
why we should be proud to be Canadians. This seminar is designed
to enhance students' appreciation of their country, its people and its
institutions. While in Ottawa, students are housed with local Rotari-
ans. The program is very broad and includes visits to embassies,
RCMP headquarters, the Bank of Canada, the National Research
Council (NRC) space agency, and Parliament Hill. Students attend
an MP dinner one night, and a reception at Government House. The
week ends with a luncheon and a ceremony at the Citizenship Court.
The program aims to attract students who are outstanding all-round
young people, who will be good ambassadors for their region. There
is no standardized way of gaining acceptance to the program, as each
club has its own procedure for choosing its participant. Not all clubs
participate each year. If you're interested we recommend that you
contact the Rotary Club in your area for further details.

Organization: Foundation for the Study of Processes of Government in Canada
Program: Forum For Young Canadians

251 Laurier Avenue West
Suite 801
Ottawa, Ontario
K1P 5J6
(613) 233-4086

Executive Director: Ms Clare Baxter

Facts at a Glance:

Age: 16 - 19

Duration: 1 week

Regional eligibility: all provinces

Cost:
- $645 registration fee (usually raised through sponsors)
- $195 for travel costs (when applicable)

That covers:
- room, board, and all activities
- return travel from home to Ottawa

Getting in:
- application forms available at high schools
- often school officials approach someone they think would profit from the experience, so if you want to go, we suggest you make your interest known to your principal or history teacher
- deadline is mid November
- somewhat competitive (900 apply for 500 spots)

Overview: Each year, Forum for Young Canadians provides 500 students with an intensive, one-week course on how the Government of Canada makes decisions. Participants come from every corner of the country, which allows each an opportunity to better understand Canada and its people. Participants also get a first-hand view of governmental process. Each year, approximately 900 students apply for the available positions.

Inside View: Forum is admittedly the most academically oriented of the four Ottawa seminars available to high school students, offering a very "hard-edged academic program". Virtually every minute of the six-day schedule is planned for you. A typical day might see you touring the parliamentary library, hearing a lecture by a senator, visiting the National Gallery, and discussing provincial rights. Each day begins at 7:30 am and winds down with an 11:30 pm curfew. We don't want to mislead the reader, all participants we spoke with remember the week as one of education, friendship, and lots of fun.

The course is given by constitutional experts, Privy Council and PMO officials, Cabinet ministers, judges, and other individuals who are currently participating in government. They speak about what they do, what their responsibilities are, where they have freedom of action and where they are limited. Each speaker has 15 minutes to make a presentation. Students then have 45 minutes to question them - and students get in line to grill them. Consequently, the success of the session depends on the quality of the speaker and the intellectual curiosity of the participants. You are expected to do your homework before arriving in Ottawa to ensure that you will know what is going on; a recommended reading list is sent to all Forum participants before they leave home. Other planned activities are tours of Rideau Hall, Parliament, and the Supreme Court. Throughout the week, you will lunch with senators and have dinner with MPs.

Participants are first chosen by their schools; a regional selection is then made based on qualifications and a provincial/territorial quota system. Candidates must be good students, usually having an A or A- average, but they must also take part in extra-curricular activities. Letters of recommendation are given careful consideration. Because much of the time in Ottawa will be spent in groups, good communication skills are required.

Alison Loat, 17, of St. Catharines, Ontario, had just returned from her week with Forum when we spoke with her in the summer of 1993. Despite the academic nature of the week, as with the other Ottawa programs, the friendships she made were a definite highlight for Alison. She told us that the 120 participants were evenly divided from all over Canada. She also enjoyed the mock elections and debates. Another bit of inside information - during her Forum session the whole group stayed in a hotel, while during other sessions the group stays in school residence dorms. If you could somehow discreetly and anonimously find out which sessions get to stay at a hotel it might be worth trying to go then. The Executive Director of Forum wrote that "Forum is a tough and demanding program which leaves the participants with a lot of satisfaction, they learn an awful lot in the space of one week."

Organization: Interchange on Canadian Studies
Program: National Conference

F.H. Collins School
1001 Lewes Boulevard
Whitehorse, Yukon
Y1A 3J6
phone: (403) 668-3898, fax: (403) 668-3885

National Director: Mr Richard Martin

Facts at a Glance:

Age: 16 - 17 1/2

Duration: 1 week (April or May)

Regional eligibility: all provinces

Cost: $500 (usually raised by schools, boards of education or service clubs)

That covers:
- return travel from home to conference site
- room and board
- all activities

Getting in:
- the process varies from province to province
- contact your provincial board of education for more information

Overview: Interchange on Canadian Studies is a week-long forum on national issues for high school students from across Canada. This conference provides students from each province with the opportunity to increase their understanding of Canada's cultural diversity and identity as a nation. Each year the conference is held in a different province or territory and students are billeted with host participants. Often, the host will visit his or her twin for a week during the summer.

Inside View: This week of academic and social activities aims to facilitate and further a knowledge of Canada. Students are given the opportunity to hear and to meet with prominent speakers from a variety of fields. The group workshops allow Canadians from every region of the country to share ideas and experiences, thereby gaining a better understanding of and appreciation for the regional and cultural diversity of Canada. In addition, tours, dances, and pin swapping are all part of the week's activities. Before students leave for the conference, they participate in a two-day orientation with the other members of their provincial delegation. This allows them to meet some other delegates and prepares them for the program of the upcoming days.

The students we spoke with said that at first they were a bit nervous about whether they would get along with their twins, but for most this fear quickly wore off. Organizers try their best to match up participants who have common interests. Many students say the best part of the experience was meeting and getting to know students from every part of Canada. One delegate wrote, "I was really surprised how much everyone had in common.... I was expecting stereotypes, but the people I met shared similar views, interests, and fears."

Tom Casey, a 16-year-old from Morden, Manitoba, added, "The confidence I have in my country has been greatly influenced by this week. Up until now I was not sure what Canada had to offer—now I know." The conference will be hosted by Newfoundland in 1994 and the following year students from across the country will head to Manitoba for Interchange.

Organization: The Royal Commonwealth Society
Program: Student Commonwealth Conference

969 Bronson Avenue
Suite 111
Ottawa, Ontario
KIS 4G8
(613) 235-9856

President: Ms Shirley Webb

Facts at a Glance:

Age: grade 12 students

Duration: one week every spring

Regional eligibility: all provinces

Cost: none

That covers:
- return airfare
- room and board
- tours and activities

Getting in:
- application forms available from above address
- applications should be received by late November

Overview: The Student Commonwealth Conference has been taking place every year since 1973. The event, which annually involves 140 secondary school students from every province, is sponsored by the Royal Commonwealth Society. The conference takes place in Ottawa where participants are billeted in the homes of local participants. The focus of the event is on group discussions, simulation games, independent tours, guest lectures and workshops. The aim is to develop in students a sense of international relations and the interdependence of nations.

Inside view: This is an Ottawa conference with a few interesting twists. Upon arrival in the capital, you and the 139 other participants will be split into groups of three. For the duration of the week you and your two "colleagues" act as the delegation of a Commonwealth country, let's say Barbados. In group discussions and mock Heads of Government meetings you take your country's stand on issues. To make the experience more real, you will be told, prior to your departure for Ottawa, which country you will be representing. You are expected to do some research into the policies, economy and political situation of your new nation.

Another interesting twist at this seminar is the way in which tours are conducted. Instead of being bussed around the city en masse, again participants are divided into small groups. Each group is provided with a list of sites to visit and a disposable camera to bring back proof that you hit all of your stops. It seems like you'll be given a fair amount of freedom and responsibility. Even meal time is a bit different at the Commonwealth Conference. At one of your banquets the theme will be "food for thought". That evening for every person who is lucky enough to dine on steak and potatoes, there'll be someone else stuck with rice or nothing at all. The point of this little exercise is to make clear that even though all Commonwealth countries share a tie to the Queen, we don't all share the same economic advantages. Sounds interesting.

This conference is designed for students, by students. The organizing committee members, all under 22 years of age, are all past participants on the conference from the Ottawa area. They know what makes for an interesting week. If you'd be interested in getting involved in Commonwealth Society activities get in touch with the people at the above address. Activities at a regional level take place in Halifax, Winnipeg, Victoria, and Vancouver.

Organization: Lester B. Pearson College of the Pacific
Program: Summer Seminar in International Development

Lester B. Pearson
Victoria, B.C.
V8X 3W9
(604) 478-5591

Program Director: Marc Abrioux

Facts at a Glance:

Age: Grade 11 students

Duration: 3 weeks in August

Regional eligibility: all provinces, quota system

Cost: $150

That covers:
- all fees, materials, room and board
- travel expenses to Victoria are often paid by the participant's school board (if not, the student must also pay this)

Where can I go? Victoria, B.C.

Getting in:
- application forms are available from the above address and requires a reference letter from the student's principal
- past involvement in international development, extracurricular, public speaking and volunteer work is helpful

Overview: This high school development seminar has been around for four years. Modelled on the 10 year old university program Discovering our Future (p. 184) it is also funded by CIDA. It aims to educate Canadian youth on development issues and highten their interest in the Third World. Each August 80 grade 11 Canadian students participate in at the Lester B. Pearson College of the Pacific in Victoria, B.C.

Inside View: This is an incredible way for any grade 11 student to spend one month of his or her summer vacation. After living with

175

80 young Canadians and 50 16-year old students from developing countries at Lester B. Pearson College's colonyyou are guaranteed to have a new outlook on life and new goals for the future. Lester B. Pearson itself is a spectacular facility of cedar buildings overloooking the Pacific Ocean and situated in a forest (see p. 246). If that isn't enough, this seminar gives you the chance to work, learn and live with students from across the country and around the world. The program uses small discussion groups, seminars and community outreach activities in its exploration of topical development issues. It provides unique opportunity for a very intense and dynamic educational, cultural and travel experience at a young age. The program is very popular, so you should spend some time preparing your application - particularly the essay on why you want to participate.

Note: This program is funded by CIDA and thus may be subject to some new funding rules. You should therefore verify that it is being offered in 1994.

STUDENT PROFILE

Name: Jeffrey Blain
Age: 19
Home: St. Catharines, Ontario

A keen interest in politics has helped open doors for Jeffrey Blain. Now entering university, Jeffrey has taken advantage of many available programs (several of which he came across in the early editions of this book!) and definitely made the most of his final years of high school.

Jeff began getting the most from his education early in his academic career. While in grade 7, Jeff applied to be and was accepted as a page in the Ontario legislature. This meant the chance to experience life in Toronto for five weeks, the vast majority of which was experienced from the legislative assembly room itself. The program is politically intense and involves spending approximately 40 hours per week scurrying around fetching water, filling binders, and passing notes to and from MPPs. On top of the long hours on work duty, Jeff and the 22 other pages spent five hours each week with a tutor. While in Toronto, Jeff, like most students on the program, stayed with relatives. The page program provides a great chance to raise your political awareness, work and study closely with a small group of other students, and get a taste of independence at a fairly early age.

The next couple of years (grades 8 and 9), while in a French immersion program, Jeff put his new language to work on two exchanges to Quebec. The following year, while involved in the yearbook, orchestra, chess club, math team, and as a peer tutor, Jeff also decided to apply for the Encounters with Canada program. Until Jeff read about this exciting opportunity no one from his high school had ever been on Encounters with Canada. It was just another program, which had been overlooked by the overworked guidance team at Jeff's school. Jeff was accepted as a participant. He asked to go when the theme was to be Science and Technology and he got his choice. (There are several themes to chose from and it is not always possible to accommodate a students' first choice). In order to raise the money for the trip, Jeff asked his school and the local Lion's Club if they would help him out (the former gave him $100, the latter $225). In exchange, Jeff gave speeches to both groups upon his return. Because of his fund-raising efforts, the entire cost to Jeff was $50. Highlights of the week in Ottawa included hanging around with kids from places as diverse as Whitehorse and St. John's, touring the Chalk River Nuclear Plant, and visiting the Science Museum and the Parliament Buildings. Most of all, Jeff remembers Encounters as "a heck of a lot of fun. The climax was the all night dance." Because the entire group is housed in a dormitory building and eat their meals together in a cafeteria the week can't help but be a very social one.

This year Jeff participated on another of the Ottawa seminar programs. This time he went with Adventures in Citizenship, administered by Rotary. Less social than Encounters with Canada, Adventures in Citizenship was found to be more politically educational. The focus was on listening to guest speakers and then asking them lots of questions. Because participants were quite politically aware and outgoing, these discussion sessions were very enlightening. While in Ottawa, Jeff lived with a Rotary family with two guys from Saskatoon. Their days typically began with a tour or lecture at 8am and didn't wind down until 9pm. By the end of the week everyone was exhausted.

Meeting people from across Canada whetted Jeff's appetite for travel. In order to expand his experiences a little further afield, Jeff headed to Bloomington, Indiana, in the summer of 1990 to spend a week with students from all over the United States as a participant on the Phi Delta Kappa Summer Camp Institute (p. 295). The program ended up costing Jeff nothing because a local chapter of the fraternity sponsored his travel expenses. Jeff had a wonderful time in Indiana meeting people from all over the United States. He describes the seminar as an action packed week with many ambitious students getting a taste of campus living. The program ended with a formal dinner and dance which is always a fun way to end a student seminar. Jeff advises that anyone interested in participating should carefully explain on the application form why they are interested in becoming a teacher.

Since Jeff had explored quite a bit of North America he set his sights on Europe. After examining the various organizations offering year abroad services, Jeff settled on ASSE (p. 268) which he found to be best suited to his needs. He lived with a family for one year in the village of LaRochelle, France located up the coast from Bordeaux. Because Jeff had participated in a French immersion program, he found it quite easy to adjust to life at the local public highschool. The regional rep. for ASSE in France called Jeff periodically to make sure things were going well which reassured his parents that he was okay. Returning home, Jeff was given some credits by his Ontario highschool. In order to get the credits, Jeff had to do some negotiating with the school board and principal both before and after his trip.

Jeff is now heading to university already armed with a wide variety of travel and education experiences. He has made the most of highschool and is well equipped to benefit from his university years.

Organization: Ontario Government
Program: The Ontario Educational Leadership Centre

Ontario Educational Leadership Course
General Delivery
Longford Mills, Ontario
L0K 1L0
phone: (705) 689-5572, fax (705) 689-6072

Executive director: Mr Jacques Riopelle

Facts at a Glance:

Age:
- Secondary Programs - 15 to 18 (grade 10, 11 or 12)
- Elementary Programs - 12 to 14 (grade 7)

Duration: 5 to 9 days (May 29 through October 1)

Regional eligibility: Ontario students

Cost:
- $85 to $200
- usually paid by the school
- travel to the Centre is usually paid by the student, but any cost over $150 is paid by the Centre

That covers:
- accommodation and meals
- materials, including uniform if required

Getting in:
- application forms are sent to the principal of each school who nominates one student to participate
- if one of these courses sounds interesting to you, we recommend letting your principal know of your interest

Overview: The Ontario Leadership Centre is located on a 175-acre site on Lake Couchiching, 150 kilometers north of Toronto. For the past 45 years the government has been running 5- to 9-day courses in leadership development for Ontario students. These courses are now partially sponsored by boards of education. Courses are offered in music, athletics, student parliament, multiculturalism, multiracialism and fine arts. Courses for elementary students in the areas of athletics, fine arts and multiculturalism are also offered. The objectives of all the courses include developing interpersonal, communication, and organizational skills. Each year approximately 1,500 students from across Ontario attend a session. Students are chosen by their school's principal and the cost of the course is shared by the government and the student. (The student's portion is normally paid by the school.)

Inside View: If you consider yourself an average musician or athlete, or if you're a key member of your student government, then a session at the Student Leadership Centre could be a really great experience. The facility is completely equipped for almost every individual and team summer sport. There are two 400-metre tracks, six tennis courts, basketball and volleyball courts, a waterfront area, archery and golf ranges, and a gymnastics hall. Whether you go to the Centre for an athletic, music, or student government session, you'll spend time each day playing a sport of your choice. All your meals will be taken in the dining hall, and you'll be housed in cabins with students from various parts of the province.

The Centre's focus is on developing leadership skills in students. For example, some weeks the leadership skills are brought out through the medium of music. So, if you're there for one of the music sessions you'll spend a few hours each day in small improvisational groups. Staff members will be around most of the time—not to teach technique, but to offer support and suggestions. You won't learn any new musical skills, but will strengthen your self-confidence and become a better speaker and leader. All students at the Centre take turns leading seminars on socially relevant topics such as native rights, drug use, or abortion. No matter what musical, social, or recreational activity you're involved in, there will always be an appointed student leader.

Sandra Pujoll, a Brock University student, spent two weeks on a music session of Ontario Leadership Centre when she was in high school and says that it was an experience she'll never forget. When her music teacher approached her about attending the course, she'd never heard of it. She thought it sounded intriguing and didn't mind paying roughly $45 for her transportation to the Centre. Sandra had a great time there. "I learned a lot from it—a lot," she told us, "I'm basically a shy person and the next year in school I knew how to organize and express myself."

This program is very efficiently run, is professionally supervised by school teachers selected from across the province, and offers students the use of some of the best facilities around. It can't hurt to drop some hints to your teachers or principal that you'd love to be

chosen to participate. The only criteria for selection is your ability
to demonstrate leadership skills within your school.

Organization: WUSC
Program: International Seminar

1404 Scott Street
Ottawa, Ontario
KIY 4M8
phone: (613) 798-7477 fax: (613) 798-0990

Executive Director: Mr Edward Barisa

Facts at a Glance:

Age:

- must be returning to post-secondary institution in the fall
- average age is 22

Duration: 5-6 weeks (June-July)

Regional eligibility: all provinces

Cost: $2,300 (most of which can be raised from your university)

That covers:

- return travel from home to Africa or Asia
- room and board
- travel and incidental expenses

Language: French and English are used on alternate years

Getting in:

- application forms available from universities or from WUSC
- interview by regional representatives
- final selection made by national committee
- deadline is mid-October
- very competitive (300 apply for 30 spots)

Overview: Every year 30 students from across the country are chosen to participate in a five-week seminar, usually held in a developing country. Participants spend their time researching social, political or economic conditions in the country which are of personal interest to them. They also work on development projects with local resource people and WUSC faculty. The official language of the seminar alternates between French and English. The 1993 seminar was conducted in English and was held in Indonesia. The 1994 seminar will be held in Benin and participants will need a very strong knowledge of French. (contact the WUSC office for details on the location of future seminars).

Inside View: If you are lucky enough to be one of the select group chosen, your five weeks in Africa, Asia, or the Americas can't help but be enlightening. Along with your individual research into some aspect of the country's development, you can expect to travel with your group to various national points of interest. Since you'll be travelling in a developing country, don't expect luxury accommodation. In fact, you'd better count on some pretty primitive conditions. Living conditions vary considerably each year, but may include staying with a family or in a dorm. Lynn McDonald, 23, from Delta, British Columbia went to Botswana with WUSC in 1991. While there she studied the effects of government education policy on income distribution. She spent five weeks travelling around Botswana learning to see the country through the eyes of the locals and gathering insights for her research paper. Now at law school at the University of Toronto, Lynn remains close to many students who were part of the Botswana WUSC team.

To have a chance of being picked, you need decent grades, but more important, you should take your studies seriously and work well in groups. Of course, a demonstrated interest in international affairs wouldn't hurt your chances. You must also agree to do three speaking engagements upon returning home.

Your fee of $2,300 represents less than half the total cost of the seminar. The rest is paid by CIDA and WUSC. Although the cost to you is already very low, you'll be asked to request sponsorship from your school and from private foundations to further defray the cost.

Organization: Trent University International Program
Program: Discovering our Future

Trent University International program
Trent University
Peterborough, Ontario
K9J 7B8
(705) 748-1626

Director: Mr Karanja Njoroga

Facts at a Glance:

Age: College and University students

Duration: 3 weeks in August

Regional eligibility: all provinces

Cost: $250 registration

That covers:

- accomodation and meals at Trent University
- travel to Trent University
- seminar materials

Where can I go? Peterborough, Ontario

Getting in:
Apply by May 31st — applications available from above address or send a letter, not exceeding 250 words, explaining why you want to participate and stating your past experience in development.

Overview: Discovering our Future is a unique seminar on international development issues which draws 100 students from across Canada, including 20 foreign students, for an intense 3 weeks at Trent University's Catherine Parr Trail College in Peterborough, Ontario. The seminar is designed to have participants learn about contemporary development issues through group discussions and other participatory activities and guest speakers. Although the seminar has been around for 10 years, it will not be offered in its current form in 1994. However, it is expectd to be available in some other form.

Inside View: Funded by CIDA, Discovering our Future has been providing Canadian students with a dynamic and exciting program designed to strengthen and enhance their skills and knowledge in interenational development policy planning and administration while at the same time giving participants a forum to exchange ideas and perspectives on development themes. The themes for the 1993 summer program were "Culture, Development and Democracy" and "Women and Popular Participltion". The main attraction of this program is its wide variey of participants, of all walks of life, from both Canada and Developing Countries. The three weeks give everyone an opportunity to exchange ideas and discuss issues facing the world.

Unfortunately, the future of Discovering our Future is in doubt. Due to changes in CIDA's funding guidelines for 1994, this program will have to offer an 8 week field phase as part of its seminar if it is to qualify for a grant. At the time of publication, the exact nature of the 1994 program had yet to be determined. However, it is probably safe to say that a modified Discovering our Future will only be able to accomodate 10-15 students and may incorporate a 3-4 week seminar in Canada with an eight week overseas placement on a development project.

If this program sounds interesting, you should write to the above address to determine what is set up for 1994 and following.

Organization: Trucks to Nicaragua

125 Concord Avenue
Toronto, Ontario
M6H 2P2
Phone: (416) 536-0414

Coordinator: Mr Harry Smaller

Facts at a Glance:

Age: all ages

Duration: normally from 2 to 4 weeks any time during the year

Regional eligibility: all provinces

Cost:
- participants share the expense of gas, food and lodging on the way down to Nicaragua
- between $300 and $600 airfare from Central America back to Canada

Where can I go? Nicaragua

Getting in:
- for the address of a group near you contact the above address
- a sincere interest in the project and the committment to help in fund raising are all that is required

Overview: Trucks for Nicaragua is a private volunteer organization, based in Toronto, which raises money to help with work and social service organizations in Nicaragua. Specifically, they use the money they raise to acquire jeeps, vans or buses which they then drive to Nicaragua and donate them to a local organization. Volunteers drive in groups of 4 or 5 (or more, or less depending on the individual project) and normally spend two weeks to get there. Once in Nicaragua participants are encouraged to spend some time in the country either on a volunteer work project or just travelling around. When participants are ready to return to Canada they are responsible for the cost of their return transportation.

Inside View: Participating in Trucks for Nicaragua allows you to travel with a group through the United States and Mexico all the way to Managua, Nicaragua for very little money. At the same time you are raising the money for, and personally delivering, a much needed vehicle to an environmental, work or social development project. Everyone gains something through this operation.

If this sounds like something you'd like to get involved with here is how you should proceed. First, call Harry Smaller at the above phone number and find out when the next vehicle is leaving for Nicaragua and from where it is departing. Even if another group has already raised the money to purchase a vehicle they may need extra drivers and you may be able to go. If there are no groups active in your area you can probably start one. This is a small grass roots group and they depend on the initiative of interested people. Starting a group would entail enlisting a few other people willing and able to help with fund raising and driving. In the past, money has been raised through raffles, selling T-shirts, benefit nights at clubs or bars etc. You could take another approach and solicit a school board or car dealership to donate a used bus or van. Once you've got the vehicle, you're ready to hit the road.

Depending on your group, you might decide to camp all the way and cook your own food (this way you could keep your out-of-pocket expenses to a minimum) or you might stay in hotels and eat in restaurants. All such decisions are left to you and your group. Obviously if you're living and driving with a group for two weeks, compromise is a crucial concept. If you feel like detouring for a quick tour of Graceland and your idea is vetoed by the group, you can't sulk - after all, you are on a volunteer mission not a pleasure tour. Anyway, so now you've been on the road a while and you are pulling into Managua. You then locate the office and drop off the vehicle. At this point you may opt to hop directly onto a plane back to Canada. We were told by past participants that it is cheapest to buy your ticket down there. Buying your ticket there should save you about 50% and should cost between $300 and $450. It really would be silly though to return right away after your lengthy journey. What you should do is go straight to a place called Casa Canadiense. This is a project centre run by a Toronto organization. They have a dormitory which sleeps 14 where you can stay (small donations are appreciated and much needed). They can also help to set you up on a volunteer work project, arrange a homestay or suggest interesting travel routes.

Concerns about safety in Nicaragua are valid. Before going you could contact the Nicaraguan Embassy in Ottawa (the address and phone number are listed in the apendix.

We spoke with Mike Pearson, a student at Guelph University who drove down to Nicaragua last summer with this program. He said he never feared for his life and gave the good advice that you must simply rely on common sense. Trucks to Nicaragua has allowed many teenagers to participate as part of larger groups, so no one is too young and it can't be that treacherous.

Once Mike and his group had dropped off their truck he stayed in hostels in Managua for a while and then participated on a work program. He told us that hitch-hiking is permitted in the country and that there are numerous hostels and bed and breakfasts. As a final note, we have been told that if you can get your hands on a small publication called *Not Just Another Nicaraguan Travel Guide* it will be quite useful. It was written by a couple of Canadians and published in Nicaragua. It's apparently near impossible to find but we thought we'd tell you anyway. (Think how excited you'll be if you find it now!).

Exchange Programs

Have you ever wondered what life is like in other parts of the world? Consider the high school student in a small fishing village in France, the 16-year-old living in rural Québec or the 18-year-old raised in Vancouver. Learning about cultural diversity can strengthen and develop our sense of unity. An exchange visit between schools, cadet corps or community groups, inside or outside Canada, is an excellent way to see another culture and to share something of your own.

Organization: The Department of the Secretary of State
Program: Open House Canada

Youth Participation Directorate
Department of the Secretary of State
Ottawa, Ontario
K1A 0M5
(819) 994-1315

Program Director: Ms Louise Vincelli

Overview: Open House Canada is aimed at youth between the ages of 14 and 19. The program's objective is to develop a greater sense of identity and unity among Canadian youth by increasing their knowledge, appreciation and respect for the diversity of Canadian society and it's institutions. To accomplish this goal, Open House Canada provides financial support to non-profit organizations which administer reciprocal group exchange programs and national forums for Canadian youth. The funding provided covers part of the participants travel costs.

Organization: Society for Educational Visits (SEVEC)
Program: School Year and Summer Exchanges and Tours

201-57 Auriga Drive
Nepean, Ontario
K2E 8B2
(613) 998-3760 Ottawa
1-800-38-SEVEC
Director of Programs: Ms Valerie Deane

Facts at a Glance:

Age: 10 - 19 depending on the program

Regional eligibility: all provinces

Duration: 3 - 30 days depending on the program

Where can I go? all over Canada

Cost:

- membership fee of $25 and a registration fee of $15 and up
- for some programs travel is subsidized, for others it is the student's responsibility

Overview: Each year over 8,000 students go on exchanges and educational trips through SEVEC. The majority of their programs are bilingual exchanges that allow students to live their learning. SEVEC offers group as well as individual exchanges during both the summer and school year to points within Canada. They also operate cultural visits to Quebec City, Ottawa, Acadia, Iqaluit and Toronto. Custom tailored visit packages can also be arranged.

Inside View: If you are looking for a short-term cultural exchange take a closer look at what SEVEC has to offer. For all exchanges, you are "twinned" with another student for both phases of the visit. Remember, with such an arrangement you risk getting stuck with someone whose idea of fun is sitting in their room picking fuzz balls off their sweaters. This is not likely to happen with SEVEC as great care is taken in matching students according to hobbies, interests and maturity level. To qualify for bilingual exchanges you must have some ability to communicate in your second language; otherwise life will be unbearably frustrating. A school that intends to undertake an exchange through SEVEC must be a member of the society. (The cost for a school to become a member is only $25).

School Year Exchange

Schools can apply to SEVEC asking to have classes twinned with other classes around the country. In this case, all students as well as teachers participate in a 4 to 10 day reciprocal exchange. Teachers twin the students. The exchanges occur between groups of English and French students. SEVEC also organizes Canada-U.S. student exchanges. However, these are much more expensive as students must pay all transportation costs. Organizing such a program takes a lot of patience and energy on the part of teachers, but if you can find a willing organizer this is a great way to go on an inexpensive and educational trip. All provinces and territories except for B.C. and Alberta are eligible for this program.

Summer Group Exchanges

This is an exchange between school boards in Ontario and Québec. Boards exchange groups of 43 students, each of whom is twinned, for a two-week stay in each community. These exchanges occur in July in a summer camp setting where students participate in well-prepared, fun, language-oriented educational activities. Each summer approximately 50 centres are involved in this program.

Interprovincial

This allows students from across Canada to participate in a cultural youth exchange during the summer. Annually, approximately 700 applications are received and 500 students are successfully twinned. Whether you get chosen depends on whether you can be twinned; a person with a wide variety of interests will probably be more easily matched. Also, since all exchanges are bilingual, the number of francophone applications will determine how many anglophone students will have an opportunity to participate in the program. Most applicants are between 8 and 18, although older students are eligible if a suitable twin can be found. Depending on where your twin lives, this can be quite a costly program, since you are responsible for 100% of you transportation costs. However, your only other expense is pocket money. While at your exchange home, your twin's family will provide your room and board, and you are expected to do the same when your twin visits. Each phase of the exchange is usually two weeks in length, although they can be as short as one week or as long as a month. These details are worked out between the two families. The travel dates are also flexible.

Organization: YMCA of Greater Toronto
Program: Visions

15 Breadalbane Street
Toronto, Ontario
M4Y 2V5
(416) 922-7765
Director: Mrs Marianne Roche

Facts at a Glance:

Age: 14-19

Regional eligibility: all provinces

Duration: 5 - 14 days

Where can I go? all over Canada

Cost:
- $95 registration fee
- fund raising covers other costs

This covers: return travel from home to exchange site

Getting in: for information, write to Visions at the above address

Overview: Visions is a nation-wide youth exchange program coordinated by the YMCA of Greater Toronto, in cooperation with the YMCA of Canada. Visions exchanges operate under the mandate and guidelines of Open House Canada and thus its format is very similar to the latter's. The exchanges involve YMCAs, YWCAs and other community groups. Each year close to 700 young people and 35 groups are able to participate on a Visions exchange. Visions always gets many more applications than it can fund, and a very long waiting list exists. In line with the mandate of Open House Canada, Visions gives priority to "target" group exchanges. Visits are for 5-14 days and usually take place during the spring or summer.

Visions offers three types of exchanges: (1) North - South, between groups from the Territories, Yukon, Labrador, and northern Québec and groups from southern Ontario; (2) East - West, between groups from different regions across Canada; and (3) bilingual. If you are a member of an organization that might qualify for a Visions exchange write to the YMCA of Greater Toronto for a brochure and further information.

Organizations

If you're looking for an extra-curricular activity as well as the opportunity to meet young people from across Canada, there are several interesting options you should read about in this section. You don't have to be content with reading about the Arctic Circle: you can do something that may allow you to earn or win a trip there some day. Although this book is primarily devoted to making you aware of specific work, travel, and study programs, interesting experiences can often be gained by involving yourself in certain activities or organizations. In particular, there are a few groups that involve students in slightly wacky yet very practical activities. Involvement in these organizations brings many opportunities to attend competitions, conferences, and exchanges across North America. Those who are fortunate enough to get in on these events usually travel free. Aside from travel, there are also the benefits of developing skills and making contacts. These amazing experiences won't jump into your lap. Students work very hard to earn the privilege of participating. But as you read on, we are sure you'll agree that the rewards can be well worth the effort!

Organizations: The Army Cadet League of Canada
The Air Cadet League of Canada
The Navy League of Canada

313 Rideau Street
Ottawa, Ontario
KIN 5Y4

(613) 991-4348 (Army Cadets)
(613) 991-4349 (Air Cadets)
(613) 993-5415 (Navy Cadets)

Overview: Cadet Corps have been active in Canada since the late 19th century. Once an integral part of the school curriculum, the cadet program is aimed at personal and social development based on military training. Students learn qualities of good citizenship, leadership, physical fitness and service to the community and nation. Today, while a few schools still have cadet corps (usually private schools), they are more often sponsored by a service club, a community group, or a branch of the Canadian Armed Forces. Opportunities exist within the Air, Sea and Army Cadets. While each is an autonomous organization, their programs are very similar. For specific information on the activities of a particular Cadet League, contact your local office or the national office for details.

Inside View: If leadership training, athletics, adventure and travel in a military setting are what you crave, you might consider joining a cadet corps. There are roughly 50,000 cadets in some 300 communities from Victoria to St. John's. Cadets meet once or twice a week during the school year to learn everything from marching to map and compass skills to first aid and public speaking. Boys and girls 12-18 can join anytime during the year, although September is the best time to enroll. There are no specific skills necessary as long as you are fairly fit. The cadet corps will take virtually anyone no matter how uncoordinated, fat, skinny, tall, or short. There is no cost for cadet training, and uniforms and equipment are provided free of charge by the Department of National Defense. Periodical weekend exercises are held where survival and adventure training are taught in a field situation.

But the cadet program does not end with the school year. Each summer, approximately 18,000 students attend a variety of two-to-six-week camps. Cadets are selected from their local corps to attend these camps and eligibility is based on past performance. If you want a pressure-free exciting activity during the school year, cadets can offer you that. If you are highly motivated and want to work hard, then there is a system of rewards and incentives that can open many new doors. These camps are a lot of fun, but they are competitive. The more involved you get, the harder you will work and the more you will be evaluated. But the opportunities are quite incredible. Cadets can attend two-week camps as well as six-week leadership and instruction camps, across Canada. All expenses are paid, and a training bonus of about $275 is received upon completion of a six-week camp. Wilderness, rifle, bandsman, parachute, and scuba camps are also run. You may have the opportunity to spend a summer in Banff, northern Québec, or Whitehorse among other places.

Once you become a senior cadet other doors open. Many senior cadets are hired and paid as assistant instructors at summer camps. Those who excel in the programs may be eligible for one of many international summer exchanges. Each year senior cadets are selected from across the country for training, tours, and competitions in Europe.

Cadets can teach you many new practical skills as well as developing your existing communication and personal skills. It can introduce you to sports and activities and also allow you to see new regions of Canada and the world. All of the programs teach self-discipline and responsibility, so that when the going gets tough (anytime during your life) you can handle it. By joining cadets you make absolutely no commitment to serve in the Canadian Armed Forces, but the skills you develop will be useful throughout your life.

To find out more about joining cadets, contact your local corps, Armory or Legion. Or contact the national office for more information.

Organization: 4-H

National Headquarters
1690 Woodward Drive
Suite 208
Ottawa, Ontario
K2C 3R8
(613) 723-4444

Executive Director: Mr Mike Nowosad

Overview: For 75 years, 4-H has provided young Canadians with a unique forum for personal growth and leadership development. Through specific projects in agriculture, outdoor living and home economics, 4-H members learn to work together, organize their time and pick up new knowledge and skills. The typical 4-H project might be composed of 10 or 12 individuals ranging in age from 12 to 21, who would be advised by an adult supervisor. If the group was undertaking an agricultural project, they might grow a crop of corn or raise chickens, getting together for a couple of hours each week to work on the project. Depending on what they were doing, the project might last anywhere from two months to a year. An integral part of most 4-H projects is displaying the end result to the public at some sort of local fair or exposition. There are 4-H organizations in every province and almost every community has its own 4-H club. Given the nature of the club, you'll rarely find 4-H in big cities; however, there's bound to be a group close by in the suburbs. If 4-H sounds like something you'd like to join, call your local agricultural office or write to the above address for information about 4-H organizations in your area.

For those 4-H members who are between the ages of 16 and 21, the organization offers a number of great conference, exchange, scholarship, and travel opportunities. Every year, various corporations provide funding to send dozens of 4-H members to seminars in Ottawa, Toronto, and Winnipeg. In addition 4-H offers a scholarship program.

Organization: Youth Science Foundation

151 Slater Street
Suite 904
Ottawa, Ontario
KIP 5H3
(613) 238-1671

Development Officer: Ms Sue Widyaratne

Overview: The Youth Science Foundation, a non-profit organization, sponsors extra-curricular science activities for youth. Along with a wide variety of publications and activities that the Foundation makes available to students under the age of 14, YSF also coordinates about 106 regional science fairs and runs the annual Canada-Wide Science Fair. These science fairs welcome competitors from grades 7 to 13 and offer excellent awards in the form of cash, travel and summer employment.

Inside View: If you're still in high school, science fairs are great activities to get involved with. International travel, a national network of friends, big scholarships, and cash can be yours if you're willing to put some work into your project. Whatever your interests—computers, weather, chemistry, insects, emotions, plants—chances are you can turn them into a first-rate project. All it takes is some creative thinking and experimentation. Your project doesn't have to be technical, expensive, or complex. In fact, some of the best projects are none of these things: the best projects are those which evolve out of original and imaginative thought.

During your primary education your school probably held an annual science fair and sent its winners to the regional fair. At the high school level, you enter your project directly to the regional fair. No matter where you live in this country, there's a regional fair within driving distance. These fairs are usually two- or three-day events and are held sometime in March or April. The fair offers the chance to conduct in-depth research and experimentation on some topic which interests you. You'll write about and display your results, and explain them to the judges and the public. All these stages of the science fair are a lot of fun and you'll learn from all of them. By talking about your project with the judges, who are professors, scientists, business leaders, and other professionals, you'll develop good interpersonal skills, as well as self-confidence. Through some of the other stages you will improve your library research, experimentation, writing and artistic skills. Each of these stages will also demand long hard work from you.

If a pure quest for knowledge isn't enough to motivate you, maybe the idea of winning excellent cash and travel prizes is! At regional fairs, first prize winners commonly receive $100 or more. Furthermore, each regional fair sends its top three or four winners to the week-long Canada-Wide Science Fair held in a different city every year. The trip to the Canada-Wide held in May is expense free for the winners: absolutely everything is covered. Over the next three years, the Canada-Wide will be held in the following cities: 1994—Guelph, Ontario; 1995—Whitehorse, Yukon; 1996—North Bay, Ontario.

The Canada-Wide Fair brings together hundreds of people between the ages of 12 and 19 from across the country. For some this is their first national competition, while others are seasoned professionals, having attended for three or four years in a row. While all have shown that they have a real talent for creating a winning science fair project, not all will opt for science as a career. For many, this is simply an extra-curricular interest. As a result, the participants are a diverse group with a wide range of other interests and experiences. Contrary to what you may imagine, competitors do not all wear three-inch-thick glasses and sport plastic pocket protectors in their lab coat!

Okay, you've decided to go for it. You've spent about 100 hours (at least) on your project—Christmas and Easter breaks gave you a chance to work on it—you've placed second in your regional fair and have won a spot at the Canada-Wide. Congratulations! Once at the Canada-Wide, the prizes you'll compete for take on new proportions. Summer jobs with IBM, Northern Telecom, and other large corporations are available. Large scholarships, hundreds of dollars in cash, computers, expense-paid trips to London, and positions at the Weismann Institute in Israel are all up for grabs. Whether or not you walk away with one of these big awards, you'll probably have a great time at the fair—everyone does! Between judging sessions and public display hours, participants can choose from a number of organized tours, lectures, and activities. You are also given a chance to test your bargaining skills through the swapping of regional science fair buttons. Participants have been known to come with three or four of their own regional buttons and end up leaving with more dozens of buttons from across the country. There are banquets and get togethers practically every night.

A final note about science fairs: competition at regional fairs differs widely. Some are highly competitive, while others are still in the formative stages. Even if you are entering for the first time, don't think that the Canada-Wide is beyond your reach. You are judged within grade categories, and most regional fairs send at least one top winner from each age category to the national. In this way, students who are still in the early stages of their own science fair careers are exposed to the cream of the crop. Most regional fairs have a large number of entries in the junior categories, but at the high school level, often as few as half a dozen competitors are entered. Also, if you're a computer whiz, your chances of making it to the Canada-Wide are quite good. Along with the best three or four projects overall, the project judged to be the best computer entry will be sent to the Canada-Wide. The computer contestants are all sponsored by IBM. If you have an aptitude for computers, why not take advantage of this excellent opportunity?

Organization: United Nations Association in Canada
Program: Model United Nations Seminars

63 Sparks Street
Suite 805
Ottawa, OntarioKIP 5A6
Phone: (613) 232-5751
Fax: (613) 594-2948
Project Officer: Ms Oddette Langlais

Overview Highshool and university students who aspire to a diplomatic career should take a second look at the Model United Nations Seminars coordinated through the United Nations Associations in Canada and the United States. The way these Model United Nations work is as follows. Each participating school is assigned a country to represent. Say you are given Somalia - you spend the seminar participating in council meetings espousing the policies and tabling the issues important to your country. This can sometimes be a stretch depending on which country you get to portray.

For example, Aaron Yarmoshuk, a 22 year old recent graduate of Dalhousie University participated in the Model United Nations program during all four years of his undergraduate career. Dalhousie attends the Model United Nations Seminar in New York each spring - this is one of the biggest seminars on the continent and attracts universities from all over the United States and Canada. In his first year, Aaron went to New York as a member of the Dalhousie delegation. The next year, Aaron was the head delegate for his school and had the dubious honour of assuming the role of Iraq. At the time the seminar was held, the Gulf War was still raging. Not only did Aaron's delegation find themselves with quite a challenge, but CBC Radio's host of Cross-Country Check-up, found it so amusing that he interviewed Aaron live from New York on the subject!

Having to represent the views of a foreign country forces you to get another perspective on major world issues. It's a great learning experience in understanding and gives you lots of opportunity to speak in public and to discuss current affairs. You also get to travel to a new city in some cases and meet people from all over North America - people who share your interests.

There are both highschool and university programs. The two biggest university seminars are held in New York and at Harvard. The largest Canadian university seminar is in Toronto. At the highschool level local seminars are currently running in Newfoundland, Welland, Ontario, Ottawa and Victoria, B.C. The highschool seminars are for grade 11 and 12 students and last 2 days. There are also some 2 day Model United Nations set up and funded by service clubs. One of the most successful is the one in Winnipeg, Manitoba run by the Rotary Club. This seminar attracts highschool students from Ontario, Saskatchewan, Manitoba and Minnesota. Participants are boarded with local Rotary families. If this sounds too great to be true, you'll be even more pleased to find out that it doesn't cost participants a lot of money. Schools fundraise to attend the seminars and UNAC helps with off-setting the costs of attending.

Model United Nations clubs are set up at universities and highschools across the country and if there isn't one at your school you can certainly take the initiative and set one up. The national organization is really encouraging expansion. They are also setting up a network for Model UN organizations and would like you to write in to let them know if there is a group in your area.

Organization: Societe Radio-Canada
Program: La Course Destination Monde

La Course
Societe Radio-Canada
Case Postale 9080, Succ. A
Montreal, Quebec
H3C 3P3
(514) 597-5970

Program Director: Jean-Louis Boudou

Facts at a Glance:

Age: 18-26 years of age

Duration: May - March (11 months)

Regional eligibility: open to Canadians from all provinces

Language:
- this program operates exclusively in french
- to be eligible you must speak french fluently and with a great degree of polish — participants tend to be those whose first language is french

Cost: none

Getting in:
- deadline mid-April
- can't be a professionalist journalist or film- maker
- complete an extensive application package which is available from the above address
- write an essay as to why you wish to participate
- make a 2-4 minute film on a subject of your choice

Overview: "La Course" allows 8 young people to make a 182 day tour of the world. Participants start and finish in Montreal and can visit countries of their choice on any continent, but along the way must make short films which they send back to Montreal to be viewed by Quebecois at 5pm every Sunday night on the Radio-Canada (the french language wing of the CBC). The films made by the participants are not designed to be travel logs or documentaries, but rather aim at bringing the world to Quebecois through the eyes of eight youths.

Inside View: Everyone in Quebec knows of this program and the films made by the participants form one of the most watched television shows in the province. This is the program, job, and travel experience of a lifetime. Just imagine someone offering to pay your way on a long and complicated trip around the world. Your dream trip. You are told that you can set your own itinerary - can visit any and every continent you wish, any countries and any specific locations. In a sense, you are a roving reporter - because the catch is — or other benefit - depending how you look at it — you have to make movies everywhere you go. The stories you film are of your own choosing. They can be on any subject that interets you, on anything you can dream up. The intention is not for you to produce a travel vidio or a country documentary - the focus of your work is left to your discretion.

You are however, under some constraints. The films you produce must be suitable for public viewing on Radio-Canada. Also, they must be of a high quality and ready to be aired once they arrive in Montreal. The other contraint of "La Course" is that you must send films to Montreal on a very regular basis (you are given a schedule to work by) and your eligibility to continue your travels is dependant on you sending regular quality videos and your keeping in touch with the Montreal office. You'll find yourself working on very tight deadlines and having to make quick adaptations to to new climates, cultures and countries. So, while it's an exciting and facinating trip, it is also alot of hard work.

As you might expect, everyone wants to do this program and as a result there are tons of applicants and a very rigorous selection process. The initial stage requires that you write an essay, fill out a lengthy application form and make a short film. Some forty students are them shortlisted and they are interviewed in Montreal at the end of May. Fifteen semi-finalists are then selected and asked to make two short films. It is from these semi-finalists that the final eight are selected.

If selected, Radio-Canada provides you with all of the audio-visual equipment you require for the year, they provide you with airline tickets for your chosen route and also give you $1050 every two weeks to cover your living and working expenses. CBC looks for articulate, adventurous, personable, adaptable, creative, energetic and intelligent candidates. For those considering applying, it would be well worth your while to purchase a book entitled *La Course Destination Monde* which tells you everything you would ever want to know about "La Course". It also includes testimonial of past participants. It's available from Radio-Canada.

Offbeat Travel Agencies

If you'd like to do some adventurous travelling, but lack the confidence or experience to go it alone, you should seriously consider joining one of the group tours featured in this section. If the idea of jumping on a bus full of strangers to blaze a trail through 15 countries in 15 days leaves you cold—read on. The agencies we highlight in this section all specialize in unique and thorough travel adventures rather than whirlwind sight-seeing. These tours test your skills by directly exposing you to different cultures. The agencies are all quality operations with established reputations and lots of satisfied customers.

If you're a first-time traveller, the programs offered by these agencies have many advantages for you. First, you'll travel with a small group of people who have interests and expectations similar to your own. Making close new friends will be an important part of your adventure. Twenty years from now you might not remember the name of that quaint guest-house in Oxford, but you'll still be friends with that exuberant young woman you shared the room with! Another advantage of these tours is the quality of the guides employed. No matter which agency you decide on, rest assured that the guides will be knowledgeable, resourceful, and organized. Invariably they'll also be just plain great people—always sincerely eager to ensure that you're having a great time. The guides take care of everything for you. You'll never have to worry about reservations, schedules, or even buying foreign currency.

The agencies listed on the following pages charge fairly high prices for their services. You can explore on your own for much less money, but travelling alone and without a structured itinerary is not for everyone. The agencies on these pages rarely receive complaints about their services.

Organization: Butterfield & Robinson

70 Bond Street
Suite 300
Toronto, Ontario
M5B 1X3
(416) 864-1354 Toll free: 1 (800) 268-8415

Overview: Butterfield and Robinson has been organizing first-rate travel adventures for students for over 25 years. Their unusual tours send young travellers all across Europe. Normally, segments of cycling and trekking are broken up by some train or boat travel. The biking and hiking portion of the trips are not too physically demanding, but you should be in reasonable shape. Tours are limited to those between the ages of 17 and 21 (Butterfield also runs junior and adult tours), and group sizes are kept to a maximum of 30.

These tours are ideal for first-time travellers, as every detail is organized by Butterfield and Robinson. Tours are lead by experienced guides who know the languages, culture, and customs of the travelled areas. They also know the best little cafés and shops along the way. The guides are competent and very resourceful and the tours are well-structured. What's really great about these tours though, is the amount of freedom travellers are given. Take for example the Biking Tour of Europe—each night participants are supplied with a map of the next stretch of road and directions to the inn where the group will be staying the following night. You decide what time you'll leave in the morning, who you'll ride with, where you'll stop for a picnic along the way, and so on. As long as you make it to the designated inn by nightfall everything is fine. By the way, the inns you stay at are quaint bed-and-breakfast cottages, stone chalets, or converted monasteries where breakfasts of croissants, muffins, and juice are served. There is absolutely no roughing it on these tours—it's pretty luxurious all around. When you're in major cities like Paris, Rome or London, you can opt either to meet up with your guides to see various museums and cathedrals or to explore on your own or with friends.

These tours offer exceptional overviews of many countries—however, these overviews come with big price tags. The month-long bike tour of Europe, for instance, will cost you close to $5,000. This price covers everything, including return airfare, all meals, all hotels, use of a 12-speed bike, and all tours, guide services, and tipping. While there are many ways to spend a lot less money to see Europe, we don't know of any way you could spend more! As we've stated, you'll receive excellent services for your money.

Note: During the summer of 1993 Butterfield & Robinson offered only one trip for people aged 17 to 21. It seems the poor economy has kept enrollment down lately. The one trip they did offer was a 31 day bike tour from Paris to Prague. The cost was $4,790. Although the variety of trips offered has been drastically cut, the price you'll have to pay has not risen over the past few years.

Organization: Earthwatch

680 Mount Auburn Street
P.O. Box 403N
Watertown, Massachusetts
02272 U.S.A.
1-800-776-0188

President: Mr Brian Rosborough

Overview: Since 1972, Earthwatch has been sending volunteers of all ages to participate on research projects around the world. They offer dozens of unusual expeditions ranging from Leatherback turtle rescue operations in the Virgin Islands to dinosaur fossil hunts in Montana, from volcano exploration in Italy to mapping coral reefs in Fiji. The great advantage to these expeditions is that they are actual research projects being undertaken by leading scientists and scholars. As an Earthwatch volunteer, you'll be working alongside the director of the project with a small group of other volunteers. You'll come away a real authority on whatever subject you study.

Before you get too excited about the great "volunteer" opportunities offered by Earthwatch, you should know that, as a volunteer, you'll be responsible for helping out with the cost of the expedition. These expeditions are not cheap. Be prepared to fork over about $100 per day for a place to sleep, all of your meals, and the chance to participate in the project. Travel expenses to the research site will further boost your total cost and these vary considerably depending on the location of the project. The total cost of the expedition (including your travel expenses) is tax-deductible, which may or may not mean a lot to you as a student—it might, however, be beneficial to your parents. Don't overlook this fact. If the cost of the expedition is just too high to handle, (since most are around two weeks long, the average cost is $1,400), Earthwatch does provide a limited number of partial scholarships for full-time high school students. Convince them that you'll be able to share your experience with others (through speaking engagements, published articles, etc.) and you might be able to get them to help cover your costs.

If this sort of opportunity interests you but the price is too high, don't give up hope. Ask around at your local university or write to universities and museums to find out about field work that various professors are planning. At every university there are professors out doing field research. If you learn of a project that interests you, write a letter to the director of the project volunteering your services. Be sure to include a resumé and maintain a professional tone. Getting yourself on a field expedition this way will be more of a true "volunteer" experience. Chances are, you'll receive room and board in exchange for the work you do; you might even receive a small salary from the professor's research grant.

If there's an Earthwatch program that really catches your eye (a complete brochure of expeditions is available from the above address), and money is no object—apply early. A very limited number of spaces are open on each project and it's first come—first served.

Organization: Ecosummer Expeditions

1516 Duranleau Street
Vancouver, B.C.
V6H 3S4
(604) 669-7741

Managing Director: Ms Jean Barbeau

Overview: For the past 17 years, Ecosummer Expeditions has organized unique exploration adventures. What sets this operation apart from others is the fact that almost all their trips feature sea kayaking. Whether you choose to see Belize, Baja, the High Arctic or the Bahamas, much of what you see will be from a specially equipped, two-person sea kayak. You don't have to be an expert kayaker to participate on these trips; in fact, you don't need any experience at all. The kayaks are seaworthy and easy to handle. The expert guides (normally 2 per group of 10 participants) have been trained in wilderness first aid and are well versed in the flora, the fauna, the boats, and the waters. As well as being experienced naturalists and interpreters, guides also serve as your cooks during the trip. Meals consist of lots of fresh local sea food, some of it no doubt caught by you. Having helped to catch your own food, there's a good chance you'll want to help prepare it—probably around a beach bonfire.

Ecosummer Expeditions offer trips year round. Some last just one week, while others are nearly a month long. Compared to similar adventure holidays, those offered by Ecosummer are quite reasonably priced—especially those which take place along the west coast of Canada. For $849 you can spend seven days paddling around Johnston Strait, the most reliable place on the coast to see orca whales. Each evening you'll find a suitable beach to pitch your tents, enjoy a feast of salmon or trout and then perhaps go for a hike, hear a talk about the customs of the local Indians, or just relax and chat about the day's events. The only thing not included in the price of the trip is transportation from your home to the departure point which is accessible by bus from Vancouver.

If the price sounds a little high for you, think of the trip as a gift to yourself after a long summer of work. Because this particular trip is offered every week during the month of August and for the first two weeks of September, it would make a perfect break between a money-making summer job and the beginning of school. Linda Dimock, of Gloucester, Ontario, went on the orca-watching expedition late last summer and had nothing but high praise for every aspect of the trip. If Ecosummer Expeditions sounds intriguing to you, by all means write to the above address and ask for their catalogue of upcoming trips—it's full of travel opportunities.

Organization: Israel Youth Program Centre

Cavendish Mall
5800 Cavendish Boulevard
Côte St. Luc, Québec
H4W 2T5
(514) 481-0218

Director: Ms Davina Shapiro

Facts at a Glance:

Age: 15-24

Duration: 4 weeks - 2 months

Regional eligibility: all provinces

Cost: approximately $4,000

That covers:
- return airfare from Montréal
- room and board
- all tours

Getting in:
- application forms available from your local branch (see Appendix for address)
- brief interview
- no entrance requirements other than maturity

Overview: The Israel Youth Program Centre has been offering a wide range of touring and kibbutz experiences to Canadian youth for the past 35 years. Because they are directly affiliated with the World Zionist Organization, Israel Youth Programs is able to rely on a large network of coordinators, counsellors, and resource people in Israel who help to ensure that visiting Canadians enjoy trouble-free vacations. Each year approximately 1,000 young Canadians visit Israel through this organization. A large number of different group trips are available for narrowly defined different age groups (15-16, 17-18, etc.), and cater to different tastes (some have a religious focus, others an educational component, some include time on a kibbutz, and others involve straight touring). There is a trip to suit everyone. Because all trips are in a group, it is important that participants be at least somewhat energetic and outgoing. Although most participants are Jewish, people of any religious background are welcome. The trips are reasonably priced and are led by competent, young, friendly guides.

Inside View: Spending a summer in Israel—a few weeks working on an experimental kibbutz, a few weeks hiking and swimming in the mountains and a couple of weeks touring the major cities—has practically become a birthright for many Canadian Jewish teenagers. Exploring Israel is exciting even if you're not Jewish. While many trek across Europe every summer, few make it as far as Israel—a country and culture quite different from anything in Europe. Because they offer such a wide variety of kibbutz, educational, religious, and touring packages, the Israel Youth Program Centres across Canada are great organizations to help you discover Israel.

One of their most popular tours is the "Student Summer Tour", which features 2 or 3 weeks living and working on a kibbutz, followed by nearly three weeks of travel throughout Israel. On the kibbutz portion you live with people from all over the world in modest accommodations. You rise early and spend five or six hours doing some sort of manual labour, possibly picking fruit in the orchards, weeding in the fields, or serving food in the dining hall. When the work is finished, you have time to swim, relax, or participate in other special programs. Once a week, field trips explore the surrounding region. After a month of kibbutz life, you spend about three weeks touring around Israel: a couple of days in each of Tel Aviv, Haifa, and Eilat, a few days hiking in the north and a full week in Jerusalem. While in the cities, you stay at hostels or hotels and, according to 18-year-old Montréaler Wendy Weiser, you have lots of free time to do whatever you want. She told us that the accommodation and meals on the trip were surprisingly good. She'd been to Israel before for a much longer period of time, but said she saw and learned more on the one-month Israel Youth Program Centre trip. For Wendy, the group leaders were a major part of the trip's success: they were young and enthusiastic, but very competent and knowledgeable. Wendy had nothing negative to say about her experience with Israel Youth, except that her flight home was booked for the wrong day and she had to correct that herself. Some of her friends also had their flights messed up—but they all managed to straighten things out themselves.

Of special interest to students is the relatively low price of these offerings. For instance, the 41-day "Student Summer Tour" costs only $3,650. This covers everything, including return airfare, accommodations, meals, tours—everything. Other trips offered include a study component by which you can earn high school or university credits.

Organization: Blyth & Co.

13 Hazelton Avenue
Toronto, Ontario
M5R 2E1
(416) 964-2569
Toll free: 1 800 387-5603

Overview: Blyth & Co. offers a wide range of travel options for young North Americans. Blyth annually leads Coast Rican safaris, Galopagos Island diving programs, European grand tours, and many other holiday packages. One nice feature of most Blyth tours is that age ranges are kept quite narrow, which ensures that you'll have much in common with your travelling companions. Maximum age for any of Blyth's student programs is 19 and no tour ever has more than 30 participants.

The Blyth tour means quality service, excellent guides and attention to detail. Guides for the bike tours have all lived, studied, and travelled widely in Europe and speak at least two European languages. For other tours, guides are experienced educators; leading scientists and professors. Accommodation varies widely on the different tours. On the European bike tour, you'll be put up in chalets, quaint inns, and small, family-run hotels, on the Costa Rican trips you sometimes sleep in tents. Meals on all tours are hearty and delicious and are mostly local specialties. One thing all Blyth adventure tours share is their hefty price. For example, the five week European tour costs about $4,695. This price includes all airfares, room and board, guide services, entry fees, and excursions.

Organization: World Expeditions

78 George Street
Ottawa, Ontario
KIN 5WI
(613) 230-8676

Overview: The people at World Expeditions specialize in arranging travel tours for healthy and adventurous individuals. Trekking in Nepal, canoeing through the Amazon Basin, or cycling from Paris to Athens are among the more exotic offerings. World Expeditions offers all these and many other opportunities. Tour groups are small—you share your adventure with just 10 or 12 others, as well as a Canadian guide. Local guides are recruited along the way to give you an inside view of the country. Cost averages about $150 per day, but that covers everything, including return air fare. Since the trips run from two to four weeks, total cost is quite high and probably out of reach for most students. You might impress on your parents what a wonderful family vacation a trek up Mount Kilimanjaro would make. Similarly, a two-week adventure in the Galapagos Islands would be a lovely graduation gift. Use your imagination and resourcefulness, and good luck getting on one of these outstanding expeditions.

Organization: Outward Bound

150 Laird Drive, Suite 302
Toronto, Ontario
M4G 3V7
phone: (416) 421-8111
fax: (416) 421-9062

109 - 1367 West Broadway
Vancouver, B.C.
V6H 4A9
phone: (604) 737-3093
fax: (604) 738-7175

Overview: Look no further for a wilderness adventure that is guaranteed to challenge you physically and personally. Outward Bound is meant to teach you new skills and expose you to unfamiliar situations, but above all it is meant to teach you about yourself. The experience is about self-esteem, risk-taking, and personal development. There are programs for any age starting with 21-day youth programs for 15- and 16-year-olds. There are 10-, 14-, and 24-day courses for people 17-25 and over 25. The program aims to engage people in such active, adventurous activities that they find themselves doing things they had never dreamt possible. The programs operate year round in both Ontario and British Columbia.

Inside View: You will be constantly on the go for the duration of these courses. In the winter you can expect to learn how to cross-country ski, snowshoe, cross frozen rivers and lakes safely, navigate in the wilderness, and mush a team of dogs. In the summer, white-water kayaking and canoeing, mountaineering, rock climbing, and sailing are part of the program. Two-thirds through the course, each student goes on a "solo" outing for two or three days. Don't be alarmed: the object is not to see if you can survive, but to give you a chance to try out your newly acquired skills and reflect on the entire experience. All courses are lead by highly qualified professionals and groups are purposely kept small. Typically, you will have two instructors in charge of six to ten students.

Make no mistake about it, Outward Bound is not a summer camp, a guided wilderness tour or a skills-training program. It is a school with a definite educational program that focuses on personal growth. The people you meet on this course are a diverse group, all with a spirit of adventure, an openness to learning, and a willingness to experiment and change. Many come to Outward Bound at a transition point in their life. This was the case with Jean-Philippe de Caen, 16, a student from Ste. Anne de Bellevue, Québec. When asked why he went on the course he replied, "I went to Outward Bound because I wanted to develop self-confidence which would be valuable for any career I chose. I was at a turning point in my life, and Outward Bound taught me a lot about myself." For others it was the sense of adventure that lured them, as with Claire Huxtable of Willowdale, Ontario. Her 10-day winter course included snow camping and dog-sledding north of Thunder Bay. She highly recommends the course to anyone interested in a new and all-encompassing experience. The average course costs in the neighborhood of $1,200.

Youth Package Tours

Once you've decided to take a trip, you must think carefully about what you want out of that trip and how you want to travel. You may decide to avoid a lot of preparation and opt for a tour. You must then do a bit of research to find out what's available and suits your needs. There is a wide variety of tours out there, depending on where you want to go, how long you want to stay, how you want to travel, and how much you are prepared to spend.

If you are a first-time traveller or if you plan to go to a completely unfamiliar area, an organized tour is something you might consider. The major strength of a tour is that everything is organized for you and you don't have to worry about transportation, accommodation, or meals. In addition, tours will take you to all major attractions, monuments, and points of interest. On a first visit this is an excellent way to get an overview of the area. Many travellers will go on a tour and then travel on their own for a few weeks. They see all the major sites as well as spending longer periods of time in the areas they find particularly interesting.

Many companies operate tours for 18-35 year olds, but their costs and itineraries differ greatly. When booking a tour, be sure that you understand what the travelling conditions will be. Also, look into how much free time you will have and how much time is spent in each city. You should also find out how large the tour group is and how many guides will travel with you. This information will allow you to compare the merits of various companies and programs.

In this section we will give you an overview of several well-advertised tour companies that cater to young travellers. All tours can be booked through a travel agent, although in some cases you must deal with an adventure agency. If you live in Toronto, West Can Treks (17 Hayden Street, M4Y 2P2) can probably help you. Most of the companies listed below offer tours of Europe, Asia, and the South Pacific with stays of 2 to 10 weeks.

Top Deck

This British company has operated youth tours for 20 years in Europe, Britain and Asia and has recently expanded into China and Southeast Asia. The unique feature of these tours is that you travel in a double decker bus. There is sleeping space on the top level and a kitchen and storage space on the lower level. Each passenger brings his or her own sleeping bag and everyone shares in the cooking. The average age of the travellers is about 22. If you are over 25 you might find the crowd a little young.

Hilary Herrero, 21, of Calgary, Alberta, went on a five-week Top Deck Tour of Europe. She said it is a very relaxed way to get around the continent. Unlike other tours, the schedule is not rigid, so if you are on a beach in Greece and everyone wants to stay an extra day or two, you can. Although trips of up to two and a half months are available, Hilary cautions that five weeks is probably long enough in such tight quarters. The bus parks in the same campsites used by Contiki and Autotours, the difference being that on Top Deck, you sleep right in the bus. You get to know the other travellers very well and in Hilary's case this was particularly fun because her fellow travellers were virtually all from Australia, New Zealand and South Africa. You are expected to travel light—a backpack is adequate—and you should keep in mind that you'll probably end up buying a lot of stuff.

The tours in China and Southeast Asia use budget hotels and hostels and are quite inexpensive. Some are adventurous and include elephant rides, stays in tribal villages and whitewater rafting. Top Deck tours of Europe are probably the most inexpensive on the market, with a five-week tour costing about $1,500, not including airfare. The price is low and the travelling conditions can be a lot of fun, but this is not the trip for everyone. Remember, the quarters are close and there is nothing fancy about the accommodation.

Encounter Overland

Encounter Overland is another British company with offices in London which organizes off-beat trips around the world. They are a very popular company for trips through Africa, South America, the Middle East and Europe. The way there trips work is as follows. The company has these big old military trucks covered with a tarp, which carry twenty people plus the driver. The truck is equiped with 10 tents, 20 cots and a trailer carrying the gear which keeps the truck nice and free for moving about. The truck also carries the food, stove, tables, staples and cooking gear. Every 10 days you and a partner are responsible for feeding all the members of the group. This includes planning the menu, buying the food and cooking the meal. Hilary Herrero was 24 when she took a 10 week Encounter Overland voyage from Egypt through Jordan, Syria, Turkey, Iran, Pakistan and India to Nepal. She told us that it is a great way to get across difficult parts of the world. Many of the countries she visited are not well organized for tourists. Going on the group trip allowed her to see otherwise inaccessible sights outside the major cities. Hilary highly recommends the company and its trips but cautions against taking one of the four or six month extended programs because it is inevitable that spending so much time with your travel companions will inevitably drive you nuts after a while.

Autotours

Autotours has offered camping tours in Europe, Russia, Turkey and Morocco for over 25 years. Although they cater to the 18-25 age group, most travellers tend to be in the 25-35 range. Accommodation is in the same campgrounds used by Top Deck and Contiki; however, on Autotours you pitch your own tent. Once again, this is a budget travel tour and all travellers contribute to a shared food fund. Tours range in length from three weeks to over two months. If you like camping, this can be a great way to get an excellent first-time overview of Europe or Asia.

Trek Europa

This American company offers camping tours in North America, Europe and North Africa. There are a maximum of 14 passengers on a tour, which means that you really get to know your fellow travellers. Once again, you can choose from trips of two weeks to two and a half months in length. To get more information on specific tours and prices write to:

Trek Europa
P.O. Box 1338
Gardena, California
90249   U.S.A.

Insight Tours

Insight allows you to explore Great Britain, Europe, Israel and Egypt with people of your own age. The trips are shorter than those offered by other companies and range in length from ten days to one month. Accommodation are comfortable since hotels are always used. Further details can be obtained from:

Insight International Tours
P.O. Box 2420
2300 Yonge Street
Suite 906
Toronto, Ontario
M4P 1E4

Contiki

After 26 years of operation, this company now carries 50,000 passengers a year. If you are looking for a comfortable and structured way of travelling around Europe, Great Britain, Russia, Australia, New Zealand, or the U.S., Contiki may provide just what you are looking for. Contiki tours use hotels or tent and cot accommodation. Breakfasts and most dinners are included and travel is by air-conditioned highway buses. The tours are large (about 50 people from all over the world ranging in age from 18-30), very structured and more conservative than those offered by Top Deck, but comfort is superior. The pace is usually very quick, covering a lot of territory in a few days. There is a wide variety of itineraries, from a 10-country, 31-day tour of Europe to a specialized tour of Scandinavia and Britain. They also offer a 14-day one-way tour from England to Athens, visiting seven countries enroute. This tour lets you conveniently combine independent travel with a tour. Tours range in length from 14 to 56 days. Contiki's tour guides are well-trained and very knowledgeable, which results in a good overview tour of the countries.

For more information see your travel agent or write to:

Contiki Holidays
415 Yonge Street
Suite 1616
Toronto, Ontario
M5B 2E7

International Student Exchange

ISE has been running Club Europa and Club Orient tours in Europe, Great Britain, Asia, The Orient, and Australia for over 25 years. Compared to some of the other student tours described, this is a fancy way to travel. All accommodation is in hotels and the price includes most meals. You have the option of booking your flight on your own or through ISE. Once again, you are led by well-trained staff and the pace is quick—usually only a day or two is spent in each country. On a few of the longer tours, you spend up to three days in some of the larger cities. Of course, the tours visit the famous sights along the way, but also include special events from time to time. These might include river rafting in Innsbruck, a Greek feast in Athens, an evening at the Kirov Ballet in Leningrad, a visit to the salt mines of Salzburg, or a ride on a Windermere steamer in Edinburgh. These events are all included in the package price. Tours range in length from 14-64 days and are usually available with optional add-on stays at a Club Med or further travel in the U.K. or Aegean. ISEs programs are neither the cheapest nor the most expensive way to travel and, depending on your tastes and budget, may be just what you are looking for. For more information write to :

Europa House
802 West Oregon
Urbana, Illinois
61801   U.S.A.
(217) 344-5863.

STUDENT PROFILE

Name: Gil White
Age: 25
Home: Effingham, Ontario

Europe on 84 Cents a Day

At the age of 16, Gil White landed in Sidney, Australia, armed with a few tennis rackets, enough money to last one year, and the phone number of a friend of a friend. He wanted to become a professional tennis player and Australia seemed like the place to get the needed training. He was serious about his goals and had the confidence to take risks.

After five months in Sidney, Gil missed home too much to stay any longer and he decided to return to Canada. Looking back, he wishes he'd stuck it out for a full year and urges first-time travellers not to succumb to feelings of homesickness. (Many of the travellers and exchange students with whom we spoke offered the same advice.) Gil wasn't home long before his urge to travel returned and he was on the road once more. This time he stayed a little closer to home and spent a semester taking tennis lessons in San Diego, California. Part time jobs, some help from his parents, and careful budgeting made his term away possible. In both Sidney and San Diego, Gil was able to fit work and study into his travels.

When he was 19, Gil went on his first long hitch-hike. Just out of high school, Gil wanted to see his own country and the only way he could afford to was by hitch-hiking and camping out. If he had listened to the advice of most people he spoke with before going he would never have gone. People spoke to him of the risks of hitch-hiking rather than its many subtle joys. Gil learned a lot about his country and, more important, he learned to trust people. On his trip, Gil thumbed all the way to South America and was constantly surprised by the generosity of total strangers. People invited him for lunch, drove out of their way to drop him at busy intersections and often offered him places to sleep.

While hitch-hiking through Europe Gil realised that other young travelers could undoubtedly benefit from his technique and philosophy. As soon as he returned from his trip he began work on his book, *Europe on 84 Cents a Day*.

According to Gil, the most important advice in the book is to try and meet local people when you're travelling. Because of this, Gil doesn't recommend youth hostels as a first choice—you'll meet people there but not locals, just other travellers. One way Gil meets people while travelling is by simply walking up to a house, knocking on the door and introducing himself. You might consider yourself a little shy to attempt this technique, but you really shouldn't. Gil has met dozens of fascinating people, enjoyed hearty traditional meals in their homes, sometimes struck up good friendships, and always come away with a special insight into the customs of the country. People often welcome the opportunity to meet a traveller from a far-away land. If you stay in people's homes be polite: make your bed in the morning, do the dishes and leave some small gift (Gil recommends Canadian stamps—they're light, easy to pack, and you'll be representing Canada well).

Other helpful hints include

- approaching a hotel manager and offering to do dishes or wait tables for a couple of hours in exchange for a bed, dinner and breakfast;
- asking to spend the night in a small-town jail;
- volunteering to act as night watchman on a private yacht in the Mediterranean in exchange for free passage between two ports: a great way to eat, travel, and cruise free of charge.

After spending a good part of the past 10 years benefiting from the educational and cultural rewards of travelling, Gil is now reaping the financial rewards of his travels. Not only did he write a book about his hitch-hiking methods, he now speaks to university and youth organizations about how to get the most from travelling.

Create Your Own Travel Tour

There are many reasons why you might want to create your own travel tour. Perhaps you enjoy spending some of your time alone. Maybe you'd rather not pay the high price of an organized "adventure tour". It's also quite possible that you'd like to have complete freedom to move around as you please. Whatever your reasons for not going on an organized tour, creating your own can be a thrilling, economical, and rewarding experience. In this section of the Travel chapter, you'll find lots of practical information on planning your own travel itinerary; tips on how to get there; sources of bargain air, bus, ferry, and train fares; and where to stay once you arrive.

Important Documents

Where ever you go, there are a number of official documents that you must get, as well as a couple that you should get. Don't wait until the last minute to make the arrangements. In fact, the moment that you decide to go abroad is the time to get these formalities out of the way.

PASSPORTS: Canadian citizens require a passport to enter most countries in the world (except for the United States). Getting a passport is pretty straightforward, but you should allow a month to receive it (especially if you're doing it by mail). If you're in a rush, it is possible to get a passport application processed in three to five days by going directly to a regional passport office. Passport application forms can be picked up at all post offices, MP's offices, travel agencies, and passport offices. To complete an application you will need two identical photographs, proof of Canadian citizenship and an application fee of $30. Passports are valid for five years. You can mail your application to:

The Passport Office
Department of External Affairs
Ottawa, Ontario
K1A 0G3

Regional Passport Offices are listed in the blue pages of your phonebook. Also available from the passport office are *Bon Voyage, But—* and *Canada Passport*; these booklets give helpful information on currency, consular assistance, visas, and passports, among other things. Both of these publications are free.

VISAS: A visa is an authorization placed in your passport by a foreign government, allowing you to visit that country for a particular purpose and for a given amount of time. You may require a tourist visa in order to enter some countries. Visa requirements can change frequently so you should check to see if one is required by the country you plan to visit. For instance, restrictions in many Eastern European countries have recently been relaxed. In order to apply for a visa, you must give your passport and the official application form to an official at the foreign consulate or embassy concerned. You must do this for each visa you require. You may need one or more extra photos when applying for a visa, so get a couple of extras taken when you get your passport photos. You often have to pay for your visa. Fees vary depending on the country and the whole process can take several weeks, so you are advised to make these arrangements well before your planned departure. It is also a good idea to double-check visa requirements just before you leave to make sure that there have been no changes in policy. In the Appendix you will find a list of foreign embassies in Canada. They can refer you to a consulate office in your area.

A company which can answer any questions you might have about updated visa requirements in Eastern Europe is Intervisa. They can also get visas for you—saving you the bother of sending your passport to Ottawa. There is a small charge for this service. They can be contacted at the address below:

Intervisa
323 Sommerset Street
Ottawa, Ontario
(613) 594-8444

International Student Identity Card (ISIC): When travelling anywhere in the world it is a good idea to have official proof of your student status. Many museums, airlines, and so on, give discounts to students and the ISIC is recognized internationally as proof of student status. It is available to you as long as you are a full-time student over 12 years of age.

In Canada the ISIC is available at Canadian Federation of Students (CFS) Travel Cuts offices (see Appendix for locations) and at your student union office. If you attend a university or college that holds CFS membership, then the card is available to you at no charge (ask your student union about this). For all other full-time students the current cost is $15. To obtain your card you must have a letter from your school (usually from the registrar's office) verifying that you are enrolled as a full-time student. You will also need a passport-size photo of yourself.

The ISIC is valid from September 1 through to the end of the following calendar year. (For example, the 1994 card is valid from September 1, 1993, through December 31, 1994.) When you are issued your card, you can also obtain a student travel catalogue and a guide which lists many of the merchants and services who give discounts upon presentation of the ISIC. Students we spoke with stressed that during their travels they were each able to save more than the cost of the card.

INternational Driving Permit Are you are planning to drive while abroad? Most countries will allow Canadian citizens 18 years of age and over to drive with a valid Canadian driver's license, but a few require the International Driving Permit as well. To find out which countries require this permit and how to obtain it, pay a visit to your local Canadian Automobile Association (CAA) office.

International Union Of Students (IUS) Card: If you are travelling in Eastern Europe you'll need the IUS card in order to take advantage of student discounts in the former socialist countries. This card can be obtained from student travel bureau offices in Eastern Europe.

Federation Of International Youth Travel Organization (FIYTO) CARD If you are under 26 years of age but not a full-time student you are eligible for this youth discount card, which costs $15 and comes with a booklet detailing the discounts available to you. It is available at all Travel Cuts offices.

Transportation

Hitch-hiking: Despite the occasional horror story, hitch-hiking remains a popular mode of transportation for many people. Of course, the most obvious benefit to hitching is that you travel for free. Hitching also gives you the chance to meet all sorts of interesting people and learn about local lifestyles, politics and history. Many travellers who could easily afford to take the train opt to hitch-hike just to meet new people. It's fun to stand at the side of the road taking in the scenery and wondering what sort of ride you'll get next. My very first attempt at hitching landed me an hour-long cruise down a Welsh country road in a red Porsche! Not all rides will be this luxurious, but you'll quickly find that any car that pulls over offering a ride looks awfully inviting. Take note, however, that every driver who decides to give you a ride has had the opportunity to look you over (albeit briefly) first—you should also take a moment to size up the driver before hopping in. He (the vast majority of drivers who pick up hitch-hikers are men) could be drunk or just a little strange looking. By opening the door and asking a couple of questions, you should be able to assess the situation. Never enter a vehicle if you are at all uneasy—there'll be another one along in no time. When hitching alone, you shouldn't usually have to wait more than half an hour for a ride, but there will inevitably be times when you'll find yourself stranded on some bad stretch of highway for much longer periods of time. At times like these, when you're desperate for a ride, be sure not to lower your "driver" standards.

There are a number of helpful guides on the market devoted strictly to hitch-hiking tips and strategies. We recommend a couple of them in the book reviews at the back of this chapter.

BUS: If you've ever wanted to explore the far reaches of Ontario and Québec, but thought the price would be a little high, the Tourpass from Voyageur is your ticket. Just $159 entitles you to 14 consecutive days of unlimited bus travel anywhere in Ontario or Québec on any of about 35 participating bus lines. (If you want to extend your pass it'll cost an additional $16 per day.) This deal is open to people of any age and runs from May 1 until October 15. With the ticket, you can go from Windsor to Wawa, from Guelph to Gaspé, all for one low price. The ticket is available from any bus terminal.

Another bus pass available at all bus terminals is the Ameripass. This ticket allows unlimited travel all over the United States and can be purchased for periods of 7, 15, or 30 days. Cost is quite reasonable, especially if you take advantage of its unlimited nature. The 7-day pass costs $250, for 15 days it's $350, and the month-long pass is $450. The Ameripass must be paid for in U.S. dollars. This pass is available all year round and has no age restrictions, but can be purchased in the United States only.

TRAIN: Train travel is still one of the most romantic and picturesque ways to travel, but in Canada, with recent schedule cuts and price hikes, it's becoming less economical.

EURAIL YOUTHPASS: For about $650 you can purchase a one-month Eurail Youthpass, or for about $900 you can keep the pass for two months. Both passes entitle you to unlimited train travel in over 25 European countries. What many people don't realize is that this pass also entitles you to use a few different ferry services absolutely free of charge—most notably those linking France to Ireland and Italy to Greece! If you use your pass for just a couple of long hauls, it will be more than worth the purchase price. Not only will you save a lot of money by using this pass, you'll save a lot of headaches. What's great about the pass is that you never need reservations for any of the trains. You never have to stand in a line to buy tickets either! If you're in Vienna, for instance, and decide on a whim to check out Florence for a few days, simply walk into any train station, find the right train and hop on. When the guy comes to collect tickets, simply flash him your Eurail Youthpass. It's a great system.

The Eurail Youthpass is available to anyone under 26 from any travel agent. When you go to buy it you must have your valid passport with you. Allow a few days for the pass to be processed and issued. The pass must be purchased in Canada before you leave for Europe.

The first time you use your Eurail Youthpass, the conductor will mark in the date. Your pass will be valid for one or two months from that date.

Many countries outside Europe also have rail passes for travellers. (For example, a Japan Rail pass can save you a small fortune in the space of one week.) For one price you are allowed unlimited travel for a specific period of time. Most of these passes must be purchased in Canada before your departure. A travel agent will be able to give you more information on availability, regulations and prices.

AIR TRAVEL: If you're under 21, you can fly youth standby to destinations within Canada. Flying youth standby means arriving at an airport with no reservation and hoping there's an empty seat on the flight. If there is, you can get it for half price. It's smart to call ahead to find out your approximate chances of getting a seat. Youth standby fares are available to all destinations in Canada and to selected U.S. cities.

Another way to save on airfare is to take advantage of frequent seat sales. Seat sale tickets are often offered at half price, but must be booked and paid for at least a month in advance. There is usually a 100% penalty for cancellation.

Courier services are yet another way to travel on the cheap. These companies pay for your round trip ticket in exchange for the use of the baggage allowance. This means that you can only take carry-on luggage. The companies use your baggage allowance to ship any number of things. Some courier services require you to book a couple of months in advance. There is usually a small fee for the service, but it's definitely the cheapest way to go. Some suggestions for you are:

F.B. On Board Courier Services Inc.
P.O. Box 23641 APO
Vancouver, British Columbia
V7B 1X8
(604) 278-1266

Swift Sure
2401 Royal Windsor Drive
Oakville, Ontario
L6J 4Z2
(416) 845-9150

TNT Skypak
6655 Airport Road
Mississauga, Ontario
L4V 1V8
(416) 678-2778

A note on booking plane tickets: never book the first fare an agent finds for you—even if they insist it's the best fare you'll find. Airlines are constantly changing their rates and introducing special deals. If you try at least three travel agents, you'll probably be shocked to hear the various fares they'll find for you. Shop around!

Where to Stay

UNIVERSITY RESIDENCES: If you're going to travel across Canada in the summer, university residences are inexpensive places to stay. There are universities in all of the major cities and almost all of them open their residences to travellers in the summer. The residences are simple but clean, and often adjacent to swimming pools, tennis courts, and cafeterias. Furthermore, they are usually located near the city centre. The greatest benefit of staying in a university residence is probably the price—usually less than $15 per night. If you'd like information about staying at universities in the Maritime provinces, write to the following address and request *Travel Atlantic Canada*, a very informative brochure with prices, addresses and telephone numbers of participating universities:

Atlantic Regional Director of CUCCOA
Conference Centre, Room 210Student Union Building
Dalhousie University
Halifax, Nova Scotia
B3H 4J2

For information about universities in other areas, write or call the school directly. You'll find that many universities in the U.S., Europe, and elsewhere also open their residences for summer travellers.

YMCA & YWCA Inexpensive lodgings are also provided by YMCAs and YWCAs. Like university residences, Ys are usually centrally located, have special sports facilities, and are, for the most part, clean. However, they are almost always more expensive than residences. In fact, you can expect to pay $30 or $40 per night at a Y. While this price is cheaper than a hotel, it is not a real bargain. Ys should probably be considered your third option after hostels and university residences. Information about Ys across the country can be obtained by writing to the following addresses:

YMCA of Canada
2160 Yonge Street
Toronto, Ontario
M4S 2A9

YWCA of Canada
571 Jarvis Street
Toronto, Ontario
M4J 2J1

Organization: Hostelling International - Canada

1600 James Naismith Drive
Suite 608
Gloucester, Ontario
K1B 5N4
phone: (613) 748-5638, fax: (613) 748-5750

Overview: If you've decided to travel on your own or with a friend, hostels can provide you with comfortable and inexpensive lodging. Hostelling allows you total freedom in your schedule—if you find you really like a certain region, then stay in all the hostels in the area and explore. If you're just looking for someplace to get a night's sleep on the way to a final destination, hostels provide a convenient and inexpensive solution. For a membership fee of $25, you can use any of the 80 hostels across Canada, as well as any of over 5,000 hostels worldwide. The average price for a night at a hostel is about $15. The size and style of individual hostels vary. You might find yourself staying in a converted castle, a floating barge, a mountain chalet, or a lighthouse. The services and facilities offered at each will also vary. Some will provide only the bare essentials of a cot and a pit toilet, while others will have modern kitchen facilities, hot showers, saunas, games rooms, and coffee shops. Separate dorm rooms are provided for males and females. All major hostels and many smaller ones do have rooms for couples but advanced reservations are strongly recommended. Hostels used to enforce curfews, but this is largely a thing of the past. Most Canadian hostels now offer full day access with common rooms, storage for luggage and in some cases reception open throughout the day. Some hostels use a combination lock system so that hostellers can come and go as they please. Be sure to verify if a curfew exists whenever you check in at a hostel. I remember arriving back to a hostel in southern England five minutes past the curfew to find that my bags had been put out on the front steps. I had no choice but to spend the night under the stars. I have been assured that this no longer happens, but check the curfew just the same. Also, because the price is so low at hostels, the manager will sometimes ask you to do a small chore like sweeping a room or taking out the garbage. This small task is likely to be requested only at a small hostel.

An added bonus of staying at hostels is that you're likely to meet up with other young travellers from all over the world. You might want to do some hiking with a new friend while you're both at the hostel, or even stick together for a week or so. At the very least, the other travellers will provide interesting suggestions and conversation.

It's a good idea to phone a couple of days ahead to see if the hostel where you wish to stay has room for you. Reservation policies vary from hostel to hostel—some won't accept reservations, some will accept reservations by mail only, many Canadian hostels now accept reservations by VISA or MasterCard. If possible, it's advisable to book ahead in large cities, especially during July and August. If you arrive in London for Wimbledon intent on finding space in a hostel you can forget it. To help you plan your hostelling holiday, comprehensive guides to all international and Canadian hostels are available from the above address or from a hostel near you. Also available at most hostels, for about $20, are sheet sacks. Most hostels require you to have one to put between yourself and the hostel's blankets. These sheet sacks are simple to make yourself by folding over a sheet and sewing it up one side.

Organization: Backpackers Hostels Canada

Thunder Bay International Hostel
1594 Lakeshore Drive, R.R. #13
Thunder Bay, Ontario P7B 5E4
phone: (807) 983-2042, fax: (807) 983-2914

Overview: Backpackers Hostels Canada is an organization of independent hostel owners affiliated with private hostels in the United States and around the world. The average price for a one night stay at a Backpackers hostel is about $13. You need not have a membership card to stay at one of these private hostels. The Thunder Bay hostel is owned and operated by Lloyd Jones who is perhaps the key hostelling guru in Canada. If you write to the above address with a self-addressed stamped envelope he will send you a list of all affiliated hostels and probably answer any questions you might have.

Organization: Servas

229 Hillcrest Avenue
Willowdale, Ontario
M2N 3P3
(416) 221-6434

National Coordinator: Mr Michael Johnson

Overview: When travelling in a foreign country, have you ever walked by a row of houses and wondered what daily life was like for those behind the closed doors? Perhaps you've never been in a foreign country, but are planning a trip and want to get a balanced view of the society while sharing your Canadian perspective. Joining Servas gives you the opportunity to do just that. By becoming a member of Servas, you are linking into a system of some 12,000 hosts in over 100 countries who are willing to let you stay in their homes for two-day visits. Those who join Servas (membership costs $40) plan their own trips, but are provided with lists of hosts in the areas they'll be visiting. Most hosts require at least a week's advance notice of your visit, while a few welcome drop-in travellers. This sort of information, along with the age, travelling background, interests, and languages of the host are printed on the lists. Hosts do not expect any payment for their hospitality, but might expect help preparing meals, washing dishes, and so on. Some hosts will want to show you around their town and others may have to work. In general, don't arrive with the intention of being entertained by your host. Your stay is a way of experiencing what life is really like in a foreign home.

Don't forget that your stay has two-sided benefits—for your host, learning about Canada will no doubt be of great interest. It is essential that you be both a good ambassador for your country and a helping hand in the host's home. To ensure that those who travel with the Servas membership card fit the above criteria, all candidates are interviewed briefly on the phone and then more thoroughly in person by a local Servas representative. You'll also be asked to provide two letters of reference from someone who knows you well, like a professor, employer, or minister. What they look for, above all, is community mindedness, your ability to listen to and learn from others and an interest in creating a more peaceful world through understanding.

For further details and a list of local interviewers write to Mr Johnson at the above address, making sure to enclose a self-addressed, stamped envelope.

BOOK REVIEWS

The books reviewed below are a small selection of those written on travel. They are all good, dependable guides that may help you in your pursuit of the great wide road. If you are travelling light it is best to read as much as possible before you go and only take one or two of the most appropriate books with you. Books are heavy and it would be a shame to have to throw away a $18.95 paperback because you were tired of lugging it about.

A cautionary note: the more detailed a book, the more quickly it will become out of date—be sure to read the latest editions. What was a lovely Cairo pension in 1989 may now be a nasty cold-water flat.

Let's Go; Harvard Student Agencies, Inc. (New York, N.Y.: St. Martin's Press, published annually)

The line of *Let's Go* travel books is written by students at Harvard University. It is updated annually with first-hand information from the student correspondents who explore the foreign sights and check out local hot spots, tourist sites, hotels and restaurants. Each book has over 500 pages full of sites, activities, practical information about accommodation, restaurants, and transportation, and is geared to the budget-conscious student. Each book starts out with useful sections entitled "Planning Your Trip", "Getting There", and "Getting Around". Although it is published in the United States, the guide is specifically written for both American and Canadian students. The *Let's Go* books are readily available from bookstores, at an average price of $20, and from libraries. Titles in the series include:

- *Let's Go: Britain & Ireland*
- *Let's Go: France*
- *Let's Go: Greece*
- *Let's Go: Spain, Portugal & Morocco*
- *Let's Go: Mexico*
- *Let's Go: Italy*
- *Let's Go: Israel & Egypt*
- *Let's Go: USA (including Canada)*
- *Let's Go: California & The Pacific Northwest*

Lonely Planet Travel Guides (South Yarra, Australia: Lonely Planet Publications)

Lonely Planet publishes a "shoestring" and a "survival kit" series. Between them, they can help you get around all five continents. Each of the approximately 35 titles is usually specific to one country, giving you information on currency, visa requirements, and local customs as well as advice on how to get there and how to get around once there. Many details and facts about the region are included with suggestions on what to see, where to stay, what to eat and what to buy. Country by country and city by city (or town by town) the books tell you how to save money and make the most of your stay. Travellers who have used the book found it to be very practical and extremely useful to refer to along the way. Lonely Planet books are available from your library or a nearby bookstore.

A Year Between by the Central Bureau for Educational Visits and Exchanges (New York, 1991)

This book is a little like the one you are reading, but is designed for American students. It features dozens of possible ways to take a year off and if very informative and comprehensive and is guaranteed to give you a few ideas.

Time Out: Taking a Break from school to Work, Travel and Study in the U.S. and Abroad by R. Gilpin & Caroline Fitsgibbons (Fireside/Simon and Schuster: New York, 1992)

This is in the same vein as the book cited above. More ideas about ways to spend a year doing something out of the ordinary. You might find the book in your local library.

How to go Around the World Overland; Michael and Theresa Savage (Surface Travel Publications, 1984)

The advice and travel hints in this book are drawn from the authors' personal experiences after years of world travel. Whether your desire is to explore the outback of Australia, ski the Swiss Alps, or trek through the rainforests of South America, this guide can provide you with a lot of very useful advice. You can probably find it in your library.

Eurail Guide: How to Travel Europe and the World by Train;
K. Turpin and M. Saltzman (Eurail Guide, Annual; 27540 Pacific Coast Highway; Malibu, California; 90265 U.S.A.)

If you are trying to figure out specific information on train routes in Europe or around the world, this guide may be of some assistance. It gives information on train schedules, tells what the sightseeing is like along the various routes and informs you of discount rail passes that may be available. We don't recommend that you use this guide to plan every hour of your trip, but it may help you learn how much travelling time you should allow between points and generally familiarize yourself with the rail service in a country or between countries. This book is available in both bookstores and libraries.

Great Expeditions (P.O. Box 46499; Station G; Vancouver, British Columbia; V6R 4G7)

This magazine is filled with first hand information from travellers, as well as free classified adds and an information exchange. Previous travel features have included "Off-beat Indonesia", "Travel While You Work", and "Exploring Zaire". A year's subscription (six issues) costs $22 and is well worth the price.

Globetrotters Club (B.C.M./Roving; London; WCIN 3XX, U.K.)

Globetrotters is a small association of travellers from all over the world. A two-year membership is about $30. Membership entitles you to receive the club's newsletter, *The Globe*, which is published six times a year. Travel tips from seasoned adventurers and recent events in low-cost travel are an integral part of each issue. Members also receive the *Globetrotters Handbook*.

Offbeat Canada; by Gerry Hall (New American Library of Canada Ltd., 1981)

This paperback guide describes about 100 unusual and little-known tourist attractions and holiday spots across the country. Highlights of the book include write-ups about whale-watching adventures in the St. Lawrence, a railway which follows the Klondike Gold Rush Trail, and Viking settlements in northern Newfoundland. After most of the write-ups address are listed to which you can write for more information. You might also consider writing to enquire about possible summer jobs that may exist for students. The book is written in a light and amusing tone and makes for fun reading even if you never get to any of these out-of-the-way sites. This book was published over a decade ago but really isn't out of date.

Jim's Backpakers Bible, P.O. Box 5650, Santa Monica, California 90409 U.S.A.

This book lists over 1100 youth hostels and gives tons of advice on backpacking through the United States. You can order it from the above address by sending $7.00 american. The book is also available from the Bookpeople mailorder company.

Europe on 84c a Day; by Gil White (Best Sellers Inc., 1981)

Written by Canada's self-proclaimed "#1 Hitch-hiker", this 140-page guide provides some useful tips for travellers intent on going away on very tight budgets. The book is full of personal anecdotes which make for inspirational reading. Especially useful are the hitch hiking tips. The back of the book is full of phrases such as "May I sleep at your house tonight?" translated into twenty languages. The book was not widely distributed, but check your library.

Hitch-hikers Manual; by Simon Calder (Vacation Work, 1985)

Mr Calder has written two books in this series, one for all of Europe and one strictly for Britain. The guides begin with about 40 pages of very useful, general hitch-hiking tips. Topics addressed include choosing a location, gimmicks, signs, and an amusing bit called "Some Types of Drivers", complete with funny illustrations. The next 100 pages are full of detailed maps of highways and intersections as well as complex instructions about how to access the best hitching positions. Consistent with the entire Vacation Work series, this is a very well produced and helpful guide. You should be able to find it in a library although we do not think that it has been recently updated.

Study

Introduction

Since most of us spend the greater part of our first two decades in school, there's a good chance that the experience will go a bit stale at times. After years of primary and high school, many students become bored or disillusioned with their education, but it doesn't have to be that way. In this chapter you'll find suggestions about how to enrich your long years of education.

Your high school years present your best chance to diversify your education. This is true for a couple of reasons. First, high schools are often more willing than universities to accept transfer credits for a student's year abroad. Second, while in high school, chances are you'll live at home and not cost your parents an outrageous amount in support. They might be more willing to pay for a special program at this stage of your education than when you're away at university. Also, most of the really exciting programs are offered to people of high school age. The first part of this chapter discusses a number of unique high schools and special high school programs available across Canada and in Europe. Programs discussed include a special International Senior High School colony in British Columbia, an advanced science semester at the Ontario Science Centre, and a Canadian private school in France. A second portion of the chapter deals with high school "year abroad" programs. We review the services offered by several agencies who provide students with the opportunity to spend a school year in Europe, Asia, Africa, South America, or Australia.

We predict you'll learn more in your year away than in the rest of your high school career. You'll come back from it refreshed, with a new outlook, and will probably get more from the rest of your education. There is also a whole section of academic summer programs, including language studies, science/research programs, and fine arts courses. Special features in the chapter include "Ivy League Exposure", "What the Provinces Offer", and some student profiles.

At the university level, there are not a lot of national study programs available. For the most part you'll have to rely on programs offered by your particular university. At the end of this chapter we offer a brief overview of scholarships available to university students, as well as a few unique post-secondary programs.

Whether you're about to enter high school or are half way through university, we hope that you'll be able to vitalize your studies by using the information in this chapter.

Organization: The Toronto French School

306 Lawrence Avenue East
Toronto, Ontario
M4N 1T7
(416) 484-6533

Registrar: Anne Ginestier

Facts at a Glance:

Age: Grades pre-school - grade 13

Duration: regular school year

Regional eligibility: all provinces

Cost:
- $10,000 (tuition only)
- $18,800 (tuition and room and board)

Language:
- to enter at high school level, a substantial knowledge of French is required

Getting in:
- application forms available from above address
- forms should be in by January
- somewhat competitive

Overview: The Toronto French School, founded in 1962, is one of Canada's largest independent schools. The school has an enrollment of over 1,200 students and places strong emphasis on enriched math, science and language courses. An interesting feature of the school is that students can take a two year International Baccalaureate course. The school sits on a 26-acre campus with a gymnasium and a playing field. Although some sports are offered, a very academic focus and limited facilities keep athletics at a minimum. Class size is usually no larger than 20. The school has no student residences, so senior-level students who come from outside of Toronto board with TFS families.

Inside View: The Toronto French School (TFS) has been described as a schoolhouse for the global village. The school's emphasis on bilingualism and international teaching techniques and its granting of both the International Baccalaureate and French Baccalaureat diplomas makes this description apt. If you'd like to be a part of this internationally inspired Toronto private school, be prepared to commit yourself to quite a bit of hard work. In fact, if you don't consider yourself at least moderately intellectual or academically oriented, this probably isn't the place for you. Students at this school tend to be bright and very eager to learn, and many take advantage of the programs which prepare them for external examination diplomas. These diplomas enable you to apply to European universities, which is an interesting option to have. TFS students often place very well at the Canadian Chemistry and Physics Olympiad. The school has university-calibre science labs and award-winning science teachers who prepare students for both of these competitions, as well as for university science courses. And you can take many of these courses in French, a huge bonus. In grades 9 through 11, more than half your courses would be taught in French, but in grades 12 and 13 it is possible to take almost no French. According to the Registrar of the school, most students leave the school fully bilingual, others leave with just a general proficiency in French—it all depends on the individual's willingness to work.

TFS is an excellent school with a good international reputation. If you live in the Toronto area the cost is perhaps bearable, at just under $10,000. However, if you're from any place else, the full cost will reach over $18,000. Don't forget, they have no residences and you'd be living with a family, which is not the typical boarding school experience.

Organization: United World Colleges
Program: Lester B. Pearson College of the Pacific

Rural Route 1
Victoria, B.C.
V9B 5T7
(604) 478-5591 fax (604) 478-6421

Director: Mr Tony Macoun

Facts at a Glance:

Age: students entering 12th grade

Duration: two school years

Regional eligibility: all provinces

Cost:
- scholarships fully fund all students
- students may have to pay their own travel expenses

Scholarships cover: room and board and tuition

Getting in:
- application forms available from your high school or from the address above
- required essays and references
- top applicants interviewed by provincial selection committees
- deadline is Feb 1
- extremely competitive (approximately 1 in 15 is selected)

Overview: The Lester B. Pearson College of the Pacific, one of eight United World Colleges, is a highly selective co-educational residential school outside of Victoria. The aims of the school are to promote international understanding and provide a special environment where students from many nations can work and study together in harmony. Students from over 70 countries come to the college on scholarship for the last two years of high school and earn the International Baccalaureate diploma. Canadian students, some from each province and territory, enter Pearson after grade 11. The academic program at the school is rigorous and includes a mandatory core of courses. For instance, all students must study a second language, social sciences, humanities, sciences, and mathematics as well as a "theory of knowledge" course. Along with the demanding academic work, students participate in both a community service project (such as visiting the elderly or sharing recreational activities with handicapped teenagers) and a college service project (which might mean working in the library or on a grounds maintenance crew).

Physically, the school is a colony of modern cedar buildings which include five residences, a large auditorium, a library, an academic building, and a swimming centre. The school has been harmoniously integrated into the forest, overlooks the ocean and is quite isolated. The site was specially designed to create a feeling of community.

Inside View: If you consider yourself to be a well-rounded, academic, and community-minded student, this is one of the best programs available to you. It is extremely competitive, but if accepted you'll be in for the most challenging two years of your life. Imagine spending your last two years of high school at a secluded, beautifully landscaped educational colony perched on a forested hill overlooking the Pacific Ocean. Not only would your surroundings be idyllic, the facilities you use would be of the highest quality. So much for the physical environment (sounds great, doesn't it?); now consider the academic environment. You'll be studying with other top students and with first-rate teachers to earn an International Baccalaureate diploma allowing you to apply for entry to practically any university in the world. Many universities will offer advanced standing to holders of the IB. While the physical and academic features of Pearson College are remarkable in themselves, it is the social aspect of the school which makes it unique. At this school you become a part of a little "global community" composed of students from all over the world. The 200 students at Pearson really get to know each other during their two years together because they share everything—from class work to community service and recreational activities. Even in the residence halls an effort is made to integrate students. Each large room is shared by four students—Canadians are always placed with three foreign students. Not surprisingly, what you'll learn from your roommates and friends will probably surpass what you'll learn in the classroom. This was true for Torontonian Dianne Butterworth: having survived a nerve-wracking interview and gained acceptance to the program, Dianne adopted an "academics are secondary" attitude and threw herself into other aspects of life at Pearson. Her life there was intensely emotional—making close friends with kids from very diverse backgrounds. Now whenever she reads news about political unrest or famine in a certain country, she thinks of her friends from those areas and the stories take on a whole new dimension. The school, according to Dianne, really changes people's attitudes, often quite radically.

If Pearson sounds like the place for you, fill out the fairly lengthy application forms and send them to the above address. By the way, there are similar schools (all United World Colleges) located in Wales, New Mexico, Italy, Singapore, and Swaziland. A very limited number of Canadians are sent to these five schools each year. Opportunities to attend vary from province to province so it is best to write to the above address for more information.

Organization: Neuchâtel Junior College
Program: Senior High School Year Abroad

Cret-taconnet 4
2000 Neuchâtel
Switzerland

(011) 41 38 25 27 00

939 Lawrence Avenue East
P.O. Box 47509 Don Mills, Ontario
M3C 3S7
(416) 484 7224
Toll free: 1 (800) 263-2923

Canadian Representative: Ms Colleen Boyer

Facts at a Glance:

Age: students in their final year of high school

Duration: one year (September - June)

Regional eligibility: all provinces

Cost:
- $18,000 or more
- varies with Swiss franc exchange rate

That covers:
- room and board
- tuition
- insurance and residence permits
- transportation to and from school

Getting in:
- obtain applications from Ottawa representative
- early application recommended
- personal essay required
- usually 80% of applicants are accepted

Overview: Neuchâtel Junior College is located in the scenic university city of Neuchâtel, Switzerland. The school is non-profit and co-educational, was founded by a Canadian, and for over 30 years has granted Ontario high school diplomas to Canadian students. Students come from all over Canada to do their final year of high school in the Swiss mountains. The school also attracts a large number of Canadian students whose parents are living and working abroad. All courses at Neuchâtel are instructed in English, but students may also choose to study German, French, or Spanish, although study of a new language cannot begin there. Students live in the homes of local families where only French is spoken.

Inside View: What a great opportunity—the chance to spend your final high school year in Switzerland! Spending it at this school would guarantee you a very memorable year. Neuchâtel has a solid academic reputation, although it is no more academically challenging than any good high school in Canada. The fact that the school is located in the university town of Neuchâtel, however, means that you'll be in an environment well suited to academic pursuits. It also provides a large population of young French- and German-speaking university students. It is from interaction with these Europeans that most Neuchâtel kids pick up a substantial portion of their French. Because all courses are taught in English, any real progress you make with your French will probably come from social interaction.

Recent graduates of Neuchâtel Junior College report that there are not a lot of extra-curricular activities while school is on. During vacation periods, however, students go on interesting vacations together. Over the course of the year, the school offers four major organized trips, which most students opt to take. The first is a 10-day overland tour through France and Switzerland. It is on this trip that the staff and students get to know each other. Then at Christmas it's off to Spain or Greece for a couple of weeks of relaxation on the slopes or the beach (the school strongly discourages students from going home for Christmas). Skiing is again the central focus of a week-long break in February, traditionally spent in Zermatt. A final organized vacation, a grand tour of Italy, is conducted at Easter. These four trips are not included in the price you (or more likely your parents) pay. According to the school, you should anticipate forking over another $8,000 if you plan to participate on the school trips.

The high price will obviously put Neuchâtel out of range for a lot of kids, but if you're in a position to take advantage of the opportunity, why pass it up? You do have the option of attending the school for just one semester at a cost of approximately $10,000. You only have one final year of high school and spending it at Neuchâtel is one way of making the most of it.

Organization: Class Afloat

450 - 1 Holiday Street
West Tower
Pointe Claire, Quebec
H9R 5N3
phone: (514) 697-3900, fax: (514) 695-0951

Director of Admissions: Mr. Jonathan N. Fortier

Facts at a Glance:

Age: 16–19

Duration:
- 5 months (September - January)
- 10 months (September - June)

Regional eligibility: all provinces

Cost: approximately $15,000 for 5 months; approximately $25,000 for 10 months

That covers:
- tuition
- room and board
- land programs

Where can I go? stops in many countries including Australia, Japan, Singapore and others.

Getting in:
- application packages available from above address
- early application deadline November 15 (encouraged)
- late application deadline March 15
- interview with a regional representative, short essay, transcript

Overview: Since 1984 Class Afloat has offered half and full year academic programs aboard a modern tallship. Course work includes a flexible curriculum of marine biology, physics, anthropology, math, journalism, literature, phys. ed. and other choices. Class Afloat is fully accredited by the Alberta and Quebec Ministries of Education and students from other provinces regularly receive credit for the program especially is pre-arranged with their Ministry of Education.

The aim of this school is two fold: to enliven the education process through international travel and to teach life skills such as tolerance, independence and initiative through the team effort of crewing the tallship. Fifty students participate each year from across Canada and the United States.

Inside View: This program seems too good to be true. Imagine that it's the end of the summer and you're getting ready to head back to school and that heading back to school means flying to Vancouver, boarding a 185 foot tall ship, learning the basics of sailing for a week and then setting off for the South Seas. That's what back to school means to 46 lucky Canadian and American students every fall. The ship they board is the S/Y Concordia, the barquentine which serves as residence and classroom for Class Afloat. Some of the students will have had some sailing experience, others will have never been on a boat before. Within weeks all students will be helping to an equal degree with the rigging, navigation and maintenance of the vessel. For Marie-Jose Naliquette, who was one of the first students to participate on Class Afloat, the six hour night watches were one of the most difficult and memorable parts of the experience. She remembers sailing through the fog at 3:00 in the morning with cold rain whipping against her face and being responsible for looking out for other boats or obstacles. It was an arduous, but character building task which she still looks back on when she finds herself in difficult situations.

By the time Christmas comes around, you've crossed miles of ocean, visited several countries and studied subjects which are rarely part of a highschool curriculum (as well as core subjects). Specific details of port stops and course offerings vary every year, but in 1993 students are encouraged to spend the Christmas holidays billeted with Japanese families. Class Afloat arranges to have you placed with a family for 10 days. The cost to students is a few hundred dollars, but on a program like this who's counting! That's the big bummer about this year on the water - it's so pricey. There are some scholarships available, but for a maximum amount of $5,000. Other excursions, all of which are included in the tuition price have included hiking through rainforests in Costa Rica, touring a Gdansk shipyard, language immersion in Africa, bird watching in the Galapagos Islands and countless other fascinating and rare opportunities.

Obviously on a program like this, with very small classes, (about 8 people), a very small campus, (185 feet), and all of the teamwork involved in the sailing of a ship, you are bound to develop close friendships over the year. It is the sort of experience which binds people together and will give you a feeling of accomplishment and confidence for years to come.

Two further notes: In 1994, to celebrate their 10th anniversary, Class Afloat is organizing a special itinerary for the school. Exact details are still not firm, but the general theme involves a world tour in 180 days which will dock on every continent. Furthermore, if you don't want to spend a whole year afloat, they do offer one month long summer experiences which follow various routes. The cost for one month is $2,175.

Organization: Blyth and Co.
Program: Lycée Canadien en France

13 Hazelton Avenue
Toronto, Ontario
M5R 2E1
(416) 926-0828
Toll free: 1 (800) 387-1387

Administrator: Mrs Margaret Aitken

Facts at a Glance:

Age: last year of high school

Duration: 1 year or 1 semester

Regional eligibility: all provinces

Cost: $19,900 for one year

That covers:
- return airfare from Toronto or Montreal to France
- room and board
- tuition

Language: some French is helpful

Getting in:
- application forms available from above address
- somewhat selective (160 apply for 100 positions)

Overview: The Lycée Canadien en France is owned and operated by Blyth and Co. and offers students entering their final year of high school the opportunity to live and study on the French Riviera. The school, established in 1985, enrolls 100 students each semester with the aim of preparing them for university through a diversified academic, linguistic and travel program that meets the guidelines set by the Ontario Ministry of Education.

Inside View: Close your eyes and imagine spending your final year of high school in a classroom overlooking the port of St. Jean Cap Ferrat, passing your weekends in Florence, making new friends from across Canada, and being taught by a group of teachers who are your friends outside school hours. If this sounds like a fairy tale, you might be interested to know that such a school exists. The Lycée allows you to earn your final-year credits in a completely new environment, employs eight teachers, and restricts classes to no more than 15 students. While many students might expect to come back bilingual, this depends on the individual effort. Some returned with fluent French, having learned the language from the families they stayed with or through community involvement. Other students found it difficult to learn French. As Alexandra Christie, a 20-year-old from the Northwest Territories, wrote: "Courses at the Lycée were instructed in English and our friends spoke English, therefore many found picking up the language difficult...the experience of living with a French family was a great benefit."

The Lycée provides instruction in mathematics, sciences, history, geography, languages, art, and drama. In addition, field trips are an important part of the curriculum. Students chosen to attend the Lycée are quite independent, and show self-discipline and organizational skill. Previous academic performance is considered and your school recommendation is important. Given the cost, relative affluence is another prerequisite. If you decide to go to the Lycée, expect to get to know sons and daughters of diplomats, industrialists, and international executives. According to Derek Keddie, 18, from Willowdale, Ontario, the best feature of the program was getting to know a completely new group of kids all of whom got along very well.

Organization: Nova Languages Inc.
Program: Ecole Loire - Atlantique

P.O. Box 2938
Windsor, Nova Scotia
B0N 2T0
(902) 678-3873 (evenings)

Co-director: Mr Grenville Jones

Facts at a Glance:

Age: 15 -18

Duration: 5 weeks

Regional eligibility: all provinces (accredited only in Nova Scotia)

Cost: $3,785

That covers:

- return airfare from Halifax to Paris
- accommodations and meals
- books, materials, insurance, and tours

Where can I go? France

Getting in: application forms available from above address

Overview: Nova Languages Inc. offers Nova Scotia students the chance to combine study and travel in France for high school credit. The operation was started several years ago by two Annapolis Valley high school teachers. Of the five weeks in France, 20 days are spent in the classroom (for three hours each day), where study is focused on culture, grammar, and literature. Marks are based on tests, assignments, and exams as well as each student's progress with the language outside of the classroom. The curriculum is supplemented by numerous excursions and tours. The school is located in St. Malo, in northern Brittany, and students live in residence at the Lycée Maupertuis, a centrally located school with small dormitories, dining hall and classrooms. After three weeks in St. Malo, the group moves on to La Baule to finish off the academic portion of the trip. The final eight days are spent staying in Paris and touring the Loire Valley.

Inside View: Nova Languages Inc. offered its first program in the summer of 1989. Jane Gould, then a grade 11 student from Halifax, was a member of that first class. Part of what drew her to sign up was the fact that it was the 200th anniversary of the French Revolution that summer. Another, more practical reason for the trip was to improve her rather spotty knowledge of French. Although Jane seemed perfectly eloquent over the phone, she claimed that she "never understood French grammar—or even English grammar!" She found the classes to be stimulating and especially enjoyed the numerous excursions and the chance to practice her French with native speakers. With only 15 students on the trip being taught and tutored by two experienced teachers, the degree of personal attention was obviously quite high. As a testimony to the value of the experience, Jane has an 85% average in French this year, a marked improvement over last year's disappointing 55%.

If you're a Nova Scotia student and can get your hands on $3,875 you might consider this program. Grenville Jones, co-director of the program, states that, "Our objective is to help students attain fluency in French and to understand more about French life and culture." Because opportunities such as this are not common in Nova Scotia and because you will receive a high school credit for the course, Nova Languages has a lot going for it. It is important to note that although, officially, only the province of Nova Scotia grants high school credit for this course, students from other provinces have managed to have credit granted by their local school boards.

Organization: Ontario Science Centre School

770 Don Mills Road
Don Mills, Ontario
M3C 1T3
(416) 429-4100
Fax: (416) 429-2934
Director of Education: Mrs Pamela Kay

Facts at a Glance:

Age: students in their final year of high school

Duration:
- 1 semester
- September - January or February - June

Regional eligibility: all provinces

Cost:
- travel to and from Toronto
- you are responsible for arranging for your own room and board (the administration may be able to offer some suggestions in this regard)
- sudents from outside of Ontario are recquired to pay out of province tuition fees
- books

Getting in:
- application forms available from your high school or from above address
- applicants may be asked to attend an interview
- deadline is end of February of the year before you plan to attend
- very competitive (approximately 1 in 3 are accepted)

Overview: The Ontario Science Centre Science School has been offering talented science students a chance to spend a semester at the Centre earning high school credits since 1982. Students can choose to take three of the following courses: physics, chemistry, biology, and calculus. As well, a credit called Science and Society is compulsory. All courses are taught at an enriched level. The school accepts about 25 students from every corner of Ontario each semester. Students are responsible for their own travel arrangements and also for their accommodations once in Toronto.

Inside View: The Ontario Science Centre is a huge complex full of fascinating displays, exhibits and collections. It also serves as a classroom to 25 lucky students every semester. If you're fascinated by science, this opportunity is a dream come true. To have a reasonable chance of being chosen, you should have good marks (at least 75%) in your science and English courses and a strong academic background. The program receives about 150 applications for the 50 available spots at the centre. We were told that the quality of the applications is very high. It is therefore essential that you give a lot of thought to filling in the application forms. Once accepted, you can look forward to an exciting semester of interaction with what quickly becomes a tight-knit group of students. Susan Ollerhead, currently a Guelph University student, considers herself very fortunate in her semester at the Science Centre. She told us that because students were highly motivated, much of what they learned was self-taught. In some classes there were no textbooks—students simply used the entire Centre as their resource lab. In other courses the class conducted experiments in special labs set aside especially for the school. Kristina Polsinelli, an 18 year old Toronto student, is currently finishing her term at the Science Centre. She was very enthusiastic about the program and said she couldn't imagine returning to a 'regular' highschool. Luckily she won't have to because she will be graduating from highschool and heading off to study sciences at university. Before attending this program Kristina's future course of study had been undecided. This is a well-organized, unique program, well worth doing even if you don't plan a career in the sciences.

Organization: Biosearch College

6401 Louvois
St. Leonard, Québec
HIP IMI
(514) 327-8337

Box 367, Station U
Toronto, Ontario
M8Z 5P7
(416) 537-9441

Principal: Mr Joseph H. Acton

Facts at a Glance:

Age: grades 11, 12, and 13

Duration:
- Spring break session — one week field study in the Bahamas (March)
- 4 months of class work in Canada (November - February)
- Summer session — three weeks field and class work in the Bahamas (July)

Regional eligibility:
- accredited in Ontario
- Québec students have received CEGEP credits for the course
- students from other provinces may participate, but may not receive credit from their school boards

Cost:
- Spring break session — $1,095 U.S
- Summer session — $1,095 U.S.

That covers:
- application fee, tuition, room and meals

Getting in:
- application forms available at above address
- must submit an official transcript and reference
- deadline for spring break session — mid-November
- deadline for summer session — May 1

Overview: The purpose of Biosearch College is to provide credit courses in a natural laboratory for the student who wishes to participate in field investigations within the marine and environmental sciences. This is accomplished under the guidance of a teacher in small tutorial groups either in the Bahamas (during the summer session) or in local high schools (for the spring break session).

260

Students have a choice of earning one of two Ontario Ministry of Education approved credits—Biology (grade 11 biology is a prerequisite to this course) or Environmental Science (which is a grade 12-level course). Field studies are carried out from the CCFL Bahamian Field Station on Watling Island. Facilities there include dormitories, cafeteria, a number of large laboratories, several classrooms, and a complete darkroom as well as sports facilities for basketball and volleyball. The price for the course does not include airfare. Budget fares are available from both Toronto and Montréal to Fort Lauderdale through an agent who has served the college since 1972. Because of airline schedules, an overnight stop is required in Fort Lauderdale—the college can arrange inexpensive accommodations (on departure and return).

Inside view: If you love biology, but the prospect of memorizing tedious class notes and perhaps dissecting a desiccated grasshopper isn't really what you had in mind as a way of earning a high school credit, you should consider Biosearch College. Don't get the wrong idea—you will be required to take notes during the classroom portion of this course. In fact, you'll be following basically the same curriculum as standard high school biology courses. The difference is that while you're learning concepts inside, you'll also be seeing them in action outside, in the Caribbean Sea. You'll capture live specimens and be able to study them in specialized labs at the field centre, while other labs will be held right on the beach. You will participate on night dives to study nocturnal animals and will have two full days of independent study—your findings will then be presented as a report. It was this hands on approach to learning which drew 18 year old Jennifer Robertson to the program. Jennifer chose the spring break session and was taught her classroom program by the principal of the school, Joseph Acton. Classes were held two days every other week from 4pm to 10pm at her high school. The amazing thing was that there was only one other student in the class—talk about personal attention! At the same time that Jennifer was taking these courses she was also taking scuba diving lessons. Scuba was a skill she had always wanted to pick up, and although it was not a prerequisite to the course, it made exploring the reef that much more interesting. Jennifer told us that it really wasn't necessary to scuba because the waters are quite shallow—students who snorkeled got basically the same experience.

If Biosearch College sounds interesting to you, why don't you write to them and borrow a video which introduces you to past participants and gives you an idea of the type of studies you'll be carrying out in the Bahamas. They loan the videos or 16mm films to schools free of charge.

Public Schools—Special Programs

You don't have to leave the country or attend an exclusive private school in order to take advantage of non-traditional educational opportunities. Interesting programs often exist in your own backyard. Today, many public high schools offer French immersion, Japanese immersion, self-pacing math, programs for gifted students, co-op programs, advanced art and music courses, and enrichment classes. At no extra cost you could enrol in one of these programs and make your high school education a bit richer and more challenging. Availability of these opportunities differs within schools and school boards; but why not consult a knowledgeable teacher or principal, ask around, or call your Board of Education and find out what specialized programs are offered in your area. You may uncover a wealth of possibilities.

What the Provincial Departments of Education Offer

While researching this book we learned that many provincial Ministries of Education have well-established exchange programs for high school students. After further investigation we discovered that these opportunities are not equally available to all Canadians. Unfortunately, depending on your location, you have either a wealth of options or very few. As one education director put it in 1987, "Alberta, Ontario, and Québec are the leading lights when it comes to offering student exchange programs." Six years later, the situation has changed somewhat. Now British Columbia is also among the forerunners in the student exchange department. Even if your province has limited opportunities, you can still, with a little effort, expand your opportunities. The next feature tells you what is available province by province. If your province does not sponsor student programs take a closer look at the programs described in our student exchange section, as well as the national student conferences. Students from all provinces are eligible for these programs.

Northwest Territories and The Yukon: Individual and group exchange trips do occur, although they are not organized by the territorial Ministries of Education. These departments help sponsor student travel, but the initiative for it must come from the teachers in a particular school. Some trips have been major undertakings, as was the Coppermine student visit to China in the spring of 1987. In this region, local initiatives and national student programs provide students with travel and educational opportunities.

British Columbia: British Columbia has a substantial annual budget to administer their Pacific Rim Education Initiatives Program.

The initiative sponsors several programs including, three month long immersion classes in Japan, three month long cultural stays in Japan, Hong Kong and Thailand and summer schools for Mandarin and Japanese language study for both teachers and students as well as helping to fund school-initiated visits to Asian countries. The Initiatives Program was established in 1987, but has recently suffered from budget cuts which has resulted in the elimination of certain programs. British Columbia also administers a reciprocal exchange with Germany similar in nature to the one run in Ontario and Alberta. New possibilities are emerging quite often. Talk to your teachers or write to the Ministry to find out the latest.

National and International Education
British Columbia Ministry of Education
Parliament Buildings
620 Superior Street
Victoria, British Columbia
V8V 2M4
(604) 356-2489

Alberta: Alberta students are members of a privileged class when it comes to high school exchange programs. Organized exchanges to China, Japan, Germany, Korea and Québec are available each year through the Alberta Education's Department of National and International Education Branch and various schools. Some are individual and others are group programs, some are short term while others are long term. Exchanges to Russia may be available in the near future. For more information write to:

National and International Education Branch, Alberta Education
4th Floor, East Tower, Devonian Building
11160 Jasper Avenue
Edmonton, Alberta
T5K 0L2
(403) 427-2035, fax: (403) 422-3014

It's also worthwhile to ask your school principal or guidance counsellor about programs through your local Board of Education.

Saskatchewan: Saskatchewan used to offer a West German Student Exchange Program for high school students. Unfortunately, they no longer do. All special project initiatives occur at the local school level. If you feel like asking your Ministry of Education why they're not offering as much as your neighbors to the west, write to them at:

Saskatchewan Education
1855 Victoria Avenue
Regina, Saskatchewan
S4P 3V5
(306) 787-6024.

Manitoba: Manitoba offers a Québec Exchange for students enrolled in grades 10 and 11 at a French high school. Individual students are twinned and each spends three months with his or her host family. The entire exchange lasts for six months. Your host family provides your room and board, and your family is expected to do the same when your twin visits you. Part of your travel costs will be covered by the Manitoba Department of Education. Information is available from your school, but not all school boards participate in this project. Manitoba now offers exchanges to Germany similar to those offered in other provinces. If this interests you, write to:

Bureau de l'Education Française (for Québec programs)
Department of Education and Training (for German)
Manitoba Education
509 - 1181 Portage Avenue
Winnipeg, Manitoba
R3G 0T3
(204) 945-6916.

Ontario: The exchanges formerly offered by the Special Projects Branch of the Ontario Ministry of Education are now administered by an independent organization called The Ontario Student Exchange Foundation. Among the offerings are three-month reciprocal international student exchange programs with France, Switzerland, Italy, Germany, Mexico and Spain. All exchanges are for students between the age of 14 and 17 and cost $1,650. The cost covers your airfare, local transportation, cancellation insurance and an orientation. Students require basic knowledge of the language of the host country and most return completely fluent. In order to participate your school board must be a member of the foundation. (90 school boards are members). Deadline for application is December/January depending on your destination. All applications should be mailed directly to your local school board. For more information contact the program manager at the following address.

Bea Harper
Ontario Student Exchange Foundation
Box 86 - 80
Bradford Street
Barrie, Ontario
L4N 3A8

Call (705) 739-7596 or contact your local Board of Education for more information.

QUÉBEC: Québec offers a wide assortment of exchange programs for high school students. The Québec Government's Ministry of Education publishes a guide to these opportunities entitled *Echanges, Bourses, Voyages 1989*. Exchanges to Alberta, Manitoba, New Brunswick, and Ontario provide students with a chance to attend school in another part of Canada for up to three months. *Echanges, Bourses, Voyages 1989* is available from:

Ministère de l'Education
Direction général des ressources informationnelles
Edifice de la Tour de la Chevrotièree
1035 rue de la Chevrotière, 6e etage
Québec City, Québec
GIR 5A5

Nova Scotia, New Brunswick, Prince Edward Island, and Newfoundland: The story on exchanges in eastern Canada reads very much like a copy of the Saskatchewan report. All program directors we spoke with at these provincial ministries of education told us that there was little available in the way of youth programs for students in the Maritimes. Students have to rely on national programs such as the Terry Fox Centre, Forum for Young Canadians, Interchange on Canadian Studies, and Pearson College. More so than in other parts of the country, these programs are highly publicized in the high schools, and students' chances of being selected are quite good.

For example, in P.E.I., each year one student is selected to go to Pearson College and each school in the province annually sends one or two students to participate on the Interchange program. The 11 individual secondary schools organize exchanges on their own, but as is the case in other provinces, the P.E.I. government does not have the personnel or resources to initiate their own student-exchange programs.

In Nova Scotia the individual schools and teachers organize intraprovincial, interprovincial and international exchanges, but on an ad hoc basis. Halifax has had city-wide student music exchanges with England and Japan in recent years and other communities have undertaken similar activities. Frank Mitchell, Assistant Director of Education for the Halifax District School Board, suggests that you phone him or ask your principal if you want to find out about organizing an exchange trip or see if plans for one exist. The best time to phone Mr Mitchell is during the summer break, when his time is more flexible. He says the province tries to encourage and support teacher endeavors and cooperate in any way possible, but they do not initiate.

In Newfoundland and Labrador the scenario is the same: your best bet for organizing an exchange is to join forces with an energetic teacher.

In New Brunswick some class twinning projects with Québec do exist. They vary in their details. For more information write to the N.B. Department of Education at the address found in the Appendix.

A Year Abroad

When you look back over your high school years, do you want to remember them as one big foggy blur? Assuming you don't, why not add some spice to your secondary career by doing one year in a foreign country? A perfect time to study abroad is during one of the those "in-between" years like grade 10 or 11—nothing much really happens in those years anyway. Think for a moment what you'd leave behind—the math teacher's foul breath, the crabby secretary, the G.I. Joe gym teacher—and then consider what you'd trade it all in for—adventure, excitement, and world travel! (Not to mention the fact that, once in your "new" country, you'll be in the socially desirable position of the new Canadian kid on the block.) Sounds intriguing already, doesn't it!

If you choose to go to a country like France, Germany, or Spain, there's an excellent chance you'll become proficient in the national language—a real added bonus. If you go to Australia or New Zealand, you won't learn a new language, but you might pick up a bit of the accent, which would also be neat.

There are a number of ways you can arrange to spend a year abroad. The Rotary Club offers high school students the chance to spend a year overseas, as do several Canadian-based exchange agencies. In this section of the Study Chapter, you can read the "Inside view" on all these agencies to decide which one is right for you. Take advantage of these programs while you can—you won't regret it! After a year away, you'll come home with a broader outlook on life, a new sense of maturity and an experience that will always stand out as the thing that made your high school years worthwhile.

A word of caution before you take off. It is important that you discuss your "year abroad" plans with your guidance councillor or principal. Whether or not your school will accept credits earned in a foreign country may well influence your plans. It is basically up to your school whether to grant credit or not, so it is really to your advantage to keep the powers that be well informed from the start.

Organization: American-Scandinavian Student Exchange (ASSE)

National Headquarters
2130 St. Joseph
Lachine, Quebec
H8S 2N7
(514) 637-5596
Toll free: 1 (800) 361-3214

Director: Mr Ben Hannan

Facts at a Glance:

Age: 15-18

Duration:
- August - June for Europe
- February - November for Australia
- March - January for Japan

Regional eligibility: all provinces

Cost:
- U.S. and Mexico — around $3,000 (airfare not included)
- Europe around around $4,600
- Japan and Australia around $6,500

That covers:
- return airfare from New York or L.A. to host country
- room and board
- comprehensive insurance package

Where can I go? U.S., Australia, New Zealand, Sweden, Denmark, Norway, Britain, Holland, Spain, Finland, France, Germany, Iceland, Italy, Switzerland, Czeckoslovakia, Poland, Japan, Thailand, Portugal or Mexico

Getting in:
- apply directly to the above address
- reference letters required
- interview with a regional representative

Overview: ASSE has had a Canadian office since 1984, and each year sends over 300 high school students abroad for a year of study.

Currently, students can be placed in most Western European countries as well as in Australia, New Zealand, the United States, and Mexico. While abroad, students live with host families who provide room, board, and a home atmosphere free of charge. The families accept foreign students into their homes for various reasons, but mainly so that their children can become acquainted with another culture and perhaps learn another language. Because the host family receives no payment, the cost of this program is quite low.

Inside View: This agency seems just the right size to be able to provide you with all of the necessary services and still give you lots of personal attention. Their main office, where you should write for information, is run by the very helpful Ben Hannan. He can put you in contact with your regional representative of ASSE. These reps are very helpful, and because each one is dealing with just a few students, you will get very thorough service.

ASSE offers an excellent choice of countries and 98% of participants are placed in the country of their first choice. Cost for these programs covers everything for the entire year. You'll be attending a local public school. Depending on where you live, you might have to add another $800 to get you to New York or L.A., where the international flights depart. Total cost of an ASSE exchange is still about the lowest you'll find.

There are no language requirements for any of the ASSE programs except Switzerland's, for which there is a prerequisite of two years of high school German. This means that you can attend school in France even if you've never studied French. It obviously won't be that easy at first, but apparently, fully 90% of those sent abroad do not have any knowledge of the foreign language before leaving. If the prospect of arriving with no previous exposure to the language freaks you out, ASSE offers one - a ten day language camp. These sessions take place upon arrival in the host country and are available at extra cost. Janet Gilbertson, an 18 year old from Brandon, Manitoba, knew very little French when she landed in France last year. She can now carry on a decent conversation, but still has lots of trouble with the written language. Janet had graduated from high school and wanted to learn another language and "see something different" before heading off to university. A few months before Janet left for France, she was given the name of the family who had chosen to take her in for the year. They wrote letters back and forth three times before she arrived in Paris for a week-long orientation with a group of other ASSE students. After the orientation, Janet's host family drove to Paris and picked her up. She got along very well with the family despite the langauge barrier. Because Janet knew very little French, the first few months were quite difficult, both at home and at school. She went to a regular French high school and admitted that she was completely lost for the first couple of months—both because she couldn't understand her teachers and because she felt lonely. She stuck it out, however, and now looks back on the experience as a real confidence builder.

Every year ASSE gives away three scholarships. One covers the full price of the program and two of them cover 90 % of the cost. When you send in your preliminary application you should request information about scolarships. The three scholarships are awarded based on three criteria - academic excellence, leadership and financial need. You'll need at least an 85 % average, you'll have to be involved in some volunteer work or extra-curricular groups and your parents will need to provide some proof that paying for the program would be a stretch for them. Each year about 20 kids ask about scholarships and three are granted. This is an excellent scholarship and well worth investigating.

Organization: Cultural Homestay International
Program: Semester and Year Abroad Programs

103 Redwood Court
Sherwood Park, Alberta
T8A 1L2
(800) 463-1061

Program Manager: Ms Vivian L. Hart

Facts at a Glance:

Age: 15 - 18

Duration: 5 - 12 months

Regional eligibility: all provinces

Cost: $4,500 - $7,500

That covers:
- return travel from airport closest to your home to host country
- room and board
- school fees and related expenses

Where can I go? any of over 20 countries on every continent

Getting in:
- applications available from local offices or from above address
- deadlines vary

Overview: Cultural Homestay International is a non-profit educational exchange program which was founded in 1988. They arrange for students to spend one or two semesters in a foreign country. While abroad students study in a public school and live with a volunteer host family. C.H.I. maintains liaison officers in each country who file monthly reports on students progress.

Inside View: C.H.I. offers essentially the same services as ASSE, CACF, Interculture Canada and other similar programs. They have been around since 1988 and originally specialized in exchanges with Japan, but now can place you in any of over 20 countries. C.H.I. is relatively small - last year they placed 10 students overseas, this year they hope to place 30. Because they are so small they can provide very personalized service. For instance, if you were spending a year at a highschool in Russia, C.H.I. would have a representative there who would check in with you on a monthly basis and send reports of your progress back to Canadian headquarters. You may or may not care that someone is there nearby to look over your shoulder and help you out in case of problems but your parents are likely to be thrilled.

If a whole semester away seems too long for you, C.H.I. also offers shorter homestays during the summer. They put together small groups of people and send them on three week long homestays. To spend three weeks in Russia or Japan might cost you a total of $2800.

Note: see the Au Pair feature for more information.

Organization: Comité d'Accueil Canada-France (CACF)
Programs: 1) high school semester homestays 2) one-year University study program 3) intensive summer programs for high School and university students

CACF - OTU / Montréal
1183 avenue Union
Montréal, Québec
H3B 3C3
(514) 875-6172

Assistant Director: Mlle Patricia Godard

Facts at a Glance:

Age:
- 1) 15-17
- 2) university students
- 3) 14 and older

Regional eligibility: all provinces

Duration:
- 1) 5 months
- 2) 1 year
- 3) up to 10 weeks

Cost:
- 1) $6,000
- 2) $6,800 - $13,000 depending on which university you attend
- 3) varies depending on program and duration

That covers:
- finding a suitable host family
- room and board

Where can I go? France

Getting in:
- apply to above address
- no set deadline, but apply as early as possible

Overview: Comité d'Accueil Canada-France has offered high school homestay programs in Brittany for the past 15 years. It was founded by the French Minister of Education to allow young people to spend four to six months living like a typical French student and learning about France. CACF is the smallest of the programs featured in this section and is the most specialized in its offerings. It is also one of the most expensive programs and admits that it caters to private school students. Pretty much anyone who applies is accepted, although you must have a good academic average.

Inside View: Those of you with a few bucks to spare and an interest in learning or improving your proficiency in French would profit from CACF. As with other programs, they find a family willing to billet you, enrol you in a local high school and make sure that you get to France and settle in without any confusion. Since they are a very small program sending only a handful of students abroad each year, you receive a lot of personal attention and will probably find CACF quite well organized. Everything will be arranged for you. Since the program is expensive, they advertise their services to private schools, many of which will give their students credit for all of the work they do in France. Don't be mistaken though, you don't have to go to a private school to get in this program.

Kim Wichs, a 16-year-old Havergal College student, spent half her grade 11 year in France. For her, the best thing about the program was the opportunity to see France as a resident rather than as a tourist. She found CACF to be well organized and said she would recommend it. However, she said that to really benefit from one semester, you must be very independent, open-minded, and able to assimilate quickly. While in Brittany, she attended a local public high school, which was a new experience in itself—and a very positive one.

There is no language requirement, but a basic understanding of the language is recommended. Otherwise, your first couple of months will be quite difficult.

CACF also offers study programs at the Université de Nantes, Angers and La Sorbonne. All enrollment and living arrangements are made for you. CACF makes the process of entering a French university easier, but remember that you can save some money by enrolling directly. Many Canadian universities now offer year-abroad programs as well.

Organization: Education Foundation (EF) Services for Foreign Study
Program: High School Year in Europe

60 Bloor Street West
Suite 405
Toronto, Ontario
M4W 3B8
(416) 927-8605
Toll free: 1 (800) 263-2825

Director: Ms Mara Pawlowski

Facts at a Glance:

Age: 15-18

Regional eligibility: all provinces

Duration: an academic year or semester

Cost:
- $5,750 for European countries
- $6,700 for Australia or New Zealand

That covers:
- tuition, room and board
- return airfare

Where can I go?: France, Germany, USA, Australia, or New Zealand

Getting in:
- applications available from your guidance office or from the address above
- to ensure that you'll get your choice of country apply by early February (applications accepted until April)

Overview: EF Services, sponsored by the non-profit Swedish Educational Foundation for Foreign Study, has been offering academic homestay programs since 1979. Their Canadian office has recently opened, and in 1993-94 they will send some 325 students abroad. Each year close to 6,000 students are exchanged worldwide through EF. Students can spend one semester or a full year studying in France, Germany, Sweden, Australia, or New Zealand. While there, they live with a host family and attend a local public high school. Students between the ages of 15 and 18 are eligible to participate, provided that they have at least a 70% academic average.

Inside View: For those of you interested in turning a year of high school into a foreign study adventure, EF Services is another organization to consider. The program aims to promote international understanding and to allow you to experience a new culture and a new language. For approximately $6,000, you can spend a year in a foreign country living with a volunteer host family who will provide your room and board. School tuition and return airfare from Toronto to Europe are included in the total cost.

The program works as follows: you apply to participate and if you meet entrance requirements and can be matched to a host family and school, you're all set. EF has an extensive network of volunteers around the world who interview all host families and they won't send you anywhere they don't have an area representative. Since EF is not very large, they can give you a lot of personal attention. They make sure that the experience is as smooth as possible and will counsel and trouble-shoot as necessary. EF provides you with a very comprehensive package of pre-departure materials and operates a 24-hour emergency telephone service to reassure both you and your parents. One of the best features of EF is that they are able to guarantee you placement in the country of your choice if you apply before February 1. Early application is especially important if you plan to go to Australia or New Zealand owing to the popularity of these two recently added destinations. Overall, their prices are very competitive and the country choice and duration allow for considerable flexibility.

To be selected, you must prove that you are enthusiastic, like to get involved in activities and are academically motivated. The average student should have little problem in qualifying, but be prepared for quite an intensive screening and interview process. EF wants to make sure that you are mature and responsible enough to handle an extended period away from home. You must demonstrate that you are flexible and independent without being a loner. Be prepared to answer situational questions which will test your ability to deal with the unexpected.

For Donna Goodwin, 15, of Alhanbra, Alberta, the year spent in Liladon, France, was definitely worth it. She couldn't believe how much she learned in such a short time. Although she found her family to be rather strict, she says she thinks this is the type of experience that everyone should have. Her advice is to jump right into all aspects of the new life. She was very shy when she went over, and didn't speak much at first. This was a big mistake, she now thinks, because all the people she met really liked meeting new people and she should have taken advantage of their friendliness from the start.

Organization: Interculture Canada

1231 Ste. Catherine West
Suite 505
Montréal, Québec
H3G 1P5
1 (800) 361-7248

National Director: Mr Claude Roberg

Facts at a Glance:

Age: 15-18

Duration:

- 11 or 12 months (winter and summer departures)
- summer programs last 6 - 8 weeks

Regional eligibility: all provinces

Cost:

- $6,000 - $8,500
- summer program $2,700 - $3,900

That covers:

- return travel from Montréal to host country
- room and board
- school fees and related expenses

Where can I go? any of over 30 countries on every continent

Getting in:

- applications available from local committees or from above address
- deadlines vary
- getting accepted depends on the availability of a suitable host family somewhere in the world

Overview: Interculture Canada, affiliated with AFS International, is the oldest exchange network in the world. It is also one of the largest, annually placing about 9,000 students from around the world in foreign homes. The aim of Interculture Canada is to provide teenagers who are curious about the rest of the world with the opportunity to spend a year studying in a foreign country. While abroad, students live with a family that provides room and board free of charge and treats the student like a new family member. Anyone between the ages of 15 and 18 and in one of the last three years of secondary school is eligible to participate in an Interculture Canada exchange. Average marks and an average maturity level are all that is required. New to Interculture are summer programs which last between 6 and 8 weeks. The summer programs operate in the same countries as the year long programs.

Inside View: If you have dreamed of living in some exotic, far-away land, but never thought you had a realistic chance to do so, Interculture Canada is your answer. The organization was set up 40 years ago to serve the needs of students just like you—students interested in enhancing their education by living and studying abroad.

For between $6,000 and $8,500, Interculture will set you up with a host family, enrol you in school, fly you to the host country and then transport you to your surrogate home. Add to that the cost of getting yourself to Montréal where most flights depart. Other agencies (ASSE, CACF, and EF) charge slightly less for their exchange programs which all work the same way. One of the advantages of going with Interculture is its large size and international scope. Because it is affiliated with AFS, Interculture has large numbers of contact and resource people worldwide. This is a comforting fact for both you and your parents. Also keep in mind that Interculture offers exchanges to over 30 countries on every continent, whereas the smaller agencies deal with a dozen or less countries. However, the smaller agencies can usually do a better job of placing you in the country of your choice. If, for instance, you really have your mind set on going to France, you might be better off going with one of the smaller agencies since they'll more likely be able to place you there. However, if you are willing to go wherever there is an opening, you might end up in Indonesia, Venezuela, Thailand, or Sri Lanka with Interculture!

To be accepted for an Interculture exchange, you should have at least an average academic record, an adaptable personality and a desire to learn another language and way of life. After spending a year with a native family and attending school in the native language, most come back with a firm grasp of that new language. A full year of complete immersion does wonders. You'll have to work hard the first couple of months to avoid frustration with the new language and new environment, as it can be a difficult adjustment, but your persistence will repay you. If you can't fit a whole year away into your life, you might consider the summer programs offered by Interculture. They have one to New Zealand that sounds really fun. You would be there for the months of July and August spending part of the time living with a family and the other part of the time at a recreation centre. At the centre you learn kayaking, trekking and other outdoor activities. It sounds like a great way to get an inside view of New Zealand. It costs $3,900 and that covers everything.

Niki Deller, a 22-year-old University of Toronto student, spent a year in Japan through Interculture when she was 17. Niki was unaware that agencies such as Interculture existed until she stumbled across a dusty, out-dated application form in a desk drawer in her school guidance office. After sending away for up-to-date information she felt that Africa would be the most worthwhile place to spend a year. It happened that Interculture was unable to place her in Africa, but after a "relaxed" interview with a regional representative, they offered Niki a placement in Japan. After a two-week orientation session in Tokyo, Niki moved in with her host family not knowing a word of Japanese. By the end of the year, thanks to the quality of the school she attended, she was quite fluent. The amount of personal attention the few visiting foreign students received sounds hard to believe. For instance, Niki would attend regularly scheduled classes, where, because of the language barrier, she would understand next to nothing. Immediately following these classes, the same teachers would repeat the lessons in the presence of a translator.

Niki has nothing but praise for Interculture and wishes more Canadian students would take a year to explore another culture. She reports that kids she met from other countries had to go through a long series of gruelling interviews and that competition was very tough for spots on "year abroad" programs. She felt that Canadians had it pretty easy when it came to getting accepted by Interculture.

If you have problems convincing your parents to finance your Interculture year abroad, write to the above address for some good ammunition—they have a brochure with a couple of very positive testimonials from parents. Also ask your parents to consider how much they would spend to feed you, entertain you, and so on, in a year. All things considered your year abroad comes out looking like a real bargain—which it is!

Organizations: Provincial Ministries of Education
Programs: International and Interprovincial High School Exchanges

1) **Ontario - Germany**
   B.C. - Germany
   Manitoba - Germany
   Alberta - Germany

2) **Ontario - France**
   Ontario - Switzerland
   Ontario - Spain
   Ontario - Italy
   Ontario - Mexico

3) **B.C. - Japan,**
   B.C. - Hong Kong
   B.C. - Thailand

For addresses see respective Provincial Ministries of Education in the appendix.

Facts at a Glance:

Age:
- 1): at least 15; 2): 14 - 17; and 3): various ages
Duration: 3 months

Regional eligibility: must be a student in a province that offers the program

Where can I go?: depending on your home province—Germany, France, Switzerland, Spain, Italy, Hong Kong, Japan and Thailand.

Cost:
- 1) (except Ontario) must pay for spending money, airfare (depending on the province, some subsidization exists), and cultural excursions;
- 2) $1,650 includes everything except medical insurance and spending money
- 3) varies depending on the program
- room and board covered by host families
Language: see "Inside View"

Getting in:

- ask your guidance counsellor for information or inquire at you local board of education.
- November application deadline for most programs

Overview: Several provinces provide high school students with the opportunity to study in a foreign country for a period of three months. Exchange students then host their twin for another three-month period. The program aims to enhance students' language skills in French, German, Italian, Japanese, Thai or Spanish as well as giving them some exposure to an unfamiliar culture. The programs vary slightly from province to province, but their basic structure is the same. Ontario's programs are now administered by an independent foundation. While on exchanges, students live with their host families and attend a local high school.

Inside View: If attending high school abroad is of interest to you, but the hassle of organizing such an exchange and arranging credit transfers seems like more work than it's worth, consider a three-month reciprocal ministry exchange. Maybe you want to go to school in a foreign country or in another province, but don't want to risk losing out on credits. These exchanges have been designed with just these thoughts in mind. First of all, while the prospect of going abroad is very exciting, you may find that being thrown into a new family, school, and country when you don't know the language is a real shock. A year-long program is great for those who adjust well, but for others it may turn out to be a very unhappy experience. This is one reason that these exchanges are for three months. It's a time period that is survivable and is long enough to allow you to become fluent if you are at all diligent. Also, since it is run by the "powers that be", you receive full credit for your courses in most cases. Sometimes you will have to arrange to do a lot of extra work before you go and may have to finish assignments and tests while away.

Unlike the other high school year-abroad programs you've read about, this is a twinning exchange. You will be matched with a student from your exchange country (or province). Your twin will live with you for three months and vice versa. This feature has its good and bad points: it's easier to meet people because you'll be introduced to all your twin's friends, but if you don't get along very well it may be a very long six months! Every effort is made to pair you with someone compatible (through a personality profile) and most participants we spoke with got along well with their twins.

In most provinces a short orientation session is provided before your departure. You fly abroad with all the participating students from your province and there is an optional, cultural excursion on both legs of the exchange. Overall, these exchanges seem to be very well organized and are becoming more popular each year.

As for language requirements, they vary depending on the country. For France and Switzerland you must be studying French. Some provinces require second-year high school French. Germany and Spain require the equivalent of second-year high school German or Spanish. If you want to go to Italy you must show an interest in Italian or Roman history, the classics, art, or music. Studying Latin also qualifies you. You don't have to speak Italian, but you will have to acquire basic ability in the language before you leave for Italy.

If your provincial Ministry of Education organizes one of these exchanges why not find out a little more about it? It's your choice: spend next year holding up the wall at your school dance, or spend it watching sumo wrestlers in Tokyo...

Organization: Rotary International
Program: High School Year Exchange

Address: contact you local Rotary Club

Facts at a Glance:

Age: 16-18 years

Duration: 11 months

Cost:
- return airfare to your destination
- you will receive a small allowance from Rotary

Where can I go?: anywhere in the world where there is a Rotary Club

Getting in: application forms available from your high school or from your local Rotary Club

Overview: Rotary International is an international network involved in a number of activities including student programs. They are found in many countries around the world. On the Rotary exchange, students are selected to attend school in a foreign country and to act as ambassadors of Canada. While there, they are billeted with Rotary families. Each local club operates its own selection process but not all clubs in Canada are involved in youth exchanges.

Inside View: Rotary international can make it possible to spend a year in Japan, Brazil, Europe, or Scandinavia, among other exotic locations. Unlike other organizations, Rotary does not promise you a choice of locations, but you are asked to state three preferences and most people get one of their choices. Rotary places one follow-up condition on your selection: you must make a presentation to your sponsoring club within one year of returning to Canada. When in your new country, since you are connected to the Rotary network, you can probably ease the adjustment process by meeting new people very quickly. Some students billet with four or five families over the year, while others remain with one for the entire stay. Although you attend school for the year, most students don't get credit for their work when they return, so you're better off looking at it as an enrichment year. One drawback: Rotary sets down ground rules which include promises not to drive, travel outside your host district, or get romantically involved.

Competition for selection varies with the district. Most clubs advertise through local high schools. Completion of a questionnaire is followed by a set of interviews.

Christie Sutherland, 18, of Effingham, Ontario, spent a year between grade 11 and 12 in Brazil as a Rotary exchange student. It was a year of much personal growth for her. Although a strong support network was available for Christie, a great deal of adjustment was called for. She said that she was able to do a fair amount of travelling, but this is not encouraged by Rotary in many countries. Although she'd jump at the chance to do it again, Christie said it was frustrating at times because it was so disorganized.

What does it take to be chosen for this exchange? There are no set criteria, but if you are self-motivated, outgoing, friendly, a solid student, involved in extra-curricular activities, and open-minded, you are exactly what Rotary is looking for. It also won't hurt your chances if you have a relative in your local chapter—the successful candidate often does.

OTHER SPECIAL PROGRAMS

Organization: Art Gallery of Ontario
Program: Advanced Studio Courses

317 Dundas Street West
Toronto, Ontario
M5T 1G4
(416) 979-6608

Head of Gallery School: Mr Steven Bowie

Facts at a Glance:

Age: secondary school students (other courses for all ages)

Duration: September-May (Saturdays 9 am-1 pm)

Regional eligibility: those able to commute to Toronto every Saturday

Cost:
- $350 for non-members
- $275 for members

That covers:
- instructor's fee
- all course materials

Getting in:
- apply any time
- portfolio review and interview/discussion
- very competitive

Overview: The Art Gallery of Ontario has been offering art courses for people of all ages for over 60 years. The Advanced Studio Course is open to high school students only and is meant to serve as a college preparation course. Students have the choice of following studio courses in drawing, painting, print making, architectural design, film and video, anatomy, or graphic design. All instruction is provided by professional artists, most of whom have exhibited nationally and internationally. Students receive credit for this course at the discretion of individual schools. Courses are designed to build strong portfolios for future post-secondary studies.

Inside View: If you have artistic ability and can get yourself to Toronto every Saturday morning, this course offers an exceptional opportunity. First of all, the facilities you will use are world class. The most up-to-date equipment is available for woodworking, sculpture, drawing, design, silk-screening and lithography. These skills are all taught by carefully chosen instructors who are also professional artists. They can help you develop your technical skills as well as offering advice on how to proceed both academically and professionally with your artwork.

In short, the course offers you a thorough immersion in art and the art scene. At a price of no more than $350, this course is also an exceptional value. You'll receive 120 hours of professional instruction, use of the best facilities, and all the materials you'll need, including paints, brushes, clay, wood, canvas, and so on. A number of scholarships are awarded on the basis of need, merit, and faculty recommendation.

The course is quite competitive with class size limited to only 15 students. Selection is based on the portfolio you submit and an informal discussion. Portfolios, evaluated in late spring and early fall, can be submitted at any time. You should be aware that you probably don't stand much of a chance of being accepted unless you are already quite a good artist. If you are not chosen for this course you could always join the Preparatory Drawing Course, which is offered for the same 30-week period, on Thursday afternoons, and doesn't require the submission of a portfolio. Space is limited, however, and it is important to arrive early on registration day.

If you don't live within commuting distance of Toronto you should investigate art courses that may be offered by a gallery near you. Your art teacher or the art department at your local university or community college may also be able to provide you with information on available programs.

Organization: Royal Ontario Museum Education Services
Program: Co-operative Education Program

Royal Ontario Museum
100 Queen's Park
Toronto, Ontario
M5C 2C6
(416) 586-5801

Head of Education Services: Mr Ron Miles

Facts at a Glance:

Age: 16-19 (senior secondary level)

Duration: school year or summer

Regional eligibility: open to those who have a place to stay in Toronto

Cost: none

Getting in:
- apply through your high school
- a small number of applications are received each year; this year everyone who applied was accepted

Overview: The Royal Ontario Museum, in conjunction with the Great Metro Region School Boards, allows students to earn high school credits by doing volunteer work at the museum. Work done by each student is tailored to his or her special needs and interests. Students chosen for the program range from gifted to general-level achievers, but all share sufficient drive to put in long hours at the museum. Students can earn several credits either during the school year (which calls for some creative class scheduling) or during the summer. Marks are determined by the student's supervisor.

Inside View: If you live in or near Toronto why not add a new dimension to your high school years and earn some credits at the museum! The work you'll do there could include building displays, teaching younger students, and translating brochures. The museum's atmosphere is very energetic and creative and everyone there seems to love what they're doing. For Greg Monzar, 19, of Toronto, Ontario, earning credits from the ROM turned his high school career around. He wasn't doing very well in his regular high school classes and lacked motivation. After some fancy timetabling, Greg arranged to spend three days a week at school and two days a week at the museum. His duties at the ROM included helping to teach a creative art studio, working on a totem pole competition, and organizing a publicity campaign. The chance to take on so much responsibility allowed Greg to develop far more than if he'd been sitting in a classroom. For you, this opportunity may even unveil an entirely new set of career possibilities.

If your school guidance counsellor hasn't heard of the program, simply call Mr Miles, the very helpful Head of Education Services. This program is going with a vengeance, the ROM had 15 students this year. Also, if you live too far away to take advantage of the ROM Program, check with your local museum or school board to see what they offer by way of co-op education.

Organization: Waterloo Centre for Creative Technology
Program: Shad Valley Summer Program

Canadian Centre for Creative Technology
8 Young Street East
Waterloo, Ontario
N2J 2L3
phone: (519) 884-8844 fax: (519) 884-8191

Manager of Administration: Mr Ron Champion

Facts at a Glance:

Age: grades 11 and 12

Duration:
- 4 weeks (normally the month of July)
- usually followed by a 6-week paid work term

Regional eligibility: all provinces

Cost:
- $500 for students with an industry sponsor
- $1,750 for unsponsored students

That covers: tuition, room, and board

Where can I go?: Acadia University, University of British Columbia, University of Calgary, Carleton University, University of Manitoba, University of New Brunswick, Université de Sherbrooke, University of Waterloo

Getting in:
- application forms available from your high school or from above address
- list of top applicants is sent to sponsoring companies, which interview the students and select for sponsorship those they prefer
- deadline is early December
- quite competitive (1,200 apply for 400 spots)

Overview: The Shad Valley Summer Program, established in 1980, offers bright, scientifically gifted high school students the chance to work with and learn from their peers, university professors and Canadian industry. Students chosen to participate in the program spend one month at one of several Canadian universities with 50 other students. There they work in small groups with university graduate students and professors to complete a diverse and stimulating curriculum. Each day there is a math lecture and a business lecture (meant to prepare students for future entrepreneurship). A wide variety of seminars are also offered dealing with such topics as robotics, computer vision, satellite remote sensing, bio-engineering, leadership, and business consulting. After the month-long program, sponsored students (about 3/4 of those attending) spend six weeks working for their sponsoring corporation. The principal aim of the program is to expose students to a wide range of career options and motivate them to make the most of their scientific and entrepreneurial potential.

Inside View: If you have strong academic standing ("Shads" are typically in the top 1-2% of their classes) and motivation, and are willing to spend a summer indoors, this program will open doors for you for years to come. The Shad Valley Program has been in operation for a decade now and many of its graduates are making names for themselves in the fields of science, technology, and business. While many are still pursuing advanced university degrees, some have started their own high-tech firms and others are still employed by their sponsoring companies. Most of the graduates with whom we spoke agreed that the Shad Valley Program opened their eyes to the wide array of career possibilities available by combining scientific and business skills.

Directors screen all initial applications and choose the top several hundred. Files of top applicants are then sent to sponsoring companies, which go through and choose one or more students they feel would be best suited to work for them. These sponsoring companies pay all but $500 of the program's cost for their chosen students. (You're required to come up with $500 to show the directors that you are committed to the program.) On completion of the university portion of the program, students go to work for the sponsoring company—as a salaried employee—for the rest of the summer. It often happens that companies rehire their Shad students for several consecutive summers.

If you're chosen, you'll spend one month at a Canadian university with 50 other students, most with interests and outlooks similar to your own. You'll live in university residence, eat meals, attend seminars and conduct research experiments together and you'll inevitably make some close friends. Student interaction is one of the great features of this program. Also, the chance to live in a university setting will prepare you for the real thing a couple of years down the line.

Your time during the month-long course will be highly structured—days, evening and weekends are full of seminars, lectures and labs, as well as many scheduled cultural and recreational activities. Your instructors will be university professors and graduate students. You'll also hear talks by successful entrepreneurs, politicians, and academics who will inspire you to shoot for great heights.

Organization: The Deep River Science Academy
Program: Summer Science Program

P.O. Box 600
Deep River, Ontario
K0J 1P0
(613) 584-4541

Administrator: Ms Carole A. Judd

Facts at a Glance:

Age: high school students with at least grade 10

Duration: 6 weeks (June 24 - August 4)

Regional eligibility: all provinces

Cost:
- $3,600 if application is received by early deadline
- bursaries of up to $2,500 are available

That covers:
- room and board
- tuition
- recreational activities

Getting in:
- application forms available from above address
- deadline April 1st
- early deadline for discount March 1st
- somewhat competitive

Overview: The Deep River Science Academy is set up to allow students from all over Canada the chance to earn two high school credits while gaining practical research experience. Located in the town of Deep River, Ontario, the Academy annually accepts 42 students from all of the provinces and territories into its summer program. Students are housed at the Petawawa National Forestry Institute situated on picturesque Corry Lake which boasts facilities for swimming, canoeing, hiking and tennis. Most meals are taken at the Institute cafeteria. This facility is a fifteen minute ride away from the teaching and research buildings. The Academy offers three program options to students. The first two are teaching/research combinations, in which students cover the classroom and laboratory work of grade 11 biology (3A) or grade 12 physics (4A) in 97 hours at Mackenzie High School. These first two options also incorporate a total of 128 hours (three days per week), spent working on a real research and development project at one of the two participating national laboratories. The third option offered is a two-credit research and development enrichment program. Students who chose this plan spend five days each week (a total of 220 hours) at either the Chalk River National Laboratories or the Petawawa National Forestry Institute.

Inside View: If you're a high school student interested in science and technology and have a month and a half to spare next summer, consider spending it at the Deep River Science Academy. It'll be hard work, but is guaranteed to be an illuminating way of earning either your grade 11 biology credit or your grade 12 physics credit. Depending which of the optional programs you choose, your schedule will be divided between classroom work and time spent in the lab on a real research project. Saturday mornings are spent back in the classroom and the rest of the weekend will be free time. Because the course is condensed you'll have to spend some of that weekend free time doing homework. Make no mistake about it, this course is hard work. The program attracts students with very strong scientific interests. With the amount of time spent doing homework, attending classes, and participating in research projects, there isn't much time left over for distractions. Ken Falkner, a 17-year-old Toronto student now entering grade 12, attended the Academy last summer and thoroughly enjoyed the experience. Ken chose to follow the option whereby he earned his grade 12 physics credit and got to work on a project at the nuclear lab. With a scientist as his supervisor, Ken helped in the testing of insulators for a super-conducting cyclotron. Participating in this research, talking with professors, scientists and other keen students has helped Ken decide to pursue engineering when he enters university.

The cost of $3,600 for the program is somewhat steep and does not include your travel costs to and from Deep River. However, a number of bursaries are available to qualified students. Money can also be raised from schools, clubs, or from the government. For instance, students who come from the Northwest Territories have their entire fee paid by their Ministry of Education.

This program is similar in some ways to the Shad Valley Summer Program. The prime goal of both programs is to open up career horizons for young scientists. Both expose you to science in a professional industrial setting and both see you living with a group of similar students. The main difference between the two is that at Deep River you can earn two high school credits, while at Shad Valley you can earn money and valuable contacts by working for a company after the course. Perhaps one way to decide which program would be best for you is to ask yourself if you're more interested in pure research (Deep River) or the business side of science (Shad Valley). Both are excellent programs and offer exceptional benefits to students who are still in high school.

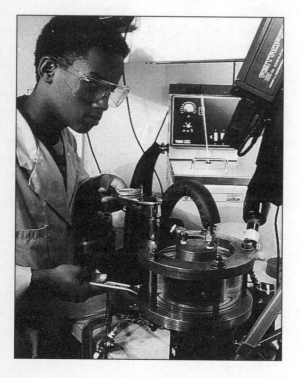

Organization: Phi Delta Kappa International
Program: Summer Camp Institute

PDK International Headquarters
Eighth and Union
P.O. Box 789
Bloomington, Indiana
47402-0789   U.S.A.
(812) 339-1156
Toll free: 1 (800) 766-1156

Facts at a Glance:

Age: students entering 12th grade the following September

Regional eligibility: all provinces

Duration: 5 days

Cost: $130

That covers:
- round trip transportation
- room and board
- materials

Where can I go?: Bloomington, Indiana

Getting in:
- not particularly selective
- application deadline February 28
- school must send official transcripts

Overview Every year Phi Delta Kappa sponsors a week long camp for high school students who are seriously considering teaching as a profession. The camp is held annually with up to 120 students being chosen to attend. Students live in residence halls and eat meals in cafeterias. The camp is designed to introduce students to the wide opportunities in education, the study of time management, problem solving, and development of leadership skills. Seminars and workshops are led by outstanding educators from across the United States.

Inside View If you've given any thought to becoming a teacher and can afford to devote a week of your summer to being in Indiana with

120 other American and Canadian students, you've stumbled across your dream program. This camp has several important things going for it. First of all, because it is basically an American program, when the admissions officers see your application they'll be all over it because having you there would make their program that much more culturally (or at least geographically) diversified. Secondly, the camp comes to you at very little cost. A hundred and thirty bucks covers everything: round trip transportation (they book your plane or train or bus—whichever is least expensive—for you), a room, all your meals, books, and other course materials. As an added bonus, some local chapters of Phi Delta Kappa provide scholarships to selected students. So, the possibility exists that this camp will be a freebie. Also, because this organization really wants to attract students who are serious about their possible futures in the field of education, you are bound to learn a few things while there. You'll probably learn as much from your co-campers as from anyone else—with 120 participating the chances are good that you'll make some friends.

Attending this camp means that you will not smoke, drink, or drive while there. Violators risk being sent home with their tails between their legs.

Organization: Antichita Archaeological Research Team
Program: Research Assistant Program

P.O. Box 156
St. Catharines, Ontario
L2R 6S4
(416) 682-8124

Director: Dr David W. Rupp

Facts at a Glance:

Age: 16 and over

Duration: 3 weeks (in June, July, or August)

Regional eligibility: all provinces

Cost: $1,495

That covers:
- accommodation and meals
- reading materials, equipment and instruction
- two excursions while on Cyprus

Getting in:
- application forms available from above address
- medical form required from a doctor
- signed release form
- not selective (eligible applicants are taken on a first-come, first-serve basis)

Overview: The summer of 1990 saw the first program for research assistants on archaeological projects in Cyprus organized by the Antichita Archaeological Research Teams. The purposes of the teams are two-fold. The first is to recruit enthusiastic participants for excavation work in Cyprus. The second is to teach novices the basic principles and methods of field archaeology. Tasks performed by research assistants include recording data, taking measurements, drawing plans, and cleaning finds. Other duties will include shovelling, sifting, and pushing wheelbarrows. Experienced archaeologists act as supervisors to each team of 12 assistants. All participants are expected to share equally in all aspects of field work regardless of age or sex. Days begin at 6am and end in the afternoon.

Participants live in a Cypniote village in simple dormitory-style accommodations where breakfasts are prepared and eaten. Lunches and dinners are eaten at simple village restaurants. All meals (except for weekends) are included in the price of the program. Air fare to Cyprus is not included in the cost.

Dr. Rupp, an experienced archaeologist who founded the program, likes to refer to it as "Downward Bound". The field work, he says, can be repetitious, tedious, and physically quite demanding. What makes the experience worthwhile is the fact that you'll learn first hand with leading scientists and historians. The program is supplemented with lectures on the history of the island excursions to other major archaeological sites and museums.

Organization: Ontario Association of Teachers of German
Program: Summer Language Enrichment Program in Germany

Thornhill Secondary School
167 Dudley Avenue
Thornhill, Ontario
L3T 2E5
(416) 889-5453

Director: Mr Robert Hart

Facts at a Glance:

Age:
- secondary school students
- must be at least 16 years of age

Duration:
- 1 month
- late June - late July

Regional eligibility: Ontario

Where can I go?: Kulmbach, Germany

Language: must have at least one year of German instruction or equivalent

Cost: $2,500

That covers:
- return airfare from Toronto
- transportation within Germany
- school materials
- room and board

Getting in:
- applications available from your local school board or from the above address
- deadline for applications is early March
- limited enrollment, but the program is not well known so it hasn't been very competitive in the past

Overview: For six years the Ontario Ministry of Education offered secondary school students summer language credit courses in Germany. However, as of January 31, 1990, the program has been run by the Ontario Association of Teachers of German in conjunction with the Federal Republic of Germany and the Ontario Ministry of Education. This intensive, month-long program is designed to develop students' ability in spoken German as well as introducing them to the culture of the new country. Formal classroom sessions, workshops, sports, and excursions are all on the agenda. The program has an enrollment limited to 25 students. A change from beforeøthis is now a non-credit enrichment program.

Inside View: Combining a little travel with a little study is a great way to spend part of your summer, especially if you're travelling to Europe. This program allows you to do just that. Before you think this is an easy way to get through that German course your parents are forcing you to take, be sure that the following sinks in.

This is not a vacation. You will go on some excursions and live in a new country, but you will work and study to learn the language. You must also depart and return with the group. Bearing this in mind, the experience is fantastic. While away, you are taught by Ontario teachers who are assisted by local employees. You attend class every morning and spend the afternoons in language workshops, attending cultural events, and visiting historical sites. While in Germany you are billeted with a family and will spend a week in Munich at the end of your stay.

Organization: Council of Ministers of Education, Canada and Secretary of State
Program: Summer Language Bursary Program

Manager of Fellowships
Summer Language Bursary Program
P.O. Box 4500
230 Park Avenue
Thunder Bay, Ontario
P7B 6G9
(see appendix for provincial addresses)
(807) 343-3205
Toll free: 1 (800) 465-3013

Provincial Coordinator: Mr Richard Jackson

Facts at a Glance:

Age: students must have completed grade 12

Duration: 6 weeks

Regional eligibility: all provinces

Cost: students are responsible for all travel expenses

That covers: the bursary covers room and board, tuition and books

Where can I go?: all over Canada

Getting in:
- application forms available from your provincial Ministry of Education
- apply directly to your provincial coordinator
- application deadline is February 16

Overview: The Summer Language Bursary Program enables post-secondary students to learn their second official language while improving their knowledge of the culture associated with that language. Courses last for five weeks and are offered at universities in all ten provinces. Students should write to their provincial Ministry of Education for a description of existing courses. Those who wish to apply for a bursary should send the forms directly back to their Ministry stating their top three program choices. Students who are able to pay the cost of the course themselves (the value of the bursary is about $1,795) should apply directly to the university of their choice.

Receiving a bursary is no guarantee of acceptance to the program of choice. Bursary criteria vary from province to province—some choose by lottery, some by need and others on a first-come, first-served basis.

The courses themselves are quite intensive, consisting of large grammar components as well as conversation and activity groups, plays and outings. Normally grammar and composition classes are held from 8:30am to 12:30am each day with special group activities scheduled in the afternoon. While on the program, students live either in university residences or with local families. Bursaries do not cover the cost of travel to and from the program site.

Inside View: If you're serious about improving your second language, this program has a lot to offer. For one thing, as long as you've completed grade 12 and you get your application in early, there is no reason why you shouldn't be readily accepted. If you apply for a bursary, you have roughly a 50% chance of getting it. The bursary covers everything but the cost of return travel to the university. That brings up another great aspect of the program—choice of course locations. Whether you want to improve your French or your English, you can choose from campuses in every province. Of course, you'll have to pay your own travel expenses, but taking advantage of seat sales or flying stand-by can keep the cost surprisingly low.

Taking this course is a great way to spend the summer before university or any summer during university—especially if you get a bursary. Depending on which university you attend, you might be able to receive credit for the course—it's up to you to check with your university and make arrangements for your transcripts to be forwarded. Never assume that you'll receive credit for this course. Also, be sure to check out the living arrangements at the program you'd like to follow. Courses at McGill and Laval, for instance, provide university residences for students, whereas in Trois Pistoles students are billeted with local families (sometimes five or six students per family). You'll have to weigh the pros and cons of each option. You'll obviously have less supervision and, according to several students, more fun living in residences. However, staying in a household where everyone speaks the language you are trying to learn is very beneficial. One student pointed out that students with very little or no French can find the experience of living with a family somewhat frustrating. It all depends on how eager you are to improve your second language.

Youtaz Irani, a 22-year-old graduate of the University of Western Ontario, went to Trois Pistoles on a bursary from this program. She chose Trois Pistoles because it was the only program that Western would accept as a credit course. For Youtaz, whose French was already quite good, the time spent in rural Québec increased her understanding of the culture more than the language. Her French didn't improve much, but she now knows what it's like to be a part of a small fishing community. Students who go into the course with less French tend to improve more noticeably, especially in their verbal skills.

A final note on this program: the McGill course for beginners fills up very quickly so apply early for this program.

Organization: Travel Cuts
Program: Eurocentres

187 College Street
Toronto, Ontario
M5T 1P7
(416) 979-2406

Facts at a Glance:

Age: 16 and older

Duration: 2 - 13 weeks

Regional eligibility: all provinces

Cost: $1,200 to $3,700

That covers:
- room and half board
- tuition

Where can I go?: England, U.S., France, Italy, Spain, Germany, or Switzerland

Getting in:
- no entrance requirements
- apply to above address or to your local Travel Cuts Office

Overview: Eurocentres is a Swiss-based chain of language schools catering to the North American market. In Canada, space in these schools can be booked through any Travel Cuts. Students can enrol in classes which last anywhere from two weeks to several months, in any of 32 cities, at levels ranging from absolute beginner to advanced courses for teachers. The courses are somewhat more expensive than many other language schools. Students can choose to live either in hotels or with local families, the latter being the more common option. Eurocentres offer such a wide range of program options that it is best to write to the above address requesting specific information. Furthermore, if you do phone them in Toronto or Montreal (and perhaps elsewhere), be prepared to spend an agonizingly lengthy amount of time on hold. This organization is in desperate need of a toll-free line. Trying to find a hostel in London or book a train reservation in Italy will seem perfectly blissful experiences compared with trying to get through to Eurocentres on the phone. Goood luck!

Ivy League Exposure

Most small, private American colleges and prep schools stay open over the summer and offer introductory-level university courses to senior high school students. If you long for a taste of the Ivy League, but don't think your parents will be interested in funding a full four years at such an institution, this is your chance to see what the Ivy League fuss is all about. The way it usually works is that you write to whatever school you're interested in attending, asking for application forms. The school will probably ask for reference letters from your guidance counsellor or principal, a complete transcript, a few short essays (topics such as "What do you hope to gain from a summer at Princeton?"), and maybe SAT scores. Generally, summer courses at these schools are much less competitive than their regular term programs. If you are a good student, you shouldn't have trouble getting in.

If you're accepted, you'll spend a month or two living in the residences, eating in the cafeterias, and attending lectures in the classrooms. Just living on campus is one of the attractions of an Ivy League summer session. Most of the buildings on these campuses actually will be covered with ivy. Well-manicured greens, formal courtyards, and huge shade trees all add to the park-like atmosphere. Your room in residence is likely to be panelled in oak and have a fireplace in the corner. The library, where you'll be able to read and relax in overstuffed, chintz-covered armchairs, might be similarly panelled. Excellent sports facilities are also guaranteed and should include numerous tennis and squash courts, at least one swimming pool, a weight room and sometimes even a golf course.

Normally your courses will be taught by regular staff members. By immersing yourself fully in the school, you'll gain a pretty good feel for what the place is all about. Sometimes it's possible to use the credits you earn towards your undergraduate degree. However, for many students, earning credit is not the most important feature of attending this sort of summer program. Most are really looking for a chance to prepare for the rigours of university life (those of an academic nature or simply those of living away from home for the first time).

Within the actual Ivy League—Cornell, Yale, Harvard, Brown University, U. Penn, Princeton, Dartmouth, and Columbia—at least the first five offer summer courses to senior-level high school students. Many other similar universities also have summer programs. A large American publication called *Peterson's Guide* has complete listings of what's available. Many U.S. and Canadian prep schools also offer pre-college courses over the summer. Schools such as Ridley College, Choate-Rosemary Hall, and Hotchkiss all offer such courses. Whichever school you decide on, expect to pay around $2,500 for a month.

This will cover room, board, and tuition, and you'll also be responsible for books, travel, and incidental expenses. The price is high, but then, these are exclusive schools.

STUDENT PROFILE

Name: Jillian Cohen
Age: 21
Home: Toronto, Ontario

Combining La Sorbonne with Passion

Four years ago, Jillian Cohen, then in grade 12, spoke only English. Despite the fact that she'd taken French every year in school, she felt dissatisfied with her verbal ability. Her grammatical skills weren't great either. Today, Jillian is completely bilingual, having no difficulty in writing or reading French and speaking with a natural, flowing accent. This transformation took place because Jillian made the effort to carefully research French language programs and to immerse herself in French culture.

It all started during the summer before grade 13, when Jillian went through the fairly simple process of applying for the Summer Language Bursary Program (p. 301). She was accepted and spent six weeks studying French grammar and conversation in the French-speaking environment of Laval University in Québec City. After the course, Jillian found her verbal skills had improved considerably. Her desire to perfect her French was also strengthened.

The next step in Jillian's path to bilingualism demanded considerably more research, writing and commitment on her part. She decided that to polish her French, she should spend some time living in an exclusively French environment. She set her sights on Paris. Because she knew she wanted to spend at least half a year abroad, but also wanted to begin university in September, Jillian took on some extra course work and finished her high school diploma in January. While at school, she wrote away to French universities to see what courses, accommodation, and so on they could offer her. She got most of the addresses for these universities from the French consulate (see Appendix). She also obtained the necessary student visa. When she'd heard back from several universities, she settled on La Sorbonne in Paris, which offered an intensive five-month course in French grammar to foreign students at all levels of proficiency. (The course level for each student was decided during the first day of classes by written exam.) Tuition for this course was roughly $500.

The lack of student residences was a drawback to study at La Sorbonne. Consequently, when Jillian arrived in Paris she had no place to live. This presented a slight obstacle at first, but as she got to know the city the housing situation righted itself. The first couple of nights were spent in a $10-per-day hotel. Through classmates, Jillian learned of a student residence which rented rooms by the month. This turned out to be an inexpensive place to live, and also an ideal spot to make friends from all over the world. After two months at the residence (which had a strict 1am curfew), Jillian, by then familiar with the workings of the city, moved in as a boarder with an elderly widow. The rent was cheap, and she gained a different perspective on Paris.

Along with her studies at La Sorbonne, scheduled mostly in the morning, Jillian wanted to get some work experience while in France. In Canada she had read copies of *Passion*, a magazine for the English-speaking community of Paris. Since Jillian had always thought journalism might interest her and since *Passion* was founded by a Canadian, she thought it might be an ideal place to work. So, as soon as she was settled into her studies, she headed out to find the *Passion* office. Although she didn't have much expertise to offer, she appeared genuinely interested and enthusiastic and the people at *Passion* took Jillian on as a volunteer. For the next five months, the *Passion* office became a focal point in Jillian's Paris existence. She basically made up her own schedule and dropped in when she could. Jillian did a lot of photocopying, typing, and filing, but it wasn't all dreary office work. Highpoints included manning a *Passion* kiosk at an exclusive prêt à porter fashion show at Les Tuilleries, where she rubbed shoulders with international celebrities; making deliveries to authors; and generally getting to know the Paris literary scene. Working at *Passion* provided Jillian with a realistic view of contemporary journalism and confirmed her interest in writing. One other student began volunteering at *Passion* the same week as Jillian—he is now an assistant editor of the magazine.

After spending seven months in Paris studying and working, Jillian's French improved 100% but her knowledge of France was limited to Paris. She felt too that her grammar could still be improved. So, once again, Jillian wrote directly to dozens of French universities enquiring about summer courses. The University of Nimes was the first to reply and Jillian enrolled in a month-long course. The cost of tuition, room, and board was about $1,000. By dealing directly with the university instead of booking the course through a Canadian summer-abroad language school, Jillian saved a considerable amount of money.

Now, four years after her first extra-curricular French course, Jillian is completely bilingual. The French and journalism skills she developed in Paris were quickly put to use at McGill where she wrote for the *McGill Daily* and *Tribune* and edited the political science journal. Jillian's creativity allowed her to gain invaluable study, travel, and work experience all at the same time.

The Post-Secondary Years

So, you're in your final year of high school and it's decision time. Yes, you're going to university, but the question is, where to apply? Before you fill out your application to the university that your friends all favour, take a minute and think about where you are at the moment. University is your opportunity to study what you want, where you want. It is your chance to meet a new group of people, maybe live in another province, or country, or if nothing else, take a few interesting courses. You should consider not only the course of study you will follow, but also the environment you want to live in for three or four years. Remember, what you now think you want to study at university stands a very high chance of changing once you get there. You'd better choose a place where you'll have a good time.

An in-depth review of your academic options from this point forward is beyond the scope of this book, but we will try to entice you with a variety of possibilities. From there, it's up to you to find out more about them, talk to a few people and spend some time in your library or guidance office flipping through school calendars.

You will have to consider the financial implications of some of these options, but there are often means of hurdling monetary barriers. Also, while some people would have no problem living at the other end of the country, you might like to be able to come home once or twice a term rather than just at Christmas. You should also ask yourself "Do I want a co-op program? Does the university offer an exchange program I may want to go on? Would I be better suited at a large or a small university? Are athletics important to me?" After pondering these considerations, you may still end up going to the same university as all of your buddies, but now because you're confident that it's really the right school for you.

Canada has some 40-odd universities, each with its own strengths and weaknesses. Some are more highly reputed than others, others offer specialized programs, and still others boast a liberal education. Some, like the University of Toronto, the University of British Columbia, and Dalhousie, are large, big-city universities, while others like Mount Allison and Bishops are small, highly residential institutions. In between these you can choose from the University of Victoria, the University of Western Ontario, or Queen's University, to name just a few.

If you're from High Prairie, Alberta, you might have wondered what all the fuss about eastern Canada was about. You can use your undergraduate years to find out the real story: apply to an Ontario or Québec university. Conversely, central Canadian students can gain an appreciation for other regions of Canada—why not go to the University of Calgary or Acadia University in Nova Scotia? True, your travel costs could be quite high, but if you take advantage of seat sales and youth stand-by fares they won't be exorbitant. Read about some of the universities in other parts of Canada before you decide. Information on courses and admission criteria are provided by the schools themselves. With a little research, you might find the very thing you hoped for but didn't know existed. Also, remember that your chance of qualifying for scholarships might be greater at one of the smaller universities.

You might also consider one of the Canadian military colleges. Royal Roads Military College, in Victoria, B.C.; Royal Military College in Kingston; and St. Jean in Québec, are degree-granting universities that combine academics with intense athletic, leadership, and military training. They offer travel, classmates from across the country and a guaranteed summer job. It is definitely not the life for everyone, but it may be for you. The price is right: the Department of Defense will pay your way through school and give you an allowance. After you graduate, you must work for the military for four years. It is a commitment; it is also a career job upon graduation. This arrangement is also available if you want to attend a regular, civilian university. The Department of Defence will pay your way through school; you work for them in the summer (and get paid) and also work for them upon graduation. If you think the idea of going to a military college is intriguing, but you don't want to commit yourself to service afterwards, the Reserve Entry Program allows you to pay your own way through RRMC or RMC. This is not as expensive as going to a regular university as it is more heavily subsidized. Before you reject these options, why not pop down to your local Armed Forces recruiting centre and talk to an officer about the details of the program and the selection procedure. It puts you under no obligation to apply and many have found that it becomes a serious option.

The United States also provides a wealth of post-secondary options for Canadians. Some, like the Ivy Leagues, are extremely costly, but others are very affordable. If you play a varsity sport, you could try for a sports scholarship to a U.S. school. Your coach or guidance counsellor might be able to give you some advice along these lines.

Another thing to remember is that many universities now have exchange programs with foreign schools. You can find out if these exist by asking at the language departments that might be involved, or by inquiring through your university admissions office. For example, Brock University offers a year at the University of Freiburg; Trent University also offers a year Freiburg, and also at Nantes (France), Grenada (Spain), and in Ecuador; York offers exchanges all over Europe; and McGill has semester exchanges with both Duke and Dartmouth in the U.S. as well as countless other programs in Europe and the north. In recent years, most Canadian universities have started exchange programs. If your university does not offer any foreign exchanges, enquire about getting on another school's program or start one yourself—it may be possible.

Organization: Laurentian University and Blyth & Co.
Program: Université Canadienne en France (year abroad program)

Université Canadienne en France
Laurentian University
Ramsey Lake Road
Sudbury, Ontario
P3E 2C6
(705) 673-6513
Toll free from Ontario: 1 (800) 461-4030

Coordinator: Denis Lauzon

Facts at a Glance:

Age:
- must have completed a minimum of 1 full year of studies at a Canadian university or two years at an American college

Regional eligibility: all provinces

Duration: 8 months, 4 months, or a 2 month spring session

Cost:
- $9,322 for 8 months; $4,757 for 4 months; $3,590 for 2 months
- students are still eligible for provincial student loans and bursaries

That covers:
- tuition fees
- return airfare Montréal/Toronto to Nice
- accommodation in university residences
- excursions in the region during the year

Getting in:
- application forms available from Laurentian University
- official transcript must accompany application
- fairly competitive (1,200 applicants for 250 positions)

Overview: The Université Canadienne en France program, established in 1987, is run by Laurentian University in cooperation with Blyth & Co. Blyth is in charge of the operation of the campus, as well as travel and extra-curricular activities. Laurentian is responsible for academic program development, staff hiring, admissions and all other academic concerns. Each year this program aims to provide 250 Canadian anglophone and francophone undergraduates from all provinces with the opportunity to earn Canadian university credits while living in the south of France. Students receive an international experience while living in a microcosm of Canada.

Inside View: The idea of studying abroad for a year appeals to many university students, but problems of language, credit transfer, and high costs often stand in their way. The Université Canadienne en France attempts to address these problems by allowing students to spend a year in Villefranche on the Côte D'Azur while still earning Canadian university credits. Students in the program are enrolled directly in Laurentian University and credits are earned through this institution. As part of the initial application process, students clear credit transfer with the registrar of their home university to prevent any complications upon their return.

The curriculum focuses on language, literature, and the humanities and highlights a special theme each year. Past themes have included "The Renaissance" and "The Mediterraneans". Half of the courses offered are taught in French and half in English. Exams can be written in the language of your choice. The school hopes that students will take a mix of courses in both languages to improve their bilingual skills. One English-speaking student we spoke with was strongly discouraged from taking all of her courses in French because they feared it would be too tough. She stuck with the idea, however, and left the school happy that she had made the most of the opportunity. She passed all courses and left with very good French. While there is no language requirement for admission, some previous instruction in your second language is recommended. Students also have the opportunity to obtain a Certificate of Bilingualism upon successful completion of a set of written and oral exams. Professors on sabbatical from universities across Canada and France make up the faculty.

Jennifer Ryan, a 22 year old recent Queen's University graduate spent the first semester of her fourth year on the program during the fall of 1992. She loved the school and was pleased with the academic offerings. The new dean of the school is set on making the program more academically rigorous. She said you have to work hard from Monday thru Thursday so that you can go on the many trips organized by the school. However, because there isn't much of a library at the school, and no computer facilities, you don't have to write many papers. Jennifer had no problem getting credit at Queen's for the courses she took in France.

Unlike the residences at French universities the dorms here are lovely villas overlooking tennis courts and a pool, and they house 12 with cooking facilities. When Jennifer went to the school there were approximately 75 students which means that you get to know everyone.

While the south of France is a beautiful vacation spot, it is not exactly the intellectual centre of France. The program is intended to be of high academic quality but don't expect the classroom to be your main focus. This program is intended to broaden your horizons and allow you to develop as a person as well as a scholar: courses are offered Monday through Thursday, providing long weekends for travel.

Most students at this university are in their second or third year, but some are graduates or postgraduates who have decided to develop fluency in their second language. Although the selection committee gives a lot of weight to student transcripts as well as letters of recommendation, achieving a representative geographic distribution is the greatest concern (although no fixed quotas exist). They aim to have representatives of each province and as many individual universities as possible.

STUDENT PROFILE

Name: Rachel Clark
Age: 25
Home: Berwick, Nova Scotia

Romantic Languages

After a first year of relatively uneventful and unfulfilling university life, Rachel Clark, now 25 decided her life needed some shaking up. Rachel had been brought up in Berwick, Nova Scotia, and was studying at Mount Allison University in New Brunswick. Maybe it was a case of too much small-town living or the fairly common first year blahs, but something pushed Rachel to move on. So, move on she did—half way around the globe, to Australia.

Rachel went over with SWAP. When she left she only planned to be away for the summer but found herself so caught up in the adventure that she stayed on a full year. During those exciting 12 months down under, she roamed from place to place doing an assortment of temporary jobs. When the odyssey was over she had crisscrossed the country and seen the Americans hold on to the America's Cup. She returned to Mount Allison that September refreshed and anxious to begin her second year of formal study in sleepy Sackville. She was majoring in modern languages and her favorite was German. Having acquired a taste for travel in Australia, it just made sense that her wanderlustful eyes next fixed on Europe. Because SWAP did not offer a German program and it was next to impossible to get a work permit on her own, Rachel began searching for a way to realize her plan. After a bit of inquiry, Rachel came across the answer in the form of the CAUTG program.

The Canadian Association of University Teachers of German has an agreement with the German government which each year allows Canadian university students to work and study in Germany. Rachel applied, was accepted and spent the summer studying at the Goethe Institute in Berlin. Rachel was a recipient of a scholarship which covered her travel, room, board, and tuition, and thus could devote all her time to honing her language skills. When the CAUTG scholarship ran out, Rachel returned to Berwick where she had just enough time to earn some money before heading straight back to Germany. You see, Mount Allison offers two international year-abroad exchanges—one with Strasbourg, the other with Tübingen. To her delight, she was chosen for the latter and spent a full year perfecting her language. The great thing about this year away from Sackville was that she earned a full year's academic credit. Another great and unexpected thing was that she met and fell in love with a German Ph.D.

candidate. Nevertheless, Rachel was true to her school and returned, somewhat reluctantly, to complete her final year of university.

After graduating with a B.A. in languages, Rachel spent six weeks studying French in Trois Rivières. This was yet another study opportunity coming to Rachel free of charge courtesy of the Summer Language Bursary Program. Upon completion of this formal study in literature and grammar (and the informal study of Quebec culture), Rachel returned to Germany—this time indefinitely. She's found herself a job teaching English in the public school system. What started as a shot-in-the-dark inquiry to the German Embassy in Ottawa, led to this firm contract offer. When that contract expired, she found work with a translation company.

At the time we went to press, Rachel was still working in Germany and will soon be married to her Ph.D. candidate husband.

When friends marvel at her travel-filled education and tell her how lucky she is, Rachel gets somewhat indignant. "Anyone can do this," she claims. "There's nothing special about me, if I can do it, anyone can." If you're willing to take a few risks along the way, Rachel is right.

Organization: Aga Khan Foundation of Canada
Program: Fellowship in International Development Management

10 Bay Street
Suite 610
Toronto, Ontario
M5J 2R8
(416) 364-2532
Fax: (416) 366-4204

Communications Assistant: Ms Sophie Lam

Facts at a Glance:

Age: university graduates under 30

Duration: 7 months

Regional eligibility: all provinces

Cost: $1,200 (a limited number of bursaries are available)

That covers:
- all travel costs in Canada and overseas
- accommodation while in Ottawa
- tuition fees

Salary: participants receive an honorarium while in Asia to cover room and board

Where can I go?: India, Pakistan, or Bangladesh

Getting in:
- applications available from above address
- deadline is March 15th
- very competitive (110 high calibre applicants for 11 positions)

Overview: This fellowship is an initiative of the Aga Khan Foundation of Canada. Support is also received from CIDA's Youth Program. The International Development Management Program (IDM) provides intensive development management training to outstanding young Canadians committed to pursuing a career in international development. Participants receive field experience in a developing country as well as practical training in field-related issues. It is hoped that these people will become Canada's leading development managers in the next century.

Inside View: This program combines an intensive three-week classroom session at the University of Ottawa with a six month field placement where students work with a local non-governmental organization (NGO) in the area of health, education, environment or rural development. While at U of O, the 11 students examine many practical aspects of grassroots development (including needs assessment, program design, community development principles, and financial management) through a case study approach. They also attend seminars conducted by experienced Canadian development practitioners. While in Asia, you are placed with an NGO which conducts work that fits with your interests and expertise. This field work allows application of the knowledge gathered during the Ottawa course and gives you a first-hand understanding of the day-to-day work of a development agency.

Shams Alibhai, now working towards her master's in Religious Studies at McGill University, completed the program in May of 1990. While in Aujarat, India, she worked with kids at several day care centres. She found that the program provided excellent practical field experience and that the Ottawa portion complemented the India portion very well. The 10 people on her program had backgrounds in nutrition, political science, economics, and education. She feels that a lot of the learning actually came from the other fellowship recipients.

Both Shams and the people at Aga Khan Foundation said that the program looks for people who are committed to a long-term career in international development. Having a master's degree is an asset but not a necessity for being chosen. If you can satisfy the requirements this could be the experience of a lifetime and may provide you with the credentials to break into the international development job market.

Organization: Centre de formation a la cooperation interculturelle du Québec

80 rue Frontenac
Rivière-du- Loup
Québec City, Québec
G5R 1R1
(418) 862-3434

Facts at a Glance:

Age: 22 to 32

Duration:
- 15 weeks in Rivière du Loup
- 15 weeks in West Africa

Regional eligibility: all provinces

Cost: $600 plus approximately $500 per month for room and board

That covers:
- return airfare from Montréal to West Africa
- course fees

Language: must speak fluent French

Getting in:
- apply directly to above address
- must have either a diploma or practical experience in forestry, health, agriculture, fisheries, or technology
- must be in excellent health

Overview: The Training Centre for International Cooperation offers a two-part program whereby students, while in Canada, learn about developing countries and then put their knowledge to use in a field project in West Africa. The course has been offered for the past seven years and begins in either September or April. Each session is limited to 20 students. Successful completion of the course (which is offered exclusively in French) earns students the Attestation d'Etudes Collegiales en Cooperation or AEC diploma.

In order to be accepted, applicants must have background in one of the following fields: agriculture, forestry, administration, health or technology. Applicants must also be creative and motivated, possess good communication skills, and be in excellent physical condition.

Inside View: Volunteering to work on a community project in a developing country might sound intriguing. However, organizations like CUSO, CARE and, to a lesser extent, WUSC, place only university graduates who have specialized training and experience in the work force. The Training Centre for International Cooperation also prefers participants with a diploma or practical experience, but they are less demanding than the larger organizations. This course is designed for people who are interested in and enthusiastic about community work in Africa, but lack such experience. The coursework done in Rivière du Loup prepares you for your stint in Africa, where you'll join a project suited to your skills.

Here is how the program works: you apply directly to the above address—the application process is not as lengthy that of the larger organizations. If accepted, you spend 15 weeks in Rivière du Loup taking courses on cross-cultural communication, the role of education in development, African history, geography, and politics, as well on as adapting to life in Africa. In Rivière du Loup you live with 19 other students in a house selected by the school. The cost of rent and food is split equally and usually comes to about $200 each per month. Living with the group and sharing responsibilities will be your first lesson in adaptability. If you can't handle sharing a house with 19 other students, you probably won't be able to handle the rest of the program. Anyway, after the 15 weeks in Rivière du Loup, it's off to West Africa for 15 weeks of work on a community project. The price of your return airfare is included in the $500 tuition fee. Once in Africa, you'll again be responsible for your room and board but these should not be more than $500 per month. When your time in Africa is up you'll return home and receive an AEC diploma. The level of the program would make it ideal for someone between high school or CEJEP and university.

Organization: The Banff Centre for the Arts

Office of the Registrar
Box 1020 Station 28
Banff, Alberta
T0L 0C0
(403) 762-6180

President: Dr Graeme McDonald

Facts at a Glance:

Age:
- no age limits
- most participants already have expertise in their particular field

Duration: 1 week - 6 months

Regional eligibility: all provinces

Cost:
- programs cost $259 per week
- room and board in shared accommodations is $278 per week

That covers: tuition

Getting in:
- application forms available from above address
- individual programs may require submission of portfolios, tapes, sample writing, etc.
- highly competitive

Overview: The Banff Centre for the Arts serves the needs of artists from a wide range of fields including dance, photography, music, media arts, theatre, ceramics, and writing. Artists at various stages of career development come to the Centre for first-rate professional training and to learn from their peers. As one participant put it, "Here, quite simply, we are artists among artists." Set apart from the rest of the world, in the spectacularly beautiful town of Banff, the Centre becomes temporary home to thousands of artists every year, all year round. If you are particularly talented in some branch of the arts and are interested in the Banff Centre for the Arts, write to them for information specific to your field. The Centre offers a wide assortment of courses, meal plans, accommodation choices, and schedules. Once you receive your information spend a few hours going over your options. There is no guarantee you'll be accepted in the program of your choice—far from it. The Banff Centre's selection process is quite rigorous. For courses in the performing arts, the Centre sends a travelling selection committee around the country to judge auditions.

If you're accepted to the Centre, get ready to use some of the best, most modern facilities around and appreciate some of the most breathtaking scenery in the world.

Courses at the Banff Centre for the Arts are somewhat pricey, but keep in mind that it is a world-renowned institution. Many scholarships and bursaries are available and are based mainly on artistic merit.

Scholarships

If you're at the point of deciding whether or not to continue your education, knowing about available scholarships may significantly affect your choice. For instance, graduate studies may not seem an option. However, if you knew of a scholarship which would allow you to earn an M.A. in a foreign country, at absolutely no cost, you might think twice about it! There are thousands of scholarships available to Canadian students at both the undergraduate and graduate level—enough to fill several books (We recommend a few in the Book Review section of this chapter). Eligibility requirements for many of the awards are quite specific (for example, "must be in third year chemical engineering") others demand proficiency in a foreign language and competition for all of them is stiff. A little research might, however, reveal a scholarship perfectly suited to your background and interests. The following few pages are meant only to give a general overview of some of the types of scholarships that exist. To find a scholarship suited to you, write away for more information and do some research.

The Canadian Bureau for International Education (CBIE)

The CBIE administers a large number of scholarships and fellowships available to Canadian students at the undergraduate and graduate level.

85 Albert Street
Suite 1400
Ottawa, Ontario
K1P 6A4
(613) 237- 4820

The Commonwealth Scholarship

All Commonwealth countries used to participate in this vast scholarship program; every year a number of them offer scholarships to Canadian students. For the 1994 academic year, Canadians are eligible for scholarships in Ghana, India, the United Kingdom, Australia, Nigeria and New Zealand. In 1993, Commonwealth scholarships were offered by all of the above as well as Trinidad and Tobago and Jamaica. As is typical of many scholarships, the Commonwealth has a very early application deadline—you have to plan at least one full year in advance for most of them. The deadline for the 1994-95 awards is October 31, 1993. Write to the CIBE to find out which countries are offering awards for 1994. Most Commonwealth scholarships are tenable for two-year periods at the graduate level and they are often restricted to certain fields of study. These scholarships are very competitive, and the application demands three reference letters, complete transcripts, and a number of essays. A Commonwealth scholarship covers your air fare to and from the host country, tuition, living and book allowances, plus money for travel within the host country.

Foreign Government Scholarships and Awards

These awards are administered by the International Council for Canadian Studies

2 Daly Street
Ottawa, Ontario
KIN 6E2
(613) 232-0417

Dozens of countries around the world offer scholarships enabling Canadian students to earn graduate degrees at their universities. Eligibility criteria, duration and value of these awards vary greatly from country to country. Generally, they are for graduate studies, are tenable for at least one year, and cover tuition and living expenses. Travel expenses may or may not be covered. Many Foreign Government awards require you to speak the language of the country and restrict the area of study. Your university guidance centre should have complete information on these awards; if not, write to AUCC and they'll send you all you need to know, free of charge.

The Association of Universities and Colleges of Canada (AUCC)

151 Slater Street
Ottawa, Ontario
KIP 5NI
(613) 563-1236

The AUCC administered awards include the Frank Knox Memorial Fellowship which pays tuition to Harvard; the Robert and Mary Stanfield Foundation Scholarships, which supplies $6,000 to study your second language at any Canadian university; and many others. The AUCC also has a list of over 100 companies which offer scholarships to the sons and daughters of their employees. Write for complete scholarship information. AUCC will send you a huge package of information—it's worth reading through.

Other Scholarships

ROTARY SCHOLARSHIPS: In addition to their high school scholarships, Rotary also provides scholarships for students at both the undergraduate and graduate level. While relatives of Rotary members seem to be favoured at the high school level, university students with a Rotary relative are ineligible. Application forms for these scholarships (tenable at any university) are available from your local Rotary Club. Beware: this scholarship has an incredibly early application deadline—apply at least a year and a half before you plan to use the scholarship.

NATURAL SCIENCES AND ENGINEERING RESEARCH COUNCIL SCHOLARSHIPS: A wide range of scholarships are available to students at the undergraduate and graduate level in most fields of science and engineering. Complete details about these awards can be obtained from the NSERC publication, "Scholarship and Fellowship Guide", available from them free of charge. (See Book Review section for address.)

SIR JOHN A. MACDONALD GRADUATE FELLOWSHIP IN CANADIAN HISTORY: Students with an honours BA who'd like to earn a master's or PhD in Canadian history, should waste no time applying for this fellowship. The award is worth $8500 for one year and is renewable for up to three years, making its total value over $25,000. The scholarship is tenable only at Ontario universities and candidates must reside in Ontario. Deadline is February 15 and applications can be obtained from the following address:

The Secretary, Committee of Selection
Sir John A. Macdonald Graduate Fellowship in Canadian History
Ministry of Colleges and Universities
Queen's Park
Mowat Block, 8th floor
Toronto, Ontario
M7A 2B4

RHODES SCHOLARSHIP: The prestigious Rhodes scholarship entitles you to study at Oxford University. It is worth approximately $20,000 per year. The scholarship program was established in the will of diamond magnate Cecil Rhodes and his bequest continues to fund the winners' study. Each year 11 awards are made across Canada. To be eligible, students must have completed three years of university study and be under the age of 25. The selection procedure occurs region by region and begins with the submission of an application package (six letters of reference, a 900-word essay, a factual list of activities and awards, and official academic transcripts). After this is reviewed, a select number of applicants are chosen for interviews. Finally, recipients are announced. The selection committee looks for excellence in leadership, academic ability, athletic prowess and concern for humanity. This is an extremely competitive award and very few even make it to the interview stage. Application forms are available from the awards office at your university or directly from the Canadian Rhodes Trust at the following address:

The Rhodes Scholarship Trust
P.O. Box 48
Toronto-Dominion Centre
Toronto, Ontario
M5K 1E6

TERRY FOX HUMANITARIAN AWARD PROGRAM: T h e Terry Fox Scholarship will be of particular interest to graduating secondary-level students and those currently studying towards a first degree or diploma in a Canadian university or college. Scholarship candidates must be Canadian citizens or have landed immigrant status. They must also be under 25 years old. The scholarship is a renewable award, subject to satisfactory progress. The value of each award is $4,000 annually, for a maximum of four years or until a first degree is obtained. For candidates attending an educational institute where no tuition fee is applicable, the award value is $2,500. Selection criteria are perseverance in overcoming obstacles, pursuit of excellence in both health and academics, ideals in citizenship, and humanitarian service. The annual deadline for application is February 1st.

For applications or information the address and phone number are:
Terry Fox Humanitarian Award Program
711 - 151 Sparks Street
Ottawa, Ontario
K1P 5E3
(613) 235-1803

BOOK REVIEWS

Study Abroad (Paris, France: Unesco, 1992-93)

Study Abroad is a comprehensive guide to international study programs, scholarships and other forms of financial aid. The vast majority of listed opportunities are offered at the graduate level. There are over 2,500 entries in the book, each one supplying all the essential information about the program—language requirements, value, address, deadlines, and so forth. If you're thinking about studying abroad, it's definitely worth your while to thumb through this densely packed guide—you might discover a way to study for free. You should be able to find Study Abroad, which is updated annually, in your local library.

Linda Frum's Guide to Canadian Universities; by Linda Frum (Key Porter Books)

This book is full of the author's first-hand observations of various aspects of student life (from drinking and drugs to sex and fashion) at every English-speaking Canadian university. It contains the type of information they don't print in official information brochures, the type of information your guidance counsellor doesn't know—in short, the information you really need to make such an important decision. Keep in mind that this book offers a very subjective view of the universities; you'll read one person's opinions. But if you can't visit each campus yourself, reading this book may prove helpful.

Commonwealth Universities Handbook (Association of Commonwealth Universities, published annually)

If you've been considering studying abroad, whether for your first, second or third degree, this four-volume set of books is a must-read. The *Handbook* lists, by country, every university in the Commonwealth and includes information on course offerings, admissions requirements, available scholarships, and even descriptions of the campus and a history of the school. If you decide to apply for a Commonwealth scholarship, these books will be an indispensible research tool. They're well organized, very complete and easy to use.

Guide to Summer Camps and Summer Schools; by J. Kathryn Sargent (Boston: Porter Sargent Publishers, Inc., 1985)

One of a series of very useful, carefully researched guides put out by Porter Sargent Publishers, this guide will be of interest to high school students. Most of the camps and schools featured in the 475-page guide are American, but there is a special section on Canadian programs. Each entry in the book offers an objective overview of the camp or school's offerings, plus age limits, costs, and an address and phone number. There are a lot of unusual opportunities listed. Computer camps, riding schools, and a three-week "Summer Whale Sail" off Cape Cod are just a few examples.

Educational Travel '93: The Canadian Guide to Learning Vacations Around the World by Vicky Busch (Athabasca University: 1993)

Athabasca puts together a helpful and thorough book on all kinds of language immersion programs, language schools, volunteer projects, study tours, eco tours, archeological digs - to name just a few.

It is now in its sixth edition and is designed for travellers who have limited time to vacation, but who want to participate in unusual programs or see a country from an unconventional angle.

It's a good resource for those looking for an educational trip.

Canadian Directory of Awards for Graduate Studies; (Published annually.)

Scholarships and bursaries offered by every university in Canada are clearly presented in this handy guide. Anyone completing their undergraduate degree who has ever given thought to continuing their education should read through this directory. The prospect of doing a second degree on a full scholarship might be quite enticing.

The New Guide to Study Abroad; by Garraty, von Klemperer, and Taylor (Harper and Row, 1980)

The authors of this 450-page guide really did their research— they traveled all over Europe conducting interviews with North Americans studying abroad. The authors' vast knowledge of their subject comes through, especially in the first part of the book where they offer lots of advice about planning your study abroad, choosing a school, settling in, travelling, and so on. Much of the rest of the book is devoted to giving very brief descriptions of dozens of foreign universities which at this point may be more or less accurate. Because these discussions are brief it's hard to get an accurate idea of the character of the schools, but this guide is definitely a good place to start your research.

Work, Study and Travel Abroad: The Whole World Handbook;
by Marjorie Cohen (New York: Council on International
Educational Exchange, 1992-93)

This guide gives details on short-term work and volunteer positions
and offers lots of useful hints for planning your time abroad. It is
organized by country and provides information about work, study
and travel on every continent. It is useful to both teenagers and young
adults.

*Exchange Opportunities: A Quick Reference Handbook of Basic
Information on Exchange Programs* (Educational Exchange; Alberta Education; 4th floor, East Tower; Devonian Building;
11160 Jasper Ave.; Edmonton, Alberta; T5K 0L3)

Although this 250-page guide was put together by the Alberta Ministry of Education, it includes information about exchanges available
to students in every province. The guide is full of addresses for many
work, cultural and study exchanges available all over the world. The
programs are organized country by country and include offerings in
Europe, Africa, Asia, and Australia. No detailed descriptions of programs are provided, but this guide, available from the above address,
is a useful reference guide to have around.

Scholarships and Fellowships Guide (Natural Sciences and Engineering Research Council of Canada; 200 Kent Street;
Ottawa, Ontario; K1A 1H5; Published annually)

This 40-page booklet, available free of charge from the above address,
describes the various NSERC scholarships offered to undergraduate
and graduate students. There are lots of good awards listed for those
in the fields of agriculture, biology, chemistry, forestry, physics, and
so on. The guide is well organized and easy to use.

Useful Addresses

Travel Cuts Local Offices

Travel Cuts Halifax
Student Union Building
Dalhousie University
Halifax, N.S B3H 4J2
902-424-2054

Voyages Cuts Montréal
Université Concordia
Édifice Hall, Suite 643
S.G.W. Campus
1455 Blvd. de Maisonneuve
Ouest
Montréal, Qué. H3G 1M8
514-288-1130

Voyages Cuts Montréal
Université McGill
3480 rue McTavish
Montréal, Qué. H3A 1X9
514-849-9201

Travel Cuts Ottawa
4th Level Unicentre
Carleton University
Ottawa, Ont. K1S 5B6
613-238-5493

Travel Cuts Ottawa
60 Laurier Ave. E.
Ottawa, Ont. K1N 6N4
613-238-8222

Travel Cuts Toronto
96 Gerrard St. East.
Toronto, Ont. M5B 1G7
416-977-0441

Travel Cuts Toronto
187 College St.
Toronto, Ont. M5T 1P7
416-979-2406

Travel Cuts Sudbury
Student Street (Room G27)
Laurentian University
Sudbury, Ont. P3E 2C6
705-673-1401

Travel Cuts Waterloo
University Shops Plaza
170 University Avenue West
Waterloo, Ont. N2L 3E9
519-886-0400

Travel Cuts Winnipeg
University Centre
University of Manitoba
Winnipeg, Man. R3T 2N2
204-269-9530

Travel Cuts Saskatoon
Place Riel Campus Centre
University of Saskatchewan
Saskatoon, Sask. S7N 0W0
306-343-1601

Travel Cuts Edmonton
Student Union Building
University of Alberta
Edmonton, Alta. T6G 2J7
403-432-2592

Travel Cuts Edmonton
10424A-118 Avenue
Edmonton, Alta. T5G 0P7
403-471-8054

Travel Cuts Calgary
1708-12th Street NW
Calgary, Alta. T2M 3M7
403-282-7687

Travel Cuts Vancouver
Student Union Building
University of British Colombia
Vancouver, B.C.   V6T IW5
604-224-2344

Travel Cuts Vancouver
Granville Island
1516 Duranleau Street
Vancouver, B.C.   V6H 3S4
604-687-6033

Travel Cuts Burnaby
Room 326, T.C.
Student Rotunda
Simon Fraser University
Burnaby, B.C.   V5A IS6
604-291-1204

Travel Cuts Victoria
Student Union Building
University of Victoria
Victoria, B.C.   V8W 2Y2
604-721-8352

Toll free numbers:
in British Columbia call:
1-800-972-4004
in Alberta call: 1-800-272-5615
in Saskatchewan call:
1-800-667-1141
in Southern Ontario call:
1-800-268-9044

Canada World Youth Regional Offices

In British Columbia
Suite 201
1894 West Broadway
Vancouver, B.C.
V6J IY9
Phone: (604) 732-5113

In the Prairies:
10765, 98th St.
Edmonton, Alberta
T5H 2P2
Phone: (403) 424-6411

In Ontario:
627 Davenport Road
Toronto, Ont.
M5R IL2
Phone: (416) 922-0776

In the Atlantic provinces:
Suite 125
1657 Barrington St.
Halifax, N.S.
B3J 2AI
Phone: (902) 422-1782

Youth Hostelling Association, Regional Offices

Newfoundland Hostelling
Association
P.O.Box 1815
St. John's, NFLD
AIC 5P9
Phone: (709) 753-8603

Prince Edward Island
Hostelling Associaton
P.O.Box 1718
Charlottetown, P.E.I.
CIA 7N4
Phone (902) 894-9696

Nova Scotia Hostelling
Association
Sport Nova Scotia Centre
5516 Spring Garden Road
P.O.Box 3010 South
Halifax, N.S.
B3J 3G6
Phone: (902) 425-5450

Quebec Hostelling Assoc.
803 Mont Royal Ave., E.
Montréal, Qué.
H2J 1W9
Phone: (514) 521-5230

National Capital Hostelling
Assoc.
18 The Byward Market
Ottawa, Ont.
K1N 7A1
Phone: (613) 230-1200

Great Lakes Hostelling
Association
223 Church St.
Toronto, Ont.
M5B 1Z1
Phone: (416) 368-1848

Manitoba Hostelling Association
1700 Ellice Ave.
Winnipeg, Man.
R3H 0B1
Phone: (204) 786-5641

Saskatchewan Hostelling Assoc.
Saskatchewan Sport and
Recreation Centre
2205 Victoria Ave.
Regina, Sask.
S4P 0S4
Phone: (306) 522-3651

CHA—Northern Alberta District
10926 —88th Ave.
Edmonton, Alta.
T6G 0Z1
Phone: (403) 432-7798

Southern Alberta Hostelling
Association
1414 Kensington Road N.W.
Calgary, Alta.
T2N 3P9
Phone: (403) 283-5551

British Columbia Hostelling
Association
3425 West Broadway
Vancouver, B.C.
V6R 2B4
Phone: (604) 736-2674

Yukon Hostelling Association
P.O.Box 4762
Whitehorse, Yukon
Y1A 4N6
Phone (403) 667-4471
(403) 667-2402

Canadian Crossroads International Regional Offices

Western Regional Office
10765 —98th St.
Suite 431 B
Edmonton, Alta.
T5H 2P2
Phone: (403) 429-2319

Atlantic Regional Office
1541 Barrington St.
Suite 315
Halifax, N.S.
B3L 1Z5
Phone: (902) 422-2933

Operation Beaver Regional Offices

B.C. & Yukon Office
Don Irving —Co-ordinator
9781 - 127 St.,
Surrey, B.C.
V3V 5J1
Phone: (604) 585-6646

Eastern Office
Marco Guzman —Co-ordinator
2622 Danforth Ave.
Toronto, Ont.
M4C 1L7
Phone: (416) 690-3930

Western Office
Ray Yellowknee —Co-ordinator
Box 1895
Slave Lake, Alta.
T0G 2A0
Phone: (403) 849-5497

Carribbean Office
Mme Lisette Casimir
Haitian Representitive
8 ruelle Alexis
Delmas 17
Port-au-Prince, Haiti, W.I.

Provincial Coordinators of the Summer Language Bursary Program

Québec:
Robert A. Savard
Direction général de l'aide
financière auxétudiants

Ministère de l'Enseignement
supérieur et de la science
1033 rue de la Chevrotière
Québec, Qué.
G1R 5K9
Phone: (418) 643-4633

New Brunswick:
French as a Second Language
David Macfarlane —Program
Consultant
Department of Education
P.O.Box 6000
Kings Place
Fredericton, N.B.
E3B 5H1
Phone: (506) 453-2771

Nova Scotia:
Gérald Aucoin
Consultant
Curriculum Development
Department of Education
Box 578 - Trade Mart Building
Halifax, Nova Scotia
B3J 2S9
Phone: (902) 424-4183

Prince Edward Island:
Mr.Ronald Rice
Director of Administration
Department of Education
P.O. Box 2000
Charlottetown, Prince Edward
Island
C1A 7N8
Phone: (902) 892-3504

Newfoundland:
Mr. Glenn Loveless
Provincial Co-ordinator
Bilingual Programs
Department of Education
P.O. Box 4750
St. John's, Newfoundland
AIC 5T7
Phone: (709) 576-2741

Candidates from the Northwest Territories and the Yukon should contact the following for information and application forms:

Mr Allain St. Cyr
Education Officer
Department of Education
Government of the Northwest Territories
Yellowknife, N.W.T.
XIA 2L9
Phone: (403) 920-8729

Foreign Emabassies and High Commissions in Canada

Embassy of Argentina
Royal Bank Centre
90 Sparks St., Suite 160
Ottawa, Ont.
KIP 5B4
Phone: (613) 236-2351

Australian High Commission
130 Slater St., 13th Floor
Ottawa, Ont.
KIP 5H6
Phone: (613) 236-0841

Embassy of Austria
445 Wilbrod St.
Ottawa, Ont.
KIN 6M7
Phone: (613) 653-1444

Bahamas High Commission
150 Kent St., Ste 301
Ottawa, Ont.
KIP 5P4
Phone: (613) 232-1724

Bangladesh High Commission
85 Range Road
Ottawa, Ont.
KIN 8J6
Phone: (613) 236-0138

Embassy of Bolivia
77 Metcalfe St.
Ottawa, Ont.
KIP 5L6
Phone: (613) 236-8237

Embassy of Brazil
255 Albert St
Ottawa, Ont.
KIP 6A9
Phone: (613) 237-1090

British High Commission
80 Elgin St.
Ottawa, Ont.
KIP 5K7
Phone: (613) 237-1530

Embassy of Bulgaria
325 Stewart St
Ottawa, Ont.
KIN 6K5
Phone: (613) 232-3215

Embassy of Burkina Faso
48 Range Road,
Ottawa, Ont.
KIN 8J4
Phone: (613) 238-4796

Embassy of Burma
The Sandringham Apartments
85 Range Road
Ottawa, Ont.
KIN 8J6
Phone: (613) 232-6434

Embassy of Burundi
151 Slater St
Ottawa, Ont.
KIP 5H3
Phone: (613) 236-8483

Embassy of Chile
56 Sparks St
Ottawa, Ont.
KIP 5A9
Phone: (613) 235-4402

Embassy of the People's
Republic of China
511 - 515 St Patrick St.
Ottawa, Ont.
KIN 5H3
Phone: (613) 234-2706

Embassy of Colombia
150 Kent St.
Ottawa, Ont.
KIP 5P4
Phone: (613) 230-3760

Commission of the European
Communties
350 Sparks St.
Ottawa, Ont.
KIR 7S8
Phone: (613) 238-6464

Embassy of Costa Rica
150 Argyle St
Ottawa, Ont.
K2P 1B7
Phone: (613) 234-5762

Embassy of Cuba
388 Main St.
Ottawa, Ont.
KIS 1E3
Phone: (613) 563-0141

Embassy of Czechoslovakia
50 Rideau Terrace
Ottawa, Ont.
KIM 2A1
Phone: (613) 749-4442

Embassy of Denmark
85 Range Road
Ottawa, Ont.
KIN 8J6
Phone: (613) 234 0704

Embassy of the Dominican
Republic
260 Metcalfe St.
Ottawa, Ont.
K2P 1R6
Phone: (613) 234-0363

Embassy of Ecuador
150 Kent St
Ottawa, Ont.
KIP 5P4
Phone: (613) 238-5032

Embassy of the Arab Republic
of Egypt
454 Laurier Ave. E.
Ottawa, Ont.
KIN 6R3
Phone: (613) 234-4931

Embassy of El Salvador
294 Albert St.
Ottawa, Ont.
K1P 6E6
Phone: (613) 238-2939

Embassy of Finland
222 Sommerset St. W.
Ottawa, Ont.
K2P 2G3
Phone: (613) 236-2389

Embassy of the West Germany
I Waverley St.
Ottawa, Ont.
K2P 0T8
Phone: (613) 232-1101

Ambassade de France
42, prom. Sussex
Ottawa, Ont.
K1M 2C9
Phone: (613) 232-1795
Ghana High Commission
85 Range Road
Ottawa, Ont.
K1N 8J6
Phone: (613) 236-0871

Embassy of Greece
76-80 Maclaren St.
Ottawa, Ont.
K2P 0K6
Phone: (613) 238-6271

Embassy of Guatemala
294 Albert St.
Ottawa, Ont.
K1P 6E6
Phone: (613) 237-3941

Embassy of the Republic of
Guinea
112 Kent St.
Place de Ville, Tower B
Ottawa, Ont.
K1P 5P2
Phone: (613) 232-1133

Guyana High Commission
Burnside Building
151 Slater St.
Ottawa, Ont.
K1P 5H3
Phone: (613) 235-7240

Holy See (Apostolic Nunciature)
724 Manor Ave.
Rockliffe Park, Ont.
K1M 0E3
Phone: (613) 746-4914

Embassy of Honduras
151 Slater St.
Ottawa, Ont.
K1P 5H3
Phone: (613) 233-8900
Embassy of Hungary
7 Delaware Ave.
Ottawa, Ont.
K2P 0Z2
Phone: (613) 232-1711

Indian High Commission
10 Springfield Rd.
Ottawa, Ont.
K1M 1C9
Phone: (613) 744-3751

Embassy of Indonesia
287 MacLaren St.
Ottawa, Ont.
K2P 0L9
Phone: (613) 236-7403

Embassy of Iran
411 Roosevelt Ave.
Ottawa, Ont.
K2A 3X9
Phone: (613) 729-0902

Embassy of Iraq
215 McLeod St.
Ottawa, Ont.
K2P 0Z8
Phone: (613) 236-9177

Embassy of Ireland
170 Metcalfe St.
Ottawa, Ont.
K2P 1P3
Phone: (613) 233-6281

Embassy of Israel
410 Laurier Ave. W.
Ottawa, Ont.
K1R 7T3
Phone: (613) 237-6450

Embassy of Italy
275 Slater St.
Ottawa, Ont.
K1P 5H9
Phone: (613) 232-2401

Jamaica High Commission
275 Slater St.
Ottawa, Ont.
K1P 5H9
Phone: (613) 233-9311

Embassy of Japan
255 Sussex Dr.
Ottawa, Ont.
K1N 9E6
Phone: (613) 236-8541

Embassy of Jordan
100 Bronson Ave.
Ottawa, Ont.
K1R 6G8
Phone: (613) 238-8090

Kenya High Commission
415 Laurier Ave. E.
Ottawa, Ont.
K1N 6R4
Phone: (613) 563-1773

Embassy of Korea
85 Albert St.
Ottawa, Ont.
K1P 6A4
Phone: (613) 232-1715

Embassy of Lebanon
640 Lyon St.
Ottawa, Ont.
K1S 3Z5
Phone: (613) 236-5825

Lesotho High Commission
350 Sparks St.
Ottawa, Ont.
K1R 7S8
Phone: (613) 236-9449

Embassy of Mexico
130 Albert St.
Ottawa, Ont.
K1P 5G4
Phone: (613) 233-9272

Embassy of Morocco
38 Range Road
Ottawa, Ont.
K1N 8J4
Phone: (613) 236-7391

Embassy of the Netherlands
275 Slater St.
Ottawa, Ont.
KIP 5H9
Phone: (613) 237-5030

New Zealand High Commission
99 Bank St.
Ottawa, Ont.
KIP 6G3
Phone: (613) 238-5991

Embassy of Nicaragua
170 Laurier St.
Ottawa, Ont.
KIP 5V5
Phone: (613) 234-9361

Nigeria High Commission
295 Metcalfe St.
Ottawa, Ont.
K2P IR9
Phone: (613) 236-0521

Embassy of Norway
90 Sparks St.
Ottawa, Ont.
KIP 5B4
Phone: (613) 238-6571

Embassy of Pakistan
151 Slater St.
Ottawa, Ont.
KIP 5H3
Phone: (613) 238-7881

Embassy of the Philippines
130 Albert St.
Ottawa, Ont.
KIP 5G4
Phone: (613) 233-1121

Embassy of Poland
443 Daly Ave.
Ottawa, Ont.
KIN 6H3
Phone: (613) 236-0468

Embassy of Portugal
645 Island Park Dr.
Ottawa, Ont.
KIY 0B3
Phone: (613) 729-0883

Embassy of Saudia Arabia
99 Banks St.
Ottawa, Ont.
KIP 6B9
Phone: (613) 237-4100

Embassy of Spain
350 Sparks St.
Ottawa, Ont.
KIR 7S2
Phone: (613) 237-2193

Sri Lanka High Commission
85 Range Road
Ottawa, Ont.
KIN 8J6
Phone: (613) 233-8449

Embassy of the Sudan
457 Laurier Ave. E.
Ottawa, Ont.
KIN 6R4
Phone: (613) 235-4000

Embassy of Sweden
441 MacLaren St.
Ottawa, Ont.
K2P 2H3
Phone: (613) 236-8553

Ambassade de Suisse
5, av. Marlborough
Ottawa, Ont.
KIN 8E6
Phone: (613) 235-1837

Tanzania High Commission 50
Range Road
Ottawa, Ont.
KIN 8J4
Phone: (613) 232-1509

Embassy of Turkey
197 Wurtemburg St.
Ottawa, Ont.
KIN 8L9
Phone: (613) 232-1577

Uganda High Commission
170 Laurier Ave. W., Suite 601
Ottawa, Ontario
KIP 5V5
Phone: (613) 233-7797

Embassy of the U.S.S.R.
285 Charlotte St.
Ottawa, Ontario
KIN 8L5
Phone: (613) 235-4341

Embassy of the U.S.A.
100 Wellington St.
Ottawa, Ontario
KIP 5TI
Phone: (613) 238-5335

Embassy of Uruguay
130 Albert St., Suite 1905
Ottawa, Ontario
KIP 5G4
Phone: (613) 235-5151

Embassy of Venezuala
294 Albert St., Suite 602
Ottawa, Ontario
KIP 6E6
Phone: (613) 235-5151

Embassy of Yugoslavia
17 Blackburn Ave.
Ottawa, Ontario
KIN 8A2
Phone: (613) 233-6289

Zambia High Commission
130 Albert St., Suite 1610
Ottawa, Ontario
KIP 5G4
Phone: (613) 563-0712

Zimbabwe High Commission
112 Kent St., Suite 1315
Place de Ville, Tower B
Ottawa, Ontario
KIP 5P7
Phone: (613) 237-4388

French-speaking Countries

Ambassade de l'Algerie
435, avenue Daly
Ottawa, Ontario
KIN 6H3
Phone: (613) 232-9453

Ambassade de Belgique
Suites 601-604
85, ch. Range
Ottawa, Ontario
KIN 8J6
Phone: (613) 236-7267

Ambassade de Benin
58, avenue Glebe
Ottawa, Ontario
KIS 2C3
Phone: (613) 233-4429

Ambassade du Cameroun
170, avenue Clemow
Ottawa, Ontario
KIS 2B4
Phone: (613) 236-1522

Ambassade de la Cote d'Ivoire
9, avenue Marlborough
Ottawa, Ontario
KIN 8C6
Phone: (613) 236-9919

Ambassade de France
42, prom. Sussex
Ottawa, Ontario
KIM 2C9
Phone: (613) 232-1795

Ambassade de Gabon
4, chemin Range
Ottawa, Ontario
KIN 8J5
Phone: (613) 232-5301

Ambassade d'Haiti
112, rue Kent, bureau 1308
Place de Ville, Tour B
Ottawa, Ontario
KIP 5P2
Phone: (613) 238-1628

Ambassade du Niger
38, avenue Blackburn
Ottawa, Ontario
KIN 8A2
Phone: (613) 232-4291

Ambassade du Senegal
57, avenue Marlborough
Ottawa, Ontario
KIN 8E8
Phone: (613) 238-6392

Ambassade de Suisse
5, av. Marlborough
Ottawa, Ontario
KIN 8E6
Phone: (613) 235-1837

Ambassade de Tunisie
515, rue O'Connor
Ottawa, Ontario
KIS 3P8
Phone: (613) 237-0330

Ambassade du Zaire
18, chemin Range
Ottawa, Ontario
KIN 8J3
Phone: (613) 236-7103

Youth Parliaments in Canada

Mr. Wayne Montgomery
National Youth Parliament
Association
36 Westwood Drive
Nepean, Ontario
K2G 2X1
Phone: (613) 226-7144

British Columbia Youth
Parliament
P.O. Box 15335, Main Post
Office
Vancouver, British Columbia
V6B 5B1

Mr. David Marriott
Chief Returning Officer
Tuxis Parliament of Alberta
506 Summit Square
Leduc, Alberta
T9E 1Z6
Phone: (403) 986-0056

Mr. Ken Millard
Youth Parliament of
Sakatchewan
P.O. Box 126
Birch Hills, Saskatchewan
S0J 0G0
Phone: (306) 749-2267

Mr. Glen Hickerson
Deputy Premier
Manitoba Youth Parliament
122 Cameo Crescent
Winnipeg, Manitoba
R2K 2W4
Phone: (204) 668-1519

Ms. Leslie Quinton
Premier
Ontario Youth Parliament
932 Auden Park Drive
Kingston, Ontario
K7M 5S1
Phone: (613) 389-1073

Parlement Jeunesse de Quebec
P.O. Box 634, Station K
Montreal, Que.
H1N 3K2

Nova Scotia Youth Parliament
P.O. Box 42
Halifax, Nova Scotia
B3J 2L4

Mr. John Barron
President
Newfoundland & Labrador
Youth Parliament
P.O. Box 2571, Station C
St. John's, Nfld.
A1C 6K1
Phone: (709) 364-6585

Ms. Karen Nielson
Yukon Territory Youth
Parliament
94 Alsek Road
Whitehorse, Y.T.
Y1A 3K4
Phone: (403) 667-4825

Provincial Ministries of Education & Other Contacts

Lorne Smith
Education Officer
N.W.T. Education
Government of N.W.T.
Yellowknife, N.W.T.
XIA 2L9

Marilyn Neily
Gordon Robertson Education
Centre
Frobisher Bay, N.W.T.
X0A 0H0
Phone: (819) 979-5281

Universities and Student
Services Division
Ministry of Education
Parliament Buildings
Victoria, British Columbia
V8V 2M4
Phone: (604) 387-4611

or

Elisabeth Dawson
Sir Winston Churchill
Secondary School
7055 Heather Street
Vancouver, B.C.
V6P 3P7
Phone: (604) 261-6334

Ms. Chris Bexte
Education Exchange Officer
Alberta Education
Devonian Building, West Tower
11160 Jasper Avenue
Edmonton, Alberta
T5K 0L2
Phone: (403) 427-2285

Mr. Frank Bellamy
Program Services Division
Saskatchewan Ministry of
Education
2220 College Avenue
Regina, Saskatchewan
S4P 3V7
Phone: (306) 787-1185

Mr. Gary McEwen
Manitoba Education
Robert Fletcher Building
1181 Portage Avenue
Suite 509
Winnipeg, Manitoba
R3G 0T3
Phone: (204) 945-6916

Paul DeSadeleer
Special Projects Branch
Ministry of Education
14th Floor
Mowat Block, Queen's Park
Toronto, Ontario
M7A 1L2
Phone: (416) 965-5605

M. Marc Champeau
Direction generale des regions
Ministere de l'Education
1035, rue De La Chevrotiere, 6
etg.
Quebec, P.Q.
GIR 5A5
Phone: (418) 643-7411

Frank Mitchell
Coordinator of Senior High
School Education
P.O. Box 370
Halifax, N.S.
B3J 2RI
Phone: (902) 421-6836

Nova Scotia Dept. of Education
Box 578
Halifax, Nova Scotia
B3J 2S9
Phone: (902) 424-5605

Ron Rice
Dept. of Education
Box 2000
Charlottetown, P.E.I.
C1A 7N8
Phone: (902) 892-3504

Mlle. Donata Theriault
Ministere de l'Education
C.P. 6000
Fredericton, N.B.
E3B 5H1
Phone: (506) 453-2326

Virginia Barrett
Dept. of Culture, Recreation
and Youth
Confederation Building
St. John's, Nfld
A1A 5T7
Phone: (709) 576-5240

Richard Martin
F.H. Collins High School
1001 Lewes Blvd.
Whitehorse, Yukon
Y1A 3J1
Phone: (403) 668-3898

Index

International Trainee Exchange, 118
International Trainee Exchange Program, 116
International Voluntary Workcamps, 108
International Workcamps, 128
Internship Program, 86
Israel Antiquities Authority, 113
Israel Youth Program Centre, 213
Japanese Exchange and Teaching Program (JET), 99
Junior Achievement of Canada, 72
La Course Destination Monde, 204
Laurentian University and Blyth & Co., 312
Legislative Intern Program, 66
Legislative Page Programme at Queen's Park, 24
Lester B. Pearson College of the Pacific, 246
Lester B. Pearson College of the Pacific, 175
Lycée Canadien en France, 254
Management Board Secretariat, 54
Manitoba Environmental Youth Corps, 30
Manitoba Legislative Intern Program, 68
Ministere du Loisir, de la Chasse et de la Pêche, 40
Model United Nations Seminars, 202
Mouvement Québecois Des Chantiers, 40
National Air and Space Museum at the Smithsonian Institute, 86
National Conference, 171
Natural Resources, 28
Natural Science and Engineering Research Council, 60
Navy League of Canada, 196
Neuchâtel Junior College, 249
Newfoundland and Labrador Conservation Corps, 28
Nova Languages Inc., 256
Nova Scotia Legislative Intern Program, 69
Nova Scotia Youth Conservation Corps, 29
Office Franco-Québecois pour la jeunesse, 111
Official-languages Monitor Program, 57
Ontario, 66
Ontario Association of Teachers of German, 299
Ontario Educational Leadership Centre, 179
Ontario Environmental Youth Corps , 30
Ontario Government, 179
Ontario Legislative Assembly, 24
Ontario Ministry of Industry, Trade and Technology, 74
Ontario Ministry of Natural Resources, 34
Ontario Ministry of Natural Resources, 36
Ontario/Québec Summer Student Job Exchange Program, 54
Ontario Rangers, 34

Ontario Science Centre, 44
Ontario Science Centre School, 258
Open House Canada, 190
Operation Beaver, 38
Outward Bound, 217
Overseas Programs, 134
Overseas Volunteer Program, 87
Page Program, 48
Parliamentary Guide Program, 52
Parliamentary Internship Programme, 64
Phi Delta Kappa International, 295
Plenty Canada, 139
Preparing Yourself for an International Career, 146
Prince Edward Island Young Environmentalist Program, 29
Provincial Ministries of the Environment and Ministries of Provincial Ministries of Education, 280
Québec, 319
Québec Legislative Intern Program, 69
Rangers 11, 36
Research Assistant Program, 297
Resource Assistant Program, 32
Rotary International, 168
Rotary International, 283
Royal Canadian Mint, 42
Royal Commonwealth Society, 173
Royal Ontario Museum Education Services, 287
Royal Tyrrell Museum of Palaeontology, 46
Saskatchewan Environment Youth Corps, 31
School Year and Summer Exchanges and Tours, 191
Secretary of State, Canada, 57
Semester and Year Abroad Programs, 271
Senate of Canada, 50
Senior High School Year Abroad, 249
Servas, 236
Shad Valley Summer Program, 289
Societe Radio-Canada, 204
Society for Educational Visits (SEVEC), 191
Special Opportunities with Religious Organizations, 151
Student Commonwealth Conference, 173
Student Conservation Association, 32
Student Summer Work Program, 120
Student Work Abroad Program (SWAP), 90
Summer Camp Institute, 295
Summer Guide, 42
Summer Language Bursary Program, 301
Summer Language Enrichment Program in Germany, 299
Summer Science Program, 292
Summer Seminar in International Development, 175
Summer Volunteer Program, 108
Summer Work Exchange, 106

Reader Response

In this, the third edition of *A World of Difference*, we have included discussions of over 100 Canadian-based work, travel and study programs available to students. We have also offered advice on creating your own opportunities. It is only after having interviewed hundreds of program directors and students that we have been able to bring you this detailed, inside information. Now you, as a reader of the third edition, can help us make subsequent editions more helpful to thousands of students nationwide. Do you know of an interesting program we've neglected to mention? Have you used your initiative to land yourself an off-beat job? What did you find particularly useful in this book? Where could we improve? Write to us and let us know. If we use your name in the next edition, we'll send you a complimentary copy. In this way you can let the rest of Canada in on your tactics and get your name in the book at the same time!

Any letters should be addressed to:

Chris Coy and Lisa Yarmoshuk
A World of Difference
c/o Broadview Press
Box 1243
Peterborough, Ontario
K9J 7H5

Thanks very much for helping make the book a more valuable tool.